Martin Luther King's Biblical Epic

RACE, RHETORIC, AND MEDIA SERIES
Davis W. Houck, General Editor

Martin Luther King's Biblical Epic

His Final, Great Speech

Keith D. Miller

University Press of Mississippi   Jackson

www.upress.state.ms.us

The University Press of Mississippi is a member
of the Association of American University Presses.

"I've Been to the Mountaintop," reprinted by arrangement with The Heirs to the Estate of Martin Luther King Jr., c/o Writers House as agent for the proprietor New York, NY. Copyright 1963 Dr. Martin Luther King Jr.; copyright renewed 1991 Coretta Scott King.

Copyright © 2012 by University Press of Mississippi
All rights reserved
Manufactured in the United States of America

First printing 2011

∞

Library of Congress Cataloging-in-Publication Data

Miller, Keith D.
　Martin Luther King's biblical epic : his final, great speech / Keith D. Miller.
　　p. cm.
　Includes bibliographical references and index.
　ISBN 978-1-61703-108-3 (cloth : alk. paper) — ISBN 978-1-61703-109-0 (ebook) 1. King, Martin Luther, Jr., 1929–1968—Oratory. 2. King, Martin Luther, Jr., 1929–1968. I've been to the mountaintop. 3. King, Martin Luther, Jr., 1929–1968—Knowledge—Bible. 4. Sanitation Workers Strike, Memphis, Tenn., 1968. I. Title.
　E185.97.K5M4898 2012
　323.092—dc22　　　　　　　　　　　　　　　　2011011331

British Library Cataloging-in-Publication Data available

To Andrew Jin Miller and Elizabeth Larson

You shall prophecy with them and be turned into another man.
—I Samuel 10:5–6

Lord they have killed thy prophets, they have demolished thy altars, and I alone am left, and they seek my life.
—Romans 11:3 (adaptation of I Kings 19:10)

CONTENTS

Acknowledgments xi

Introduction
And Then I Got into Memphis 3

Chapter 1
I Left Atlanta: King's Religious Rhetoric 27

Chapter 2
A Certain Man Fell among Thieves:
King and the Parable of the Good Samaritan 51

Chapter 3
I'm Delighted to See Each of You Here Tonight:
Pentecostalism and Mason Temple 62

Chapter 4
Across the Red Sea: The Exodus Continues 71

Chapter 5
Fire on the Streets and in the Bones:
King Revives Hebrew Prophecy 89

Chapter 6
If I Do Not Stop, What Will Happen to Them?
King's Rhetoric of the Body 112

Chapter 7
Mine Eyes Have Seen the Glory:
Julia Ward Howe, the Bible, and Memphis   129

Chapter 8
If I Had Merely Sneezed, I Would Have Died:
King's Biblical Interpretation   158

Appendix A:
Text of "I've Been to the Mountaintop"   175

Appendix B:
The Parable of the Good Samaritan, as Told in Luke 10:25–37   183

Appendix C:
The Murray/Buttrick Intertext   184

Appendix D:
The Luccock/Buttrick Intertext   185

Appendix E:
The Buttrick/King Intertext   188

Appendix F:
The Murray/Buttrick/King Intertext   191

Appendix G:
The Luccock/Buttrick/King Intertext   193

Appendix H:
Liberal Protestant Commonplaces in "I've Been to the Mountaintop"   195

Appendix I:
Parallels for Segments of "I've Been to the Mountaintop"   201

Notes   203
Bibliography   223
Index   237

ACKNOWLEDGMENTS

Many people helped make this book possible. For help, support, encouragement, and criticism, I thank Ted Coonfield of paella fame, Meg Nightingale, Joel Berning, Matt Berning, Mike Ponder, and other Oregonian beachcombers. I am grateful to Dale Billingsley, Lin Billingsley, zigzagging Steve Wright and Sue Wright, Joshua Horwitt, Nehoma Horwitt, Rebecca Horwitt, Peter Wilf, Jeff Bartow, Barbara Geis, Michael Hayton, Melissa Meredith, Elaine Alvear, Phyllis Fetzer, Vince Vitullo, and Irene Vitullo. Rev. Max Grubb, Patty Barrett, and many other fine people at First Christian Church, McAllen, Texas, supplied encouragement, as did Rinda Janney, Chris Guy, Julie Guy, Gretchen Puente-Reinhardt, and other sojourners at Tempe Friends Meeting in Arizona. I tip my hat to Nancy Gretzinger and other amigos in our adoption community. Fortunately, Laura Godwin told me to stick to this project.

I thank many people at Arizona State University: Maureen Daly Goggin and Neal Lester, who supported my applications for sabbatical leave and senior leave; Sally Kitch of the Institute for Humanities Research; Linell Cady and Carolyn Forbes of the Center for the Study of Religion and Conflict; and other colleagues and former colleagues, including Kyle Longley, Roxanne Doty, James Foard, Matthew Whitaker, Tracy Fessenden, Juliann Vitullo, Diane Wolfthal, Randy Helms, Alyssa Robillard, Dan Gilfillan, Aaron Baker, Angelita Reyes, Stanlie James, and Pam Sterling. Cecilia Menjivar, Victor Agadjanian, Kathy Kyle, and other fanciers of white elephants helped. Daniel Ramirez first suggested that I explore the Pentecostal setting for "I've Been to the Mountaintop." I appreciate current and former colleagues in my area: Patricia Boyd, Alice Daer, Peter Goggin, Kathleen Lamp, Barry Maid, Duane Roen, Shirley Rose, Karen Dwyer, Jackie Wheeler, and Sharon Crowley. Fortunately, Elizabeth Horan exhibited much patience while listening to me talk about this project. So did

Karen Adams. So did Mark Montesano and Claudia Sadowski-Smith. I thank them. I raise a toast to other department mates, including Cora Fox and Ayanna Thompson (coordinators of the nonpareil Cupz Seminar), Eddie Mallot, Dan Bivona, Taylor Corse, Paul Matsuda, Django Paris, Elly van Gelderen, Joni Adamson, Joe Lockard, Risha Sharma, Sheila Luna, Demetria Baker, Ruth Johnston, Phillip Karagas, Karen Silva, and Kristen LaRue. Simon Ortiz is always splendid. All of my current and former graduate students have stimulated and challenged me. Many thanks! Among my former undergraduates, I pour a libation for Natalie Nicol, Samantha Jensen, and Katrina Anderson. Cindy Cowles helped with the index.

Professors and graduate students at other universities have provoked me while encouraging this project. Keith Gilyard and Jack Selzer proved especially useful. Clare Colquitt graciously supplied felicitous conversations. Also supportive have been Kevin Browne, Kelton Cobb, David Green, Ersula Ore, Glen McClish, Melissa Pearson, Tom Miller, Roxanne Mountford, Tom Farrell, Kelton Cobb, Elizabeth Vander Lei, Vincent Wimbush, and J. Kameron Carter. Gaynelle Wethers offered her support. David Holmes, Stephen Schneider, Cedric Burrows, and Davis Houck help carry the torch for the study of the oratory and the literacy practices of the civil rights movement.

I celebrate other civil rights scholars who spurred me to think harder. They include Tony Badger, Stewart Burns, Clayborne Carson, David Chappell, James Cone, Charles Eagles (who lent me a sweater on a cold night), Sue Englander, Glenn Eskew, Catherine Fosl, Elizabeth Jacoway, Ralph Luker, Charles Marsh, Ted Ownby, Jonathan Rieder, Kerry Taylor, Brian Ward, and Juan Williams. David Garrow serves as an indispensable resource for me and many other researchers.

I learned from conversations with a number of civil rights veterans, including Chuck McDew, Vincent Harding, Julian Bond, Bob Zellner, and (especially) Ed King and Lawrence Guyot.

For their help in Memphis, I thank Michael Osborn, Antonio de Velasco, and Calvin Burrows. Michael shared his memories of 1968 and kindly drove Beth Larson and me to Mason Temple. There she graciously photographed its sanctuary. I also applaud Clyde Milton for his tour of Mason Temple and for information about the tomb of C. H. Mason and about the small changes at the temple since 1968. Led by Ed Frank, the staff of the Special Collections of the University of Memphis Library were congenial and helpful.

I applaud everyone at University Press of Mississippi, especially Walter Biggins, Sophia Halkias, and a very capable, anonymous outside reviewer.

I remain grateful to my late parents, Doris Miller and Ernest Miller, and thank the whole Miller circle, including Steve Miller, Janma Miller, Kirk Miller, Diane Miller, Faith Miller, Darren Maple Leaf of Team McLean, Drew Miller, Alicia Miller, Smiling Jessica Garcia, Simon Garcia, Katie Guild, Justin Guild, Ron Miller, Pam Miller, Alverna Cobb, Shann Cobb, Lori Kragor, Cheri Rogers, Harvey Rogers, Robin Gonzales, Irma Darphin, and Eugene Brink.

Finally, I congratulate Lili Chen for the world's greatest dumplings and praise Nancy Erickson for the world's greatest graduation party. I am very glad that Beth and Andrew brighten my life every day.

Martin Luther King's Biblical Epic

INTRODUCTION

And Then I Got into Memphis

On the night of April 3, 1968, Martin Luther King Jr. entered Mason Temple in Memphis and unfurled "I've Been to the Mountaintop." It was his final speech and possibly his greatest.[1] It also barely happened.

Joan Beifuss explains the baleful weather that night in Memphis:

> By early that evening storms were . . . tossing across the city, piles of white-streaked gray and purple clouds, storm light deepening the green of grass and shrubs, then heavy sullen blackness. Thunder could be heard off to the west, down the bluff, across the river, the first rain running ahead of the lightning.[2]

Although rain often drenched Memphis, this thunderstorm proved unusually muscular. After a while, it stopped tossing across the city; instead, it was tossing the city. It hurled parts of Arkansas, Tennessee, and Kentucky along with it. Beifuss explains: "Tornado warnings were out now, the eerie wail of civil defense sirens sounding across the city as the storms swept out of Arkansas and across Tennessee and Kentucky, leveling houses, barns, utility lines, trees."[3] A tornado lifted a sizable piece of asphalt and dropped it on several cars, killing seven people.[4] Only twenty miles from Memphis, a twister ripped a trailer court. Electricity disappeared in places. All told, the storm killed twelve and injured more than a hundred.[5]

Ralph Abernathy, King's boon companion, recalls that, when riding through Memphis that evening, he heard "loud explosions" of thunder accompanied by "as bad a wind and rain as we'd seen in months." Driving proved virtually impossible, Abernathy relates, as "sudden sheets of water washed across the windshield of the car and rendered the frantic wipers useless."⁶ Civil defense sirens were blasting, a tornado was brewing, winds were flattening the landscape, and drivers couldn't peer through windshields. Nature was telegraphing a simple message: "Stay home, everyone!" Why would Abernathy or any other sane person venture to Mason Temple on such a night? Why, especially, would a civil rights icon go there?

King hadn't wanted to visit Memphis in the sunshine. In spring 1968, he was trying to mobilize the Poor People's Campaign, a large, multi-ethnic demonstration that he was orchestrating for Washington, D.C. Despite the vigorous objections of most of his upper-level staff, he insisted on the pivotal importance of staging a huge protest in Washington.⁷

The Poor People's Campaign was now everything. Memphis was not on the schedule.

Then Rev. James Lawson, a veteran activist and stalwart Gandhian, contacted King about the prospects of African American garbage workers in Memphis, the blues capital of the universe and the largest city in the Mid-South. Lawson began his commitment to nonviolence as a teenager. During the Korean War, he spent time in federal prison for resisting the draft. He then traveled for three years to India, working as a teacher and as a Methodist campus minister. After meeting King in 1957, he served as a catalyst for the sit-in movement in Nashville, training many young people—including John Lewis, Diane Nash, James Bevel, and Bernard Lafayette—who would exert important leadership during the Freedom Rides and later civil rights struggles. King liked and greatly respected Lawson.

By February 1968, thirteen hundred garbage workers galvanized the attention of Lawson and everyone else in Memphis. They joined the Local 1733 affiliate of the American Federation of State, County, and Municipal Employees (AFSCME) and launched a wildcat strike against Memphis and its mayor. Many of these city employees had gravitated to Memphis from rural counties, especially those in the nearby Mississippi Delta, where improved agricultural machinery had eliminated their jobs.⁸ Their work in Memphis was decidedly arduous. Homeowners in Memphis positioned fifty-gallon drums in their backyards and routinely placed their garbage into the drums. Sanitation laborers lifted and set these barrels of debris into tubs before shouldering, carrying, and emptying the tubs into garbage trucks. Because garbage disposals had yet to invade the underside of kitchen sinks, household trash regularly included scraps of unwrapped, half-eaten, rotting vegetables and meat. As the workers hauled their loads, they battled flies and sweltering humidity in the summer, daylong rain in the fall, and cold in the winter. James Robinson describes his assignment: "We had to pick up trash out of the backyard. You had to tote it on your head in a tub. The tub's full of water, rain, garbage, maggots, everything else running out. ... If you'd get a hole in it the water'd run all out the tub down on ya."[9] He adds:

> You had to stay out there as long as it would take you. You'd work, ten, twelve hours a day. But you didn't get paid but for eight. You stayed out there until you'd get through. We were out there sometimes till dark. You'd start at seven o'clock in the morning, no extra for overtime.[10]

Another garbage collector, Clinton Burrows, remarks:

> It was worser than being in the penal institution. The [supervisors] didn't want you to enter the office to get a drink of water. ... Eating without washing your hands, working in the snow without [heat]. These are inhumane treatment.[11]

Yet another sanitation laborer, Nathaniel Broome, remembers: "People used to laugh at us. They called us 'walking buzzards' because we picked up the trash."[12]

For this work, the city paid a salary that could not be called a living wage. Robinson explained, "I wasn't making a damn thing. ... [In 1968] I'd been there fifteen years and I made $1.65 an hour."[13] Another man lamented, "There is no worse job. I would take anything."[14]

One day two workers dodged heavy rain by entering the large barrel of their outmoded garbage truck. They died tragically when the faulty trash-compacting mechanism of the truck crushed them. In his capacity as city commissioner and head of the Public Works Department, Henry Loeb had purchased the defective truck.[15] Weeks before the deaths of the two men, T. O. Jones, a dedicated AFSCME organizer, had complained to the city, now headed by Mayor Henry Loeb, about their outdated trucks. Loeb refused to listen. Failing to provide benefits to workers, penny-pinching city officials now assisted the two bereaved families only by granting one month's extra salary per family plus five hundred dollars to help with burial costs.[16] As King's lieutenant Andrew Young explained, the two deaths and the city's response to the families "were symptomatic of the disrespect with which garbage workers were treated."[17] For years Jones had tried to coax the workers to strike, but to no avail. Shortly after the two men died, however, the laborers spontaneously defied their mayor by idling their garbage trucks.

Even though working led nowhere, a walkout did not seem promising either. The union lacked a strike fund. Some white unionists in Memphis supported their African American counterparts, but others did not. Unable to secure well-paying jobs, which were reserved for whites, most local blacks could hardly afford to assist the strikers. Further, far from urging a labor confrontation in Memphis, national leaders of AFSCME dreaded one. P. F. Ciampa, field services director of AFSCME, initially groaned, "'I wouldn't have called that strike—not in February.... And, my God, what in the hell am I going to do with a strike in the South?'"[18] He recognized that Memphis and its whole region generally lacked a tradition of public sympathy for organized labor. The two large Memphis newspapers fiercely opposed unions, as did many powerful white Memphians, including Mayor Loeb, who had successfully fought unionization at his Loeb's Laundry Cleaner Company.

Yet, despite hostility from city hall and wariness from the national office of AFSCME, garbage workers saw little choice but to strike. Taylor Rogers explains that he and others reached

> the point that we had to do something. You didn't have no benefits. You didn't have no say-so about what you did and how you did it. You did it like they said to do it. That's why we wanted a union, we wanted somebody to represent us, so that we could have some say about our hours and working conditions.[19]

The wholehearted devotion of Rogers and other strikers eventually impressed AFSCME officials and many others. Led by Maxine Smith and Jesse Turner, the local National Association for the Advancement of Colored People (NAACP) rallied behind Jones and the walkout. The indefatigable Cornelia Crenshaw mobilized women to provide logistical assistance for the strike and to raise money for the cause. The white president of the United Rubber Workers allowed the strikers to meet regularly at his union hall. In addition, numerous African American pastors heartily endorsed the strike and aided the workers. Loeb, however, insisted that he would never recognize the union as a bargaining agent.

On February 17, approximately two thousand trash collectors and supporters gathered at Mason Temple to hear preachers and labor leaders.

Having encouraged his congregation to contribute food and money to the strikers, Bishop J. O. Patterson Sr., pastor of Mason Temple, asked the crowd to help bag the food.[20]

National reporters missed Patterson's words. Despite increasing tension in Memphis, the outside press yawned at the strike. After providing a steady diet of turbulent racial dramas for over a decade, the news media could hardly keep claiming that every conflict warranted attention, especially one in a medium-sized city. Garbage piling high provided a new variation on the theme of racial confrontation; but mounds of debris did not attract much notice, especially when journalists on the East Coast did not have to smell it.

On February 23, following a second, exasperating encounter with the city council, garbage workers, union leaders, and supportive ministers marched nonviolently from the council chambers toward Mason Temple. Nearby, white police officers carried a new weapon—aerosol cans filled with mace. Combining tear gas with a chemical that sandpapers human skin, mace causes temporary blindness and renders its victims helpless. Assertive police soon began spraying mace on peaceful dissenters, including T. O. Jones and P. J. Ciampa, leaving Ciampa semi-conscious. Police also maced several ministers, including James Lawson and Ralph Jackson. Despite this reception from the police, the bedraggled protestors resumed their march until they finally stumbled into Mason Temple. Jones and Jackson then delivered fiercely polemical speeches as they railed at the police and city hall.

The next day Lawson, Patterson, and others announced that one hundred ministers were creating a new political organization. In addition to donating food and agreeing to join picket lines, the pastors demanded more jobs in careers that whites denied to African Americans. The preachers also announced a boycott of downtown white businesses, adopting the slogan, "No new clothes for Easter."

One hundred fifty ministers and several hundred others convened that evening at Mason Temple. Infuriated by the insensitivity and outright racism of the two leading newspapers in Memphis, Lawson demanded that their reporters speedily exit the church. Then speakers lifted the crowd with oratory and sparked a songfest of hymns and civil rights anthems.[21]

Even after the macing incident, the national press corps ignored Memphis. Eager journalists had persistently related many episodes of police assaults against peaceful marchers a few years before in Birmingham, Danville, and Selma. Banner headlines had publicized the ugly murders of three civil rights activists in Mississippi and the appalling slaying of four girls in a church bombing in Birmingham. A massive race riot three years earlier in Los Angeles garnered rivers of ink and many hours of television images. So did an even larger conflagration in Detroit in 1967, less than a year before the Memphis strike. After such crises, Memphis seemed insignificant.

As reporters slumbered on the East Coast, activists managed to convince two prominent civil rights figures to fly into Memphis. On March 14 Bayard Rustin, organizer of the March on Washington, and Roy Wilkins, president of the NAACP, arrived at Mason Temple to headline a large, exuberant gathering on behalf of the city workers. Thousands of people cheered an excited Rustin, who celebrated the "profound importance" of the strike.[22] He finished by transforming himself into a musical conductor and his entire audience into a choir as they sang rhythmical labor lyrics together. Striking an uncharacteristically militant note, the usually restrained Wilkins lambasted the police macing and saluted the black community for its unity. He urged workers "to stay here and fight until hell freezes over" and insisted on "new pay scales, new security, new life for the people."[23]

King had ventured to Memphis before. In 1959, endorsing a slate of African American political candidates, he joined Rev. Fred Shuttlesworth, Daisy Bates, and Mahalia Jackson for a large rally at Mason Temple. One speaker urged "the burial of Uncle Toms."[24] Congratulating the community for its "magnificent unity," King ignited the crowd with a call-and-response rhythm so inspiring that, in the words of one participant, he touched his audience "like a brain relating to the limbs."[25] As outgoing city commissioner, Henry Loeb responded to these candidates by organizing a "white unity" ticket. Loeb's candidates defeated the black aspirants, and Loeb was elected mayor of Memphis.

King again returned to Memphis in 1966 to address the Metropolitan Baptist Church—a year before Loeb's re-election as mayor.

In 1968, when Lawson implored King to revisit the city perched along the Mississippi River, King, like Wilkins, at first declined. Finally, after repeated urging from Lawson, King landed in Memphis for the purpose of kindling another rally. On March 18, four days after Rustin and Wilkins had aroused those in Mason Temple, organizers corralled many into the same church. Thrilled that King had returned, admirers jammed every open space in the large sanctuary, many standing along the walls. Andrew Young accurately observed, "This was a larger crowd than we could ever have assembled in one hall in Birmingham or Selma."[26] Indeed King had rarely attracted such a huge live audience.²⁷ With many of his allies balking at his plans for the Poor People's Campaign, blue-collar workers in Memphis were generating the kind of vibrant, nonviolent movement that had fueled King's reputation. Many thoughtful people believed that such protest was no longer possible in the current, volatile national atmosphere.

When King entered Mason Temple on March 18, the large throng supplied resounding cheers and applause. In this oration, "The Dignity of Labor," he hailed the garbage workers and excoriated city authorities.²⁸ Explicating Jesus's Parable of Dives and Lazarus, he inserted the sanitation laborers into the biblical narrative. He bemoaned the "'starvation wages'" that they received, maintaining that they were "'just as significant as the physician'" in preventing "'disease'" from becoming "'rampant.'" Poised to exert maximum economic pressure on Mayor Loeb, he declared:

> You may have to escalate the struggle a bit. If they keep refusing . . . I tell you what you ought to demand. And you're together here enough to do it. In a few days you ought to get together and just have a general work stoppage in the city of Memphis.²⁹

He elaborated:

> And you let that day come and not a Negro in this city will go to any job downtown, not a Negro in domestic service will go to anybody's kitchen, black students will not go to anybody's school.³⁰

King again reached his audience like a brain relating to the limbs: the crowd responded with jubilation. Rev. Billy Kyles observed that listeners "'were whooping up everything [King] would say.'"³¹ They shouted so loudly that listeners could not hear King's closing words. The reception was so electrifying that King—coaxed by Lawson, Young, and Abernathy—agreed on the spot to return to Memphis to lead a protest march.

Members of King's quarrelsome executive staff, however, proved difficult to convince. King had already leaned on them to jettison their own projects to work on the Poor People's Campaign. Now, switching directions, he asked them to concentrate on Memphis instead. Even though several of his lieutenants proved self-centered and wayward, they were also understandably frustrated that their leader was redirecting their focus, again. Yammering at the man they often called "Doc," they ventilated their unhappiness that he was picking Lawson's strike, not one of their own prized projects. Although they respected Lawson, he was not even a member of King's staff, and they were King's staff. Further, they implied, King was addressing a mere local complaint. Who cared about a mid-sized city in Tennessee? Exasperated by their criticism, King erupted in anger, insisted on loyalty, and informed them that the Poor People's Campaign might begin beside the Mississippi River in Bluff City. In Memphis.

Others African Americans also questioned King's leadership. The Invaders, a group of youthful militants, embraced neither Lawson's nonviolent philosophy nor his goal of racial integration. Even though Lawson had proven himself a highly skilled leader of workshops on Christian nonviolence, no one trained the Invaders in nonviolence or screened participants for the march slated for March 28. On that day, by the time King's plane landed from New York City, no one had told King that the Invaders—plus an assortment of petty criminals and hooligans—had infiltrated the ranks of the marchers he was about to lead. After King's arrival, the demonstration began innocently. But soon tempestuous young men began shattering store windows and ransacking merchandise. Police wielded mace, teargas, and batons indiscriminately—against rioters, looters, and respectable marchers alike. Worried that King would be hurt or killed, Lawson prompted him to exit the melee. King's aide Bernard Lee flagged a random car and coaxed the owner to let him drive King safely to a hotel. Meanwhile, with bullhorn in hand and teargas swirling around him, Lawson attempted to restore order, urging protestors to return to Clayborn Temple, where they began their star-crossed march. Following his instructions and guided by his assistants, most activists reversed directions and headed toward the church.

Despite Lawson's efforts, the chaos and conflict spread. Wearing helmets and gas masks, rampaging police chased the demonstrators while macing and pummeling them. Many frantically tried to escape the police while others cowered in doorways. NAACP leader Maxine Smith, however, calmly chose to walk, not to run, from the police.[32] As they clubbed the protestors, some police were also injured. Enraged, they swarmed into restaurants and bars, indiscriminately pounding and macing customers who were simply eating and drinking there. As the demonstrators reached Clayborn Temple, police unceremoniously invaded the church and continued to beat and mace those who sought refuge inside. Teargas from the police wafted through the sanctuary, and gas casings stained the floors and walls. When violence spilled into other parts of the city, tragedy struck as police killed a black teenager named Larry Payne.

The maelstrom in downtown Memphis aroused the national press. After ignoring the garbage workers' strike, reporters and editorial writers—including many who had previously supported King—now assailed him, blaming him for the window-breaking and looting. They explained that the ill-fated march badly tarnished his reputation as a heroic problem solver and Gandhi-like avatar of nonviolence. After retreating from Memphis for six days, King returned to the city, shaken, but determined to redeem the possibilities of nonviolent dissent—and his own leadership. He insisted on leading a new, exemplary march that could help the laborers win their strike.

Organizers scheduled an evening rally at Mason Temple on April 3, shortly after King's return. But the formidable thunderstorm seemed to preclude a sizable turnout. Many of those who heard King on March 18 made the prudent decision to stay home, thereby dodging high winds, a tornado, lightning, and flooded streets. Yet stout-hearted unionists and their supporters would not be deterred. Between 2,500 and 3,000 people braved the cloudburst to huddle in Mason Temple.[33]

But King wasn't coming. Memphis wasn't supposed to happen. Neither was this speech.

Anticipating that only a tiny number of folks would defy the tempest and reach Mason Temple, King dispatched Abernathy to talk in his stead. Why would King speak to a nearly empty house? If he were to do so, the press might decide that no one wanted to hear him. Plus, he remained deeply unhappy about the calamity six days earlier. Over the phone he voiced anxiety that day to his friend Stanley Levison, wondering aloud whether critics of nonviolence were right. His anxiety was keen, but it certainly was not new. Abernathy, Levison, Andrew Young, and others close to King had noticed that, over at least a year, he often seemed moody and depressed. In private he smoked cigarettes and sometimes drank moderately. Year after year he hopscotched the nation, slipping into airports, then boarding, riding, and exiting planes several times per week, almost every week—all in an effort to resolve a knot of national dilemmas that often seemed insoluble. Following month after month of endlessly wearying travel and stress—his entire life a blur—King felt exceedingly depleted. Young observed that King suffered from a sore throat on April 3 and was "physically feverish."[34] He definitely needed to rest at the Lorraine Motel.

But, arriving at Mason Temple alongside Young and Jesse Jackson, Abernathy quickly discovered an audience much larger and more passionate than he and King anticipated. In addition Abernathy noticed television cameras that stood ready to record King's speech. He also correctly judged that the crowd wanted King. Locating a phone in the vestibule of the church, he dialed his companion and implored him to speak. King reluctantly agreed.

As Bernard Lee edged King's car through the thunderstorm, wind and rain lashed the roof of Mason Temple; its high, plain amber windows clattered. Hung from a rafter was a large white banner emblazoned with these words from the Bible:

> "Not By Might, Nor By Power, But By My Spirit
> Saith the LORD OF HOSTS" Zechariah 4:6[35]

Reluctant to allow the crowd to sit in silence, several ministers, in turn, rose, stepped under the banner, and spoke from the pulpit. Lawson sternly charged that police had murdered Larry Payne. The student body president of a high school promised that well-disciplined teenagers would abandon their classrooms to march nonviolently with King. The crowd filled the sanctuary with vibrant, melodious songs.

Around nine o'clock, wearing a black rain jacket with a red inner lining, King finally arrived. As he walked from the vestibule and into the sanctuary in full view of the crowd, listeners strained to glimpse him, stamping their feet, and cheering lustily.[36] One minister observed, "It was an overwhelming spirit in Mason Temple that night."[37] Approaching the chancel, King quickly noticed Abernathy, Lawson, Young, and Jesse Jackson sitting there. Several other ministers aligned beside them, all arranged in a slight curve behind the pulpit. The clapping grew louder and louder. Impeccably attired in a very dark brown suit; white shirt; and copper-tinged, dark brown tie, King soaked in the applause.

Under the rafters and a relatively low ceiling, King heard rain tattooing the metal roof and shutters slamming. He gazed at those who occupied almost all of the 1,969 seats that were bolted onto the floor, facing the pulpit.[38] He also glimpsed two side balconies and a back balcony that, together, held 739 bolted seats. Many of those seats were also full, especially those in the back balcony. Others chose among the 435 seats in the one chancel, almost entirely eschewing the 591 seats behind it. Looking directly ahead, King easily spied the faces of Memphians who occupied the last row of seats on the floor. Those listeners sat only 120 feet away from him. Others at the farthest, back corner of the floor rested only 150 feet away from him. Sections of the back balcony held, at most, seven rows of seats. No one—repeat, no one—in the whole sanctuary perched more than 175 feet from the pulpit, and almost everyone was considerably closer.³⁹ The architect of Mason Temple enabled between 2,500 and 3,000 people to hear King's speech, and each of them sat literally close to the preacher.⁴⁰ For his part, King could clearly see everyone facing him and beside him. And everyone could easily hear everyone else.

But King hardly seemed able to talk. Young, who knew the orator quite well, remembered that on this day, he "was as depressed as I'd ever known him to be." Even as King took a seat near the pulpit, Young still sensed that his friend looked "tired and depressed."⁴¹ A local pastor, who also sat close by, observed that King "'looked harrowed and tired and worn and rushed.'"⁴² Introducing King, Abernathy spun an uncharacteristically long narrative that summarized King's life and recalled his many accomplishments—some of which King would relive in his speech. Abernathy's long-windedness granted King roughly a half hour—or perhaps even an hour—to will himself out of his exhaustion.⁴³ When Abernathy finally left the pulpit, he states, King "turned and with a grin on his face and said, 'You took a terribly long time to introduce me.'"⁴⁴

Immediately after teasing his friend, somewhere between 9:25 and 10:00, King entered the pulpit. In a city he did not want to distract him, at a time he did not want to speak, in a state of semi-exhaustion and depression, with possibly a sore throat and a slight fever, he surveyed his listeners. Competing with noise from heavy, intermittent rainfall, thunder, and banging shutters—silenced at some point by loud, rumbling ceiling fans—he delivered "I've Been to the Mountaintop," his final speech and possibly his best speech.

Although millions of Americans know something about "I've Been to the Mountaintop," relatively few understand it well. Repeated endlessly on television and YouTube is a snippet of its final two minutes. Millions have noticed *only* this snippet, in which, especially in hindsight, King appears to offer an eerily accurate prediction of his assassination the next day. But the entire hour-long speech obviously matters, not merely its closing two minutes. Inasmuch as a conclusion always finishes *something*, one can *only* grasp the conclusion of *any* oration by pondering the *entire* oration. Otherwise, why would anyone deliver a whole speech? Like any other orator, King used the final two minutes to *conclude* what he had been *developing* throughout his address.

Perhaps Americans refuse to consider the entire hour because, as numerous scholars and civil rights veterans have noted, Americans strongly prefer to treasure the earlier King while ignoring his later years. Millions who dutifully honor King on the annual national holiday commemorate the King of the Montgomery Bus Boycott of 1955–1956 and the King of "I Have a Dream" from 1963 while almost entirely bypassing the King of 1966–1968, whose major speeches proved more radical and more disturbing.[45] This little-remembered, later King realized that heroic, nonviolent campaigns to repeal legalized segregation in Mississippi and Alabama had failed to ameliorate de facto segregation in the North. So he commuted to Chicago, where he fought segregated housing, and to Cleveland, where he helped elect an African American mayor. He keenly recognized that overthrowing racist laws did not alleviate southern poverty. So he crusaded against starvation in the Mississippi Delta. Aiming to spur Congress to eradicate poverty, he planned massive civil disobedience that would disrupt government proceedings in Washington, D.C. And he urged schoolchildren and workers to shut down the entire city of Memphis.

Further, exasperated at devastating violence in Southeast Asia, King railed at the Vietnam War, thereby alienating much of the press corps that, a few years earlier, had communicated his protests and celebrated his Nobel Peace Prize. His denunciation of American war-making prompted civil rights allies—including Roy Wilkins, Bayard Rustin, and Jackie Robinson—to publicly disavow his position. So did Ralph Bunche, another African American who had won the Nobel Peace Prize.

More importantly, King's antiwar stance deeply offended and alienated his most vital political ally—President Lyndon Johnson, the commander-in-chief responsible for the American presence in Vietnam. In response to massive protests against southern segregation, Johnson had proposed—and skillfully coaxed Congress to approve—the Civil Rights Act of 1964 and the Voting Rights Act of 1965. King fully recognized that Johnson had aided African Americans more than any president since Lincoln. Yet the later, radical King failed to remain silent about Vietnam. Not only did he repudiate the war, he came close to encouraging young men to violate federal law and court years of imprisonment by refusing the draft.[46] He also demanded a halt to the nuclear arms race—a cause that most antiwar dissenters considered secondary to the immediacy of Vietnam. The later King espoused all these ideas—about poverty, nonviolence, civil disobedience, Vietnam, nuclear weapons, and peace—in important, yet largely forgotten speeches, some of which anticipated later, highly controversial orations by Rev. Jeremiah Wright.[47]

Clearly, King's later years proved so radical that, for most Americans, lauding King means prizing a truncated, likable version of the earlier King while discarding the later, disconcerting King.

But Americans might dismiss the later King for another reason as well: he used the Bible in ways that make them feel uncomfortable. During the triumphant years of Montgomery, Birmingham, and Selma, he reinvigorated a mainline African American oratorical tradition by blending appeals to American civil religion.[48] In "I Have a Dream," for example, he stood in front of a gigantic, white marble statue of Abraham Lincoln and used the Emancipation Proclamation, the Declaration of Independence, and the Bible as touchstones to demand the repeal of segregation.[49] As Richard Lischer explains, following the Selma March of 1965, King appealed less frequently to patriotic benchmarks and leaned more heavily on the Bible.

King made this argumentative shift in a number of orations. Consider "Where Do We Go from Here?" which he delivered in 1967 to a national gathering of his Southern Christian Leadership Conference (SCLC). He began by saluting the monumental gains of the civil rights movement. Next he enumerated the multifaceted work of SCLC to combat racism and poverty throughout much of the South: registering voters, educating community leaders, teaching literacy, and orchestrating "farm cooperatives, business development, tutorials, credit unions." Next he announced "a four-million-dollar rehabilitation project" for rental housing in Chicago. Then he applauded an SCLC affiliate that had created thousands of new jobs in Chicago, nurtured African American–owned banks there, and ensured fair hiring for electricians and masons. In addition, he detailed a SCLC-organized boycott of Sealtest Milk in Cleveland, which, he charged, treats "the ghetto" as "a domestic colony." And he hailed SCLC efforts to spawn new jobs and new housing in Atlanta.

He then defended nonviolence as the weapon of love against what he termed the interrelated "triple evils" of poverty, racism, and war. After favorably quoting two socialist economists—Henry George and John Kenneth Galbraith—he joined Galbraith in advocating a "guaranteed annual income" for all Americans, including those whom he deemed "the discouraged beggars in life's marketplace." The money that fueled the war in Vietnam, he insisted, could instead fund such a program. Promoting what he called "a broader distribution of wealth," he told listeners to ask such provocative questions as "'Who owns the oil?'" and "'Who owns the iron ore?'"

While detailing the work of his organization and espousing a guaranteed annual income, King made what might strike some readers today as an odd move: he drenched his entire oration in the Bible. Alluding to the biblical books of Exodus and Joshua, he likened recent campaigns for civil rights to the Exodus of the Israelites from Pharaoh's Egypt and their eventual arrival in the Promised Land. He also explicated passages of biblical prophecy—specifically from Amos, Isaiah, and Micah—that address life in Israel centuries after the episodes related in Exodus and Joshua. Then, shifting to the gospel of John, he interpreted the words of Jesus to Nicodemus, "You must be born again!"[50] Finally he provided hope by summoning familiar lines from I Corinthians and Galatians. Thus, in the same address he explicated not only disparate biblical texts, but also disparate biblical genres—a Pentateuchal narrative (Exodus), early prophetic history (Joshua), later prophecy (Amos, Isaiah, and Micah), gospel (John), and Pauline epistle (I Corinthians and Galatians). Again, he performed this feat of biblical interpretation while cataloguing the recent achievements of SCLC and promoting "a broader distribution of wealth."

"Where Do We Go from Here?" is one of King's more noteworthy speeches. But its blend of economic radicalism, antiwar protest, and biblical exegesis was not that unusual for King in 1967. During King's lifetime, most Americans either never heard this argument or readily dismissed it. They certainly failed to elect a Congress that would enact a guaranteed national income or quickly withdraw troops from Vietnam. If members of the Christian Right were to read or hear the later King today, they would, I suspect, revile his words as unpatriotic and dangerous. Today, while some liberals still attend synagogues and churches, many other progressives and intellectuals have become Buddhists, agnostics, atheists, post-Christians, or postmodernists and have little or no use for the Bible. King's reliance on the Bible to forward progressive causes might, therefore, for different reasons, seem odd today to many on both the right and the left.

Fortunately, the nation now memorializes King. Yet, through some strange alchemy, many now remember the most controversial figure of the 1960s—a decade overflowing with controversies—as little more than a walking marble statue or an African American Santa Claus. The greatest tribute anyone could ever pay to King is not to monumentalize his current, oversimplified image, but, rather, to understand him. Studying King is valuable for anyone. Comprehending King's oratory is particularly important for organizers undertaking other large-scale mass movements aimed at, for example, preventing genocide, dismantling nuclear weapons, ending global warming, halting ill-conceived wars, feeding masses of starving children, preserving endangered species, or stopping HIV-AIDS. Because national governments normally show little evidence of their ability to achieve these goals strictly by themselves, pressure from mass movements is usually necessary to spur sufficient government action to accomplish them. Even though King's courageous and fierce orations of 1967 and 1968 will still unsettle many, those addresses merit and reward scrutiny. Conservatives who breezily dismiss his economic analysis should reflect on the Wall Street debacle of 2008 and reconsider his critique of capitalism and earnest determination to end poverty. Progressives who view Christianity as the private property of the Christian Right should reconsider his use of the Bible to subvert, rather than bless, the inequities of the status quo.

During the 1960s, print and broadcast journalists undeniably exaggerated King's importance to the southern struggle for racial equality. Thankfully, recent historians compensate for this exaggeration by uncovering and spotlighting the gigantic contributions that Fannie Lou Hamer, Ella Baker, Ruby Doris Robinson, Daisy Bates, Aaron Henry, T.R.M. Howard, Fred Shuttlesworth, and other noteworthy leaders made to the triumph of racial agitation. At such key sites as Albany, Birmingham, Selma, and St. Augustine, other protest organizations provided the groundwork for King's interventions. Yet, as King crisscrossed the nation almost every week on a speech-making marathon, his oratory obviously mattered. While his leadership in the Montgomery Bus Boycott and later campaigns was undeniably significant, his rhetoric served as his greatest contribution to the centuries-long African American struggle. The single most important question that people should ask about King is, *What made his orations so eloquent, so mesmerizing, so persuasive?* Probing his use of the Bible helps answer that question.

In this book I do not investigate King's whole rhetorical career or even his entire later career. Nor do I examine his complete relationship to the Bible, either earlier or later in his public life. Instead, I focus on King's final speech, "I've Been to the Mountaintop." (For the sake of convenience, the entire text of this speech appears in Appendix A of this book.) As I explore this oration, I concentrate on King's ability to interpret the Bible in support for the garbage workers as they grapple to overcome poverty and seize dignity.

"I've Been to the Mountaintop" is, by all accounts, one of King's supreme oratorical achievements. Except for "I Have a Dream," his last oration is more familiar to the public than any of his hundreds and hundreds of other addresses. While his final speech is very accessible, it is also exceedingly rich and sophisticated; it certainly warrants and repays careful attention by scholars and anyone else. Yet, despite its richness and importance, very few researchers examine "I've Been to the Mountaintop" in any detail. No one has written a book about it. King scholars normally concentrate instead on his political leadership or his theology, usually paying scant (and sometimes literally no) attention to most of "I've Been to the Mountaintop."

While analyzing King's last address, I concentrate on his use of the Bible for two primary reasons. First, throughout his entire career, King continually treated the Bible as the Holy Book, the text above all other texts. He reflected on the Bible during his childhood and adolescence— sometimes disagreeing with his Sunday School teachers—and continued to wrestle with the Bible during his many years as an undergraduate, a seminarian, and a doctoral student. From the time of his ordination as a minister in 1946 until his death in 1968, he constantly explained the Bible, mining its passages to create foundations for literally hundreds of sermons. In addition, he cited the Bible as an authoritative text when delivering "I Have a Dream" and literally hundreds of other speeches.[51] Instead of randomly spinning a pinwheel of biblical allusions, he engaged the Bible thoughtfully. Someone else might have carelessly flipped through hundreds of biblical pages in search of an extractable line that could slide easily into a call for a boycott. But, like other conscientious Jews and Christians, King constantly grappled with crucial biblical themes and worked to translate those themes into the present.

Second, King scholars largely skip his relationship to the Bible.[52] Of course, researchers know that King was a Baptist minister who often discussed Jewish and Christian scripture. But, instead of looking *closely* at the Bible and *closely* at his explication of it, investigators almost invariably mention his biblical citations very briefly and casually. They almost entirely fail to address two *primary* questions: What *overall* interpretation of the Bible does King provide? How does that interpretation contribute to his magnetic appeal and his persuasiveness?

Embedded in queries are other important questions. What interpretation of the Bible does King offer in a single speech? That is, how does he coherently relate seemingly disparate biblical passages in, say, "I Have a Dream"? Also, does he interpret the Bible consistently when he moves from one oration to another? Is his interpretation of the Bible consistent, for example, in the fourteen sermons featured in his homiletic collection, *Strength to Love?* Or does he shift his interpretive stance from one sermon to another within the collection? Does he alter his interpretation when he moves from one city to another? Or from a church to an NAACP Convention? Or from a predominantly white audience to a predominantly African American audience? Or from his early orations to his later ones? In 1967 and 1968, how does his biblical exegesis illuminate and undergird his provocative, radical arguments about race, poverty, and war?

Other related questions arise. How and why does King depart from the approach to the Bible that he learned while studying with noted professors in his seminary? Why does he invariably treat the many books of the Bible, composed by myriad authors and editors, as a single, unified text? Which traditions of biblical interpretation does he tap? Does he use African American experience to probe the Bible and the Bible to frame African American experience? Does he supply principles of interpretation that others could employ in future decades? Why does he repeatedly quote and interpret certain biblical books while typically bypassing others? Why does he often preach on certain biblical characters, such as Moses, and rarely on others, such as David, even though David is a major biblical figure? Why does he quote the prophetic books (especially Amos) so often? How does he relate the Hebrew Bible to the Christian Bible? More specifically, how does he negotiate the tradition of evangelists (starting with Paul) who attempt to minimize the importance of Judaism to Christianity? Does he imitate Paul and many others by claiming or assuming that Christianity supersedes Judaism? Or does he navigate differently the vexed relationship between Christianity and Judaism? And how in the world does the relationship between different genres of an ancient book impinge on a current labor dispute in Memphis?

From the pulpit and the podium, King never approaches the Bible in a piecemeal or scattershot fashion. Instead, he adapts specific oratorical traditions to construct his own highly imaginative interpretation of the Bible. He consistently blends his biblical appeals with his advocacy of African American rights in Montgomery, Birmingham, Selma, and Memphis. Yet, in spite of his arguments for specific reforms in specific circumstances, he supplies a biblical interpretation that is cohesive, organized, even methodical. Because this interpretation is loosely systematic, it deserves to be called a biblical hermeneutic. Grasping his loose system of interpretation (or hermeneutic) is important for understanding many of his earlier speeches and later addresses alike. In some ways his biblical hermeneutic remains relatively consistent throughout his career; but it also evolves, especially late in his life as his rhetoric grows more radical. His later orations generally promote radical ideas housed within a framework constructed from myriad biblical genres and texts. "I've Been to the Mountaintop" is simply the most brilliant and the most fully realized of these orations.

Instead of propounding a single, commanding biblical motif, as he often does in sermons, King creates a bright tapestry in his last speech, weaving important threads spun from many different biblical books. After a brief introduction, he discusses the parting of the Red Sea—the jaw-dropping wonder of the Exodus. Later he refers to the oppressive pharaoh. After reiterating and adapting one declaration from Jeremiah and two from Amos, he adjusts a passage from (Third) Isaiah that resurfaces in Luke before devoting thirty-nine sentences to explicating the Parable of the Good Samaritan (also in Luke). Alluding to his own possible assassination, he finishes by openly comparing himself—a thirty-nine-year-old man—to the elderly Moses who, Deuteronomy explains, has reached Mount Pisgah and lies on the verge of death. King thus uses his last oration to interpret a series of characters and themes from Exodus, Deuteronomy, (Third) Isaiah, Jeremiah, Amos, and Luke while simultaneously inspiring protestors in Memphis.

For his final sentence, King quotes the first line of Julia Ward Howe's familiar "Battle Hymn of the Republic," whose extended lyrics he recited in an important speech following the march from Selma to Montgomery in 1965. Writing her anthem at the height of the Civil War, Howe reworked images of judgment and eschatology that appear in many biblical texts, including Joel, (Third) Isaiah, Jeremiah, Ezekiel, and Revelation. The first line of Howe's song—and the entire lyrics, for that matter—clearly refers to the Second Coming of Christ, the culminating theme of Christian scripture. Both in 1965 and in his final speech, King does not sample this beloved hymn simply to rouse his audience. Rather, he uses the lyrics to point toward nothing less than the Kingdom of God, the Second Coming, and the end of history.

In his last address, King interrogates and interprets many of the most important rhetorical forms and genres of the Bible: Pentateuchal narrative, Hebrew prophecy, testimony, parable, judgment, and eschatology. He does so for the purpose of analyzing local, national, and international race relations and cheering blue-collar workers in Memphis.

Each of King's biblical quotations and allusions, however brief, arrives heavily freighted with associations. When addressing the heavily churched African American community, King, like other preachers, does not tediously explicate every biblical reference. Instead, he counts on a certain level of biblical familiarity—of biblical literacy, if you will—among his listeners, who normally include many faithful churchgoers and Christian ministers as well. He recognizes that many of his religious listeners thoroughly comprehend an array of biblical plots, characters, symbols, ideas, and motifs. So when he mentions the Egyptian pharaoh, he does not note the pharaoh's obduracy or detail his misdeeds. Everyone already knows about that obduracy and those misdeeds. For him, simply to mention Pharaoh is to evoke listeners' associations with the Egyptian ruler. In order to approach King's last speech, one must understand the many biblical associations that he summons for his audience. To miss these associations is to miss the speech. To understand these associations is to grasp his biblical hermeneutic, which still speaks to us today.

In this book I argue that, in "I've Been to the Mountaintop," King's biblical hermeneutic enables him to reimagine the strike in Memphis. In other words, I claim that, by developing his system of interpreting the Bible, King gains the capacity to reinvent a labor dispute and an entire city. I maintain that he defines and enacts his last speech as biblical narrative and biblical prophecy—a definition and an enactment that empowers him to reconfigure the strike. I further contend that his interpretation of the Bible reanimates and reconceptualizes the interpretation that numerous biblical authors themselves supply for earlier biblical narratives. In addition I explain that King's interpretation revives earlier African American interpretations of biblical narratives, especially the Exodus, while strongly challenging fossilized views of Moses, Hebrew prophecy, Jesus, and the Second Coming.

This book also explores the setting for King's final speech—Mason Temple, the national headquarters for the Church of God in Christ, a large denomination of African American Pentecostals. Unfortunately, Mason Temple has been largely ignored and sometimes outright misrepresented by those who write about King. I argue that it is an absolute marvel of design made possible by Pentecostal loyalists and crafted by an amazing architect who deserves kudos rather than the obscurity that he has received. African Americans controlled no other building in the entire South that could rival Mason Temple as a venue for a speech. None. As I explain, the often unnoticed devotion of Pentecostal loyalists and the stunning talents of this unsung architect made Mason Temple possible and also made King's speech possible. Without the uniquely suitable setting of Mason Temple, King would have merely stayed in his room at the Lorraine Motel that night. He would never have given any speech at all.

Further, this book reveals, for the first time, published sources for an important portion of King's last speech—liberal Protestant texts that he borrows for his explication of the Parable of the Good Samaritan.

Here I also weigh King's rhetorical relationship with Judaism—an extremely important topic that very few scholars have contemplated.[53] I maintain that King strongly and unequivocally affirms that Judaism serves as the secure and indispensable foundation for Christianity. His rhetorical interpretation of Judaism matters enormously because it reverses long centuries of efforts by many Christian leaders to trivialize the richness of Judaism and to dismiss its importance, often with tragic consequences.

Chapter 1 explores King's route to Memphis. I analyze the religion of King's boyhood and a speech by King's father. I investigate a centuries-old tradition of African American biblical interpretation that extended from American slaves and abolitionists to such important twentieth-century figures as C. L. Franklin and Fred Shuttlesworth. Further, I consider King's career-long rhetorical relationship to that tradition, especially in such key works as "I Have a Dream" and "Our God Is Marching On."

Chapter 2 considers King's relationship to a largely white, liberal pulpit tradition, especially in regard to the explanation of the Parable of the Good Samaritan that King offers in a 1963 sermon and in "I've Been to the Mountaintop." I unveil King's unacknowledged and unnoticed source for most of the long explication of the Parable of the Good Samaritan that appears in "I've Been to the Mountaintop."[54] Just as King borrowed from this author, so did this author borrow from his predecessors. Several of these writers—including King—replayed liberal Protestant commonplaces about this famous parable. As I explain, these commonplaces began to appear in print at least as early as 1841. King delivered "I've Been to the Mountaintop" without notes. Even so, I demonstrate that, *at least as early as 1841*, a whole string of Protestant authors began *composing* a portion of King's final oration. Although they wrote about the parable before King was born, their contribution to his final speech is important and deserves to be recognized. Despite the tendency of some King scholars to ignore or downplay the sources for his oratory, these sources matter because his audiences listened to their words. In much of King's discourse, including his last oration, his use of others' words contributed importantly to his persuasiveness. While describing King's relationship to this material, I also explain how he *transformed* it for a decidedly new purpose.

Chapter 3 considers Mason Temple, the location for "I've Been to the Mountaintop." As I explain, because this facility accommodated a larger crowd than any other available facility, Ralph Abernathy was able to lure King out of the Lorraine Motel that night to speak. The large, yet paradoxically compact sanctuary in Mason Temple enabled King's exuberant audience to push him into greater eloquence than he normally achieved. This chapter explores Mason Temple and the African American men and women who, despite racism and severe economic hardships during the Great Depression, succeeded in constructing their stellar edifice. I also examine its ingenious design.

In addition, Chapter 3 relates King's oratory to the Pentecostal setting for "I've Been to the Mountaintop." Drawing on the scholarship of Cheryl Sanders and Anthea Butler (among others), I examine King's speech alongside the Pentecostal beliefs and practices of some of his listeners, whose religious customs and language helped shape their understanding of the speech. I further argue that, among some listeners, the memory of a Pentecostal bishop—and the sight of his tomb—also inflected their reception of "I've Been to the Mountaintop."

Chapter 4 investigates King's oratorical use of Exodus imagery as he imagines traveling in a time machine to visit sublime historical events. As I explain, this fantasy of time travel enables King to summon the stupendous, multifaceted importance that biblical writers assign to the Exodus. Journeying in a time machine also helps him treat the Bible as an ongoing drama that shaped the Protestant Reformation and American emancipation. Finally, venturing through time helps him refashion the Exodus as a frame for contemporary events, especially the Memphis strike.

Chapter 5 examines King's quotation of passages from Amos and Jeremiah for the purpose of constructing himself as a contemporary prophet. Although many people label King a "prophet," they treat that designation as self-evident and fail to justify or explain it. But, failing to treat prophecy as a simple phenomenon, the many authors of the Hebrew Bible composed fifteen prophetic books (including three very long books) that treat hundreds of years of prophecy and history. (Prophets appear in other books as well.) Those who call King a prophet rarely, if ever, address these two questions: How can King or anyone else evoke biblical prophecy after the Scientific Revolution, the Enlightenment, and modernity? Can anyone claim to be a biblical prophet in the twentieth century? What interpretation of history would someone need to provide in order to render biblical prophecy? Here I supply the first detailed explication of the rhetorical dynamics of prophecy that King invokes as he claims the mantle of prophet. I also address his ability to evoke biblical prophecy for the purpose of reinventing the sanitation workers' strike and Memphis itself.

Chapter 6 turns to King's use of two passages from Luke—both of which he cites in order to reconstitute the relationship between Judaism and Christianity and to reframe Memphis. The first passage is lines from (Third) Isaiah that the author of Luke reworks and that King revives in the process of explaining his own role in Memphis. The second is the Parable of the Good Samaritan, which King interprets, in part, by defining the trash collectors as the newest roadside victims in need of a Good Samaritan. I also probe the relation between King's interpretation of the parable and his recollection of the nearly fatal stabbing that he suffered in 1958. King's account of these victims—the wounded traveler in the parable, oppressed garbage workers in Memphis, and himself when he was stabbed—builds toward, informs, and shapes his concluding words about his own possible death. To lop off the conclusion and only listen to it is to misconstrue the speech. One can only grasp his concluding theme of victimization and death by comprehending the *entire* interpretation of victimization and death that he has provided throughout the address.

Eyeing this conclusion, I devote Chapter 7 to exploring King's dramatic reconfiguration of the Exodus, Hebrew oracles, Revelation, and the lyrics of Julia Ward Howe's "Battle Hymn of the Republic."

Chapter 8 explores King's general interpretation of the Bible in "I've Been to the Mountaintop" and throughout his career. I argue that King wholeheartedly affirms that Judaism serves as the indispensable wellspring for Christianity. This chapter also considers the implications of King's explication for biblical interpretation today.

One could ask, why does King's speech still matter? Literary critic Mikhail Bakhtin argues that stellar poems, plays, and novels surpass what the authors' contemporaries are able to understand. Such literature, Bakhtin explains, lives in what he calls "great time," which allows, in his words, "the infinite and unfinalized dialogue in which no meaning dies."[55] Bakhtinian scholar Juliana Claassens declares, "According to this principle, great works such as Shakespeare continue to live in the distant future." Claassens adds, "The fullness of these works" cannot be understood immediately, but "is revealed only in great time."[56]

One certainly understands a sterling oration, in part, by plumbing a speaker's relationship to an immediate audience. In this book, I probe specific dimensions of the speaker-audience relationship at Mason Temple, including numerous, important dimensions that other writers have overlooked. Yet one cannot confine the significance of a speech to the reactions of its immediate listeners. Like extraordinary literary works, addresses by Pericles, Cicero, Queen Elizabeth I, and Abraham Lincoln also live in "great time." Frederick Douglass attributes his astonishing oratorical prowess to his experience devouring a collection of addresses by people who had died long before he was born. Those speeches definitely live in great time. Of course, one understands Douglass's great speech "What to the Slave Is the Fourth of July?" in part by examining the atmosphere and audience in Rochester on the day that he delivered it. But that oration is so rich and so sophisticated that its meaning exceeds even what Douglass's most informed and most sympathetic contemporaries could grasp.

Almost everyone who heard "I've Been to the Mountaintop" was sympathetic to King and extremely well informed about events in Memphis. His listeners were the strikers and marchers, their friends and family members, supportive clergy, members of the NAACP, and civic leaders. They read the newspapers, watched television, and listened to each other and to the mayor. And they cared enough to drive through a heavy rainstorm in order to hear King. Many of them also dove into the Bible at home, studied it at weekly Sunday School classes, and heard Bible-based sermons in weekly worship services. In those services, church leaders read directly from the Bible; and biblical passages, phrases, and concepts were often adapted and repeated in hymns, spirituals, gospel songs, testimonies, litanies, responsive readings, and prayers. Many of King's auditors understood his biblical references and associations and reacted passionately to his speech. Yet, although his audience was knowledgeable and passionate, his speech did not end when he ignited Mason Temple with his last public words. His address continues to live in great time, and we can and should expand the unfinalized dialogue about it.

In an attempt to extend such a dialogue, I analyze "I've Been to the Mountaintop" by adapting rhetorical theories and rhetorical analysis from Kenneth Burke, Paul Ricoeur, Walter Brueggemann, and Mikhail Bakhtin, among others. Although Bakhtin developed his theories mainly to interpret novels—not the Bible or oratory—his ideas, when adjusted, help explain the biblical interpretation that King developed, in part by reimagining a popular form of African American oratory known as the jeremiad.

King and the civil rights movement began to pry open hermetically sealed windows, allowing new breezes to freshen the air inside the cloistered walls of academic biblical criticism. Scholars have yet to weigh many of the gigantic contributions that he and other civil rights agitators have made to understanding the Bible. In particular, King scholars and biblical scholars fail to notice his emphasis on the body as an important principle for interpreting the Bible. Further, he implicitly, but strongly, challenges many insular biblical scholars to acknowledge that they do not maintain exclusive rights to scrutinizing the Bible. Instead, King implies, researchers speak in dialogue with many other stakeholders, including African American pastors and congregations.

King's heavy reliance on the Bible also challenges secular liberals and leftists to reconsider the role that Judeo-Christian rhetoric can sometime play in promoting social, economic, and political change in the United States.[57]

As King asks his audience to revisit scripture from Exodus to Revelation, he constructs himself as a biblical prophet who depicts a garbage strike not as a mere local squabble, but as nothing less than the latest enactment of the centuries-old clash between good and evil. He does so by arguing, in effect, that, while incidentally an account of events in the ancient Middle East, the Bible is not a frozen testimony to God's mighty deeds in the dusty past. He contends, in effect, that the Bible is only incidentally a book. Instead, he claims, the Bible is an ongoing drama that engulfs all human life in Memphis and everywhere else. In this view, a labor conflict in a mid-sized city amounts to nothing less than the newest manifestation of a titanic biblical struggle and God's newest opportunity to rejuvenate those crushed by American pharaohs.

CHAPTER I

I Left Atlanta

King's Religious Rhetoric

Not far from downtown Atlanta, people milled around grocery stores, banks, insurance companies, churches, and funeral parlors that clustered around Sweet Auburn Avenue. On Sunday mornings, some folks dressed in their finery and bustled toward Ebenezer Baptist Church, where they anticipated hearing the "powerful, thundering style" of their preacher, Rev. A. D. Williams.[1] The formidable Williams headed the Atlanta Missionary Baptist Association and served as branch president for a nascent organization with a long title—the National Association for the Advancement of Colored People. He once traveled to Cleveland to deliver an address to an early national convention of the NAACP.[2]

During those same years, James King labored as an impoverished sharecropper in rural Georgia. Unable to escape the straitjacket of white supremacy, he remained on a farm and, in his frustration, turned to alcohol. His son's hardscrabble childhood included a meager education and teasing from other children because he sometimes slept in a mule barn. Barely able to read and write, the boy took to the pulpit at age fifteen in a tiny rural church whose deacons did not know the alphabet.[3] As Michael King matured, he gravitated to Atlanta in search of a congregation for his folk preaching and in quest for more education. There he met and courted Alberta Williams, the daughter of A. D. Williams.

When the couple married, A. D. Williams embraced Michael King and welcomed him into his relatively large house. After a few years, Williams died; soon, the young King assumed the position of minister of Ebenezer Baptist Church. The lives of the Williams and King family revolved around Ebenezer, which, like other African American churches, served as a haven from white supremacy. Despite the catastrophe of the Great Depression, Michael King held his congregation intact and eventually changed his name to Martin Luther King Sr. His son became Martin Luther King Jr. As her husband preached, Alberta King played the organ and helped lead the choir while their children attended several hours of worship services and Sunday School each week. King Jr. grew up listening not only to the sermons of his father, but also to those of guest ministers at Ebenezer Church, William Holmes Borders of nearby Wheat Street Baptist Church, and other pastors of note in Atlanta.

In this chapter I consider the religious roots of King Jr. in Atlanta, focusing especially on an oration that his father delivered there in 1940. I also concentrate on slaves' and later African Americans' tendency to narrate their own lives by shoving the Exodus and other biblical stories out of the past and into the present. Further, I weigh the African American jeremiad, a durable rhetorical form developed by abolitionists that enables orators to decry racism while issuing an updated version of biblical prophecy. As I note, King extends the jeremiad into the 1960s through such speeches as "I Have a Dream." I end this chapter by analyzing "Our God Is Marching On," the address that King delivered at the conclusion of the fifty-mile march from Selma to Montgomery. I maintain that King used passage after passage of this speech to explain the civil rights struggles of 1965 as a continuation of the biblical Exodus.

Like Williams and many others, King Sr. adopted the rhetorical fireworks of folk preaching and conservative positions on most matters of evangelical Christian doctrine. Like Williams, King Sr. also embraced a Social Gospel and emerged as a community leader who labored against racism and segregation. For example, in 1939 he led a march of protestors seeking the right to vote.[4]

By almost all accounts, churches have been (and may still be) the most important African American institutions, partly because whites could not directly control them. By almost all accounts, preaching and singing have been vital in defining African American religious life and in binding congregations—and the entire race—together. But, whereas many old and beautiful spirituals, hymns, and gospel songs have been preserved, relatively few African American sermons before the 1950s have survived. Thousands and thousands of sermons were preached, but only a tiny percentage of them were published or recorded. Lost forever are thousands of homilies by many reputable preachers who contributed mightily to sustaining their communities during the weed-choked decades of auction blocks, overseers' whips, rape, lynching, disfranchisement, poverty, and segregation.

Scholars would like to know more about the sermons that King Jr. may have heard during his childhood and adolescence. But, unfortunately, very few of these sermons appear to have survived. King Sr.'s keynote address to a conference of the Atlanta Missionary Baptist Association in 1940 is an extremely rare exception. In this oration, the elder King interprets lines from (Third) Isaiah and Luke:

> Quite often we say the church has no place in politics, forgetting the words of the Lord, "The spirit of the Lord is upon me because he hath anointed me to preach the Gospel to the poor, he hath sent me to heal the broken-hearted, to preach deliverance to the captives, and the recovering of sight to the blind, to set at liberty them that are bruised." ...
> In this we find we are to do something about the broken-hearted, poor, unemployed, the captive, the blind, and the bruised.
> How can people be happy without jobs, food, shelter, and clothes? ...
> God hasten the time when every minister will become a registered voter and a part of every movement for the betterment of our people. ...
> As ministers a great responsibility rests upon us as leaders. We cannot expect our people to register and become citizens until we as leaders set the standard.[5]

Responding, one imagines, to the impact of the Great Depression, King Sr. here explains that the Bible refuses to separate the spiritual from the physical. Rather, he notes, Jesus testifies that "the spirit of the Lord" compels a ministry to those who are broken-hearted, captive, blind, bruised, hungry, or homeless. Further, not only does the elder King choose scripture that articulates concern for the poor, he also rejects handouts as a solution. Instead of pleading for charity, he contends that the deprived need jobs so they can become self-supporting. In addition he explicitly rejects the view that the church should function simply as a private agency that offers social services. Instead, he argues, scripture demands that the church should directly involve itself in politics. He criticizes African American ministers who fail to register to vote—a failure that indicates the refusal to join "every movement" to improve the lives of "our people." He thus intertwines the goal of ending poverty with the goal of eradicating segregation.

Significantly, King Jr. quotes this same passage from (Third) Isaiah and

Luke in "I've Been to the Mountaintop," a speech in which, like his father, he blends the goals of ending poverty and eradicating segregation.

Although scholars cannot pinpoint many of the details of the young King's earliest training as a preacher, much of his oratory relates strongly to pulpit practices that are identifiably African American. Some of these practices can be traced to slavery, and understanding them contributes greatly to understanding "I've Been to the Mountaintop."

During the eighteenth and nineteenth centuries, white southerners interpreted the Bible and Christianity as pillars of slavery. In addition they often prohibited slaves from learning how to read and write. Despite such a formidable obstacle, slave preachers and lyricists managed not only to read the Bible, but also to re-envision it. They often prized biblical heroes, including the Hebrew slaves in Egypt, whom they viewed as contemporaneous with themselves. In "Go Down, Moses" and many other spirituals, they depicted southern aristocrats as autocratic pharaohs and themselves as anguished Israelites. Slaves also construed Harriet Tubman, Abraham Lincoln, and the Union army as Moses figures who were guiding an Exodus.[6] Wishing that slaves would pay more attention to Jesus, a white chaplain in the Union army unhappily noted, "There is no part of the Bible with which [slaves] are so familiar as the story of the deliverance of Israel. Moses is their ideal of all that is high, and noble, and perfect." The chaplain explained that slaves longed for "a second Moses who would eventually lead them out of their prison-house of bondage."[7] Albert Raboteau comments: "Exodus functioned as an archetypal myth for the slaves," for whom the "sacred history of God's liberation of his people would be or was being reenacted in the American South." He adds:

> In the ecstasy of worship, time and distance collapsed, and the slaves became the children of Israel. With the Hebrews, they traveled dry-shod through the Red Sea; they, too, saw Pharaoh's army "get drownded"; they stood beside Moses on Mount Pisgah and gazed out over the Promised Land; they crossed Jordan under Joshua and marched with him round the walls of Jericho. Their prayers for deliverance resonated with the experiential power of these liturgical dramas.[8]

As James Cone explains, "A separate faith emerged among black Christians in the United States because they believed that the God of the Exodus, the prophets, and Jesus did not condone the mistreatment they received from whites."[9]

In addition northern abolitionists sometimes invoked the Bible as a touchstone against slavery. Sojourner Truth, for example, reflected on the Bible as she constructed highly sophisticated and witty arguments against slavery and in favor of women's equality. Likening American slaves to Hebrews subjected to Egyptian bondage, Frederick Douglass, Henry Highland Garnet, Absalom Jones, Frances Ellen Watkins, and other stellar African American orators yearned for a new Exodus.[10] Phillips Brooks and certain other white abolitionists also wondered aloud about a possible American Exodus.

After the Civil War, orators and ordinary African Americans continued to treat the Bible as a lens for interpreting their own condition. Former slaves who moved to Kansas christened themselves "Exodusters." In the early decades of the twentieth century, African Americans sometimes viewed their Great Migration to the North as another Exodus. Through their interpretation of the Exodus, entire generations of blacks chose, as J. Kameron Carter explains, "to inhabit Israel's covenantal story."[11]

African Americans sometimes explained other immediate experiences as biblical as well. William Seymour, the sparkplug of the Azusa Street Rival in 1906, C. H. Mason, and other African American and white Pentecostals commonly interpreted their own intense worship experience—often marked by "speaking in tongues"—as the rebirth of the original Pentecost as recorded in Acts.[12] For Pentecostals, the biblical Pentecost becomes a vivid, immediate experience.

As many African Americans migrated north during the late nineteenth and early twentieth centuries, they developed more varieties of Christianity. Some ministers ignored social conditions and propounded relatively simple versions of sin and salvation to those mainly concerned about entering heaven after death. Yet, beyond the middle of the twentieth century, other African American churchgoers continued to identify with characters from the Hebrew Bible. In the mid-1950s, Rev. C. L. Franklin, who later allied himself with King, asserted that a new Moses would eventually lead those thwarted by segregation. During the early 1960s, some African Americans in Mississippi revered one civil rights pioneer, Robert Moses, as the leader of a new Exodus. When introducing Robert Moses to give a speech, Dave Dennis elaborately paralleled him to the biblical Moses.[13] In 1963, delivering a eulogy for Medgar Evers, Rev. Fred Shuttlesworth lauded Evers as a Moses who "saw from afar that Promised Land into which his people must enter."[14] Others hailed King as a Moses. "Go Down, Moses" proved popular among song leaders, including Fannie Lou Hamer. In 1963, organizers distributed song sheets for "Go Down, Moses" at the March on Washington—the largest single protest of the civil rights movement.

Shuttlesworth, King's close ally during the crucible of Birmingham, often linked African Americans to the biblical Hebrews. In 1956 he was at home in bed when racists tossed a bomb against the outside wall of his bedroom. Even though the explosion demolished the bed and most of the room, Shuttlesworth somehow emerged from the incident unscathed. He portrayed his survival as a miracle straight from scripture: "Well, God just brought the Bible up to date. You don't have to go back to Daniel in the lion's den or the boys in the fiery furnace."[15] Six years later he developed a lengthy equation between Birmingham and Babylon:

> Can we discern any difference between today's Birmingham and yesterday's Babylon? Nay, except that Babylon's might was her army, and Birmingham claims her strength in the sinews of coal and steel. Babylon thought more of her swinging gardens than the God of the universe; Birmingham prides her zoo more highly than she values her Negroes. Babylon held God's chosen people captive and demanded of them mirth while inflicting misery. For it is written, "They that carried us away captive required of us a song; and they that wasted us required of us mirth, saying 'Sing us one of the songs of Zion.'" (Psalms 137:3) Birmingham and Alabama persecute us because we fight segregation and demand that we be happy. . . . But Negroes have read that the "Earth is the Lord's and the fullness thereof." And we—even though persecuted and cast down—don't mind singing the Lord's song in strange circumstances. And for six long dreary years, we have walked and talked with Him who "giveth songs in the night." Babylon became mad and was destroyed. Alabama and Birmingham have become drunk off the wine of the Southern way of life and have become mad with power.[16]

When James Bevel, King's aide and movement strategist, spoke at a memorial service for Jimmie Lee Jackson near Selma, Alabama, he equated Jackson with James, a biblical martyr whose death is recounted in Acts. In the same eulogy, Bevel proposed a fifty-mile hike from Selma to Montgomery, the state capitol, to demand voting rights. In Montgomery, Bevel declared, the marchers could confront a powerful ruler, Governor George Wallace. Identifying with the biblical Esther, the excitable Bevel insisted: "'I must go to see the king!'"[17]

A few years earlier, Rev. Kelly Miller Smith, a King acquaintance and catalyst for the Lunch Counter Sit-Ins in Nashville, told his congregation that activists were now re-enacting the last week in the life of Christ:

> The students sat at the lunch counters alone to eat, and when refused service, to wait and pray. And as they sat there on that Southern Mount of Olives, the Roman soldiers, garbed in the uniforms of Nashville policemen and wielding night sticks, came and led the praying children away. As they walked down the streets, through a red light, and toward Golgotha, the segregationist mob shouted jeers, pushed and shoved them, and spat in their faces, but the suffering students never said a mumbling word. Once the martyr mounts the Cross, wears the crown of thorns, and feels the pierce of the sword in his side, there is no turning back.[18]

White agitators sometimes soaked immediate events in the Bible as well. In his eulogy for James Chaney, a civil rights martyr in Mississippi, Ed King announced:

> The cross means that we will have a new beginning, a new resurrection, a new birth. That over this blood which is mingled with the blood of the children of Birmingham, the people killed by the Klan in southern Mississippi, of Medgar Evers, John Kennedy, and of Jesus Christ and all who have died for the love of their brothers, this blood can free us all and we must share this freedom and forgiveness with the white people of Mississippi, and from Mississippi with all of America.[19]

A number of crucial activists—notably, Ella Baker, Ruby Doris Robinson, and Robert Moses—disdained the top-down, patriarchal model of leadership implied in the yearning for a single, Moses-like leader authorized by God. And some civil rights advocates, especially within the Student Nonviolent Coordinating Committee—preferred secular language. But, as Shuttlesworth, Bevel, Ed King, and other orators recognized, southern blacks often responded to contemporary, Bible-based narratives about racial equality. The community did so, in part, because of what Shuttlesworth's biographer, Andrew Manis, calls a "characteristically African American theology that made no distinction between the sacred and the secular or between the churchly and the civic."[20]

During the 1950s and 1960s African American also noticed Revelation. In 1963 James Baldwin raised an apocalyptic warning when he penned his best-selling treatise on race, *The Fire Next Time*. In such speeches as "God's Judgment on White America," Malcolm X summoned imagery from various biblical texts, including Revelation, when he proclaimed the imminent demise of white exploitation. Reflecting on eschatological metaphors from Revelation, gospel diva Clara Ward sang "Twelve Gates to the City." Spying other visionary motifs in Revelation, William Herbert Brewster, renowned gospel composer and choir director, contributed "The Book of the Seven Seals." White songwriters and folk singers lent a sense of urgency to the racial movement by injecting images of the biblical endtime. Peter, Paul, and Mary sang "If I Had My Way" and "Very Last Day" while Bob Dylan added "When the Ship Comes In" and "A Hard Rain's Gonna Fall." Barry McGuire's apocalyptic "Eve of Destruction" rocketed to the top of the Billboard charts.

Within the civil rights movement, most gospel singers, popular singers, orators, and writers did not devote much time to theorizing or justifying their interpretations of the Bible. White activist Robert Spike, however, did explain the importance of viewing the Bible as a contemporary document. A King ally, he served for several years as head of the Commission on Religion and Race, sponsored by the National Council of Churches. In 1963, noting that civil rights provided new challenges for conscientious preachers, he declared:

> All the theological study that can be managed surely ought to be encouraged. Questions, however, have to be raised about the nature of the theological study. I personally know of men who are whizzes in Biblical studies in their Sunday School classes, who also head units of [a white supremacist organization].... Christian theological study is not defined alone by its content—that is doctrines, and expositions, spun in a vacuum.... Christian theological study is basically an attempt to find an answer to two questions: "What is God doing in the world?" and "What should my brethren and I be doing in response to his deeds?" The awakening that is needed among many laymen is the awakening to the fact that God is moving in these moments of history. He is in the struggle for freedom in every corner of the world. He is shaking the nations.

In an apparent critique of modern biblical scholarship, Spike added, "The Bible can really only be read when it is read as commentary on our times as well as ancient Judea."[21]

Like many of his African American predecessors and contemporaries, King sometimes places contemporary actors into the coordinates of biblical plots. He invokes the Exodus so often that one scholar, Gary Selby, wrote an entire book about his use of the Exodus narrative. He spoke at least twice at a church named "Mount Pisgah"—the peak from which Moses spied the Promised Land just before dying.[22] After being convicted for violating a law during the Montgomery Bus Boycott, he summoned the Exodus: "You don't get to the Promised Land without going through the wilderness."[23] In his 1957 homily, "The Birth of a New Nation," he interpreted Egyptian slavery as a common, albeit temporary condition and observed that oppressed people "cannot be satisfied with Egypt."[24] Lauding the overthrow of British rule in Ghana, he extolled Kwame Nkrumah, an anti-colonialist leader whose new nation was "breaking aloose from Egypt" until it "crossed the Red Sea" and would soon "confront its wilderness."[25] King then described African Americans as "breaking aloose from an evil Egypt trying to move through the wilderness toward the promised land of cultural integration."[26] In the same sermon he paralleled the travails of Egyptian bondage to the crucifixion of Christ and compared the arrival in the Promised Land to the glory of Easter.[27]

In 1956 King debuted "Death of Evil on the Seashore," a sermon on Exodus that he adapted from Phillips Brooks and later included in his homiletic collection, *Strength to Love*. In this homily King likened Moses to Mahatma Gandhi and other anti-colonialist rebels:

> In nearly every territory in Asia and Africa a courageous Moses pleaded passionately for the freedom of his people. For more than twenty years Mahatma Gandhi unrelentingly urged British viceroys, governors general, prime ministers, and kings to let his people go. Like the pharaohs of old, the British leaders turned deaf ears to these agonizing pleas.[28]

King continued: "Twenty-five years ago there were only three independent countries in the whole continent of Africa, but today thirty-two countries are independent.... The Red Sea has opened."[29] He added that after American "pharaohs" ignored "many a Moses" who protested American segregation, the US Supreme Court finally "opened the Red Sea" in its landmark *Brown* decision that mandated racial integration in all public schools. Noting the effectiveness of King's oratory, activist Septima Clark remarked, "As [King] talked about Moses, and leading the people out, and getting the people into the place where the Red Sea would cover them, he would just make you see them. You believed it."[30] After King's death, two Memphis strikers compared him to Moses.[31]

In private conversations, King also used biblical categories and stories to explain current events. After mentioning the house bombing incident that somehow left Fred Shuttlesworth unharmed, his biographer observes, "In a later conversation with Fred, Martin Luther King offered the opinion that if surviving the bomb 'wasn't God making himself plain, there's no way he can.'"[32] According to Stewart Burns, King, in a staff meeting, narrated by memory a story from Numbers. In this passage, Moses dispatched a dozen spies to explore Canaan, only two of whom, upon their return, truthfully championed Canaan as a land of milk and honey.[33] Burns explains that, upon hearing this story, one staffer declared that Alabama would become a land of milk and honey when everyone could vote. At that point, Burns adds, King directed two loyalists to spy in dangerous Lowndes County, a possible site of agitation for voting rights.[34]

King's typological interpretation of the Exodus in "The Birth of a New Nation" and "Death of Evil on the Seashore" extends and reconfigures a traditional African American biblical interpretation that depicted blacks as slaves groaning in the Egypt of the slave-owning South. In his final speech King adapts both hermeneutics.

On occasion Ralph Abernathy and King directly summoned eschatological imagery from Revelation in relation to events in the civil rights movement.[35] Recruiting participants for the Poor People's Campaign, King declared: "And I can hear somebody else sayin', 'I see 'em coming. How many?'... And pretty soon I hear a voice, 'I looked and I watched and it seems to me it's a number that no man can number.'"[36] In Revelation the phrase "a number that no man can number" refers to souls in eternity waving palm branches before the throne of heaven. By re-employing the phrase "a number that no man can number," King cast an aura of holiness around volunteers for his new crusade.

Although the white chaplain in the Union army noticed African Americans' fascination with the Exodus, many whites—both before and after the Civil War—did not. For their part, a few well-known researchers grumbled that ministers and parishioners grossly neglected sacred Hebrew texts, treating them almost as though they did not matter. In 1966 James Barr complained that churchgoers "doubted" the importance of the entire Hebrew scripture.[37] Similarly, in 1979, Brevard Childs growled at Christian pastors and congregations for ignoring the Hebrew Bible altogether or for treating it merely as "background material" for the Christian revelation.[38] Focusing on white churches, Barr and Childs utterly failed to notice that many African Americans had, for well over one hundred years, placed enormous emphasis on the story of the Exodus and on other Hebrew narratives. Joining Barr and Childs, others also ignored African American perspectives on the Bible. For many generations, nineteenth- and twentieth-century experts on ancient Hebrew and Greek held forth in the cloistered chambers of liberal, largely white Protestant seminaries, privileging themselves as knowledgeable interpreters of scripture. They neglected other views on sacred texts, including African American perspectives. Ordinary white clergy and laity generally joined white academics in bypassing African American treatments of the Hebrew Bible.

During the early and middle twentieth century, Walter Rauschenbusch, Harry Emerson Fosdick, and other influential Protestants (often in the Northeast) advocated a powerful Social Gospel aimed at poverty and other social ills. But many white pastors and workaday Christians—especially in the South, Midwest, and West—froze prophecy and petrified the Exodus. As Barr and Childs observed, white preachers and congregations often treated Moses and the prophets as background figures. Whites were obviously not enslaved, so they did not identify with the Hebrews trapped in Egypt. In addition, whites sometimes viewed the prophets simply as eccentric precursors to Jesus. During the 1950s and 1960s, Billy Graham, a young evangelist, and other Southern Baptists emphasized individual salvation through Christ, not Hebrew themes, as the heart of Christianity. Many white preachers and congregants, in effect, treated Christian prophecy as a phenomenon that ended right after the Christian Bible was written—or, if not then, then certainly by the end of the Protestant Reformation or the Pilgrims' landing. And many apparently viewed the Second Coming of Christ—an electrifying topic of early Christian prophecy—as an event that God had emplotted thousands of years earlier. They assumed that the Second Coming had nothing whatever to do with American race relations.

Such views reflect the overall conservative tone that prevailed in most of the United States between 1945 and the early 1960s. Despite such exhilarating phenomena as Beat poetry, Abstract Expressionist painting, and bebop jazz, the 1950s were a time when Americans often glorified conformity. Facing a nuclear standoff with the Soviet Union that followed the shock of World War II, younger and older generations alike frequently sought middle-class lives that were respectable and predictable. Carol Polsgrove explains that the conformist atmosphere of the Cold War fell like a blanket on many of the nation's most gifted intellectuals and writers. During the period of McCarthyism, many parishioners had no desire to hear their rabbis, priests, and ministers invoke Hebrew prophecy or criticize anti-communist excesses, Dwight Eisenhower, or America.

Instead, when many devout whites attended to the Hebrew scripture, they often focused on its most highly memorable tales, characters, and motifs. After the account of the conquest of Jericho, biblical narratives about the religious and political history of the Israelites frequently become complicated and vexed. Responding to the intricacies of Middle Eastern history, the Hebrew Bible relates many decidedly jumbled plots about royal brinkmanship, territorial disputes, border flashpoints, tectonic power shifts, and convulsive wars. These narratives feature sizable historical chasms and editorial fault lines as well as overlap and congruence. Sermonizing on the meaning of the Bible is easier if one can avoid explaining frequently convoluted, decidedly incomplete storylines about a bewildering variety of tribes and nations. Preachers and Sunday School teachers could wax more easily on Noah's ark, Jacob's ladder, David's wandering eye, or Samson's haircut than on the reign of Omri, Jehoahaz, Hezekiah, Sennacherib, Jereboam II, or Tiglath-Pileser I, not to mention Tiglath-Pileser III.

African American church leaders often seized the same stories. At other times black ministers and other public figures constructed themselves as inheritors of the Mosaic tradition and as prophets. They did so mainly by generating and honing an oratorical form that was named after Jeremiah— the African American jeremiad. Frederick Douglass, Henry Highland Garnet, Frances Ellen Watkins, and John Mercer Langston all wielded the African American jeremiad for the purpose of bitterly assailing slavery. The most famous of all abolitionist speeches, Douglass's "What to the Slave Is the Fourth of July," is a scintillating jeremiad. During the postbellum era, Frances Ellen Watkins Harper, Robert Elliot, Francis Grimke, Ida B. Wells, and Douglass updated the jeremiad as they acidly decried the systematic evils of lynching, sharecropping, and racial oppression. The routine eloquence of Douglass's jeremiads enabled him to become the most prominent black person in the world.

As David Howard-Pitney explains, Douglass and many other speakers filled their jeremiads with three basic components: promise, failure, and fulfillment. Before the Civil War, they attacked slavery by offering three claims: first, the founders established America on the promise of democracy and godliness; second, slavery grossly violated the promise; and third, the Declaration of Independence and the Bible articulate the promise and warrant its eventual fulfillment. By appealing to scriptural and patriotic authorities, orators invoked and reinforced American civil religion, which fuses allegiance to God and allegiance to the United States.

Of course, the underlying pattern of the jeremiad—promise, failure, and fulfillment—reflects a common discursive structure and theme in the Bible. Douglass and others simultaneously cite the Bible as their touchstone; pattern their speeches after the promise-failure-fulfillment arrangement in the Bible; and, like Hebrew prophets, decry the mighty because they plunder the poor. The biblical dimensions of the jeremiad enabled its most eminent practitioners to frame themselves as authoritative and prophetic. Many biblical texts indicate that the suffering of the Israelites can eventually yield to fulfillment and bliss. According to the jeremiad, African American suffering can eventually yield to fulfillment and bliss.

At age fifteen King entered an oratory contest and, surprisingly, this speech, "The Negro and the Constitution," was preserved. It is a straightforward jeremiad organized around promise, failure, and fulfillment. In it, he lambastes segregation by appealing to touchstones that were familiar to jeremiad orators, namely, the Bible, the Declaration of Independence, and the Emancipation Proclamation. The mature King delivered many eloquent jeremiads, including his first oration during the Montgomery Bus Boycott.[39] "I Have a Dream" is a classic jeremiad that closely resembles many efforts by Douglass, Harper, Grimke, Wells, and other sterling orators. In a number of ways, "The Negro and the Constitution"—delivered years before King attended graduate school—anticipates and strikingly parallels "I Have a Dream." Like his predecessors (and like himself at age fifteen), King constructs his jeremiads by fusing appeals to the Bible and to American civil religion.[40]

Those jeremiads often emphasized ultimate triumph. Throughout most of his career—from 1955 until 1966—King frequently expounded the theme of salvation by embracing Hebrew prophecies of hope. He often repeated the following memorable oracles:

> The lion and lamb shall lie down together.
> ([First] Isaiah 11:6; [Third] Isaiah 65:25)

Nations shall beat their swords into plowshares
And their spears into pruning hooks.
Nation shall not lift up sword after nation.
They will study war no more.
 ([First] Isaiah 2:4; Micah 4:3-4)

Every man will sit under his own vine and fig tree
And none shall be afraid.
 (Micah 4:4)[41]

Weeping may spend the night, but joy comes in the morning.
 (Psalms 30:5)

Every valley shall be exalted.
The mountains and hills will be laid low.
The rough places will be made plain.
The crooked places will be made straight.
The glory of the Lord shall be revealed
And all flesh shall see it together.
 ([Second] Isaiah 40:4-5; Luke 3:4-6)

King's absolute favorite lines Hebrew prophecy—indeed, from the entire Bible—present twin metaphors of beautiful simplicity:

Let justice roll down like waters
And righteousness like a mighty stream.
 (Amos 5:24)

King slid Amos 5:24 into his first oration during the Montgomery Bus Boycott; installed it as the cornerstone for his "How Should A Christian View Communism?"; cited it in "I Have a Dream" and "Letter from Birmingham Jail"; and replayed it again in such important, subsequent speeches as "Our God Is Marching On," "Beyond Vietnam," "Where Do We Go from Here?," and "The Dignity of Labor." Yet again he cited Amos 5:24 in "I've Been to the Mountaintop."

King's tendency to brighten his speeches with biblical visions of bliss and promise, rather than despair and loss, is especially evident in his continued reiteration of Amos 5:24. He constantly bypasses the preceding verse in

Amos:

> Shall not the day of the Lord be darkness and not light?
> Even very dark and no brightness in it?
> (Amos 5:20)

When repeating Amos 5:24, he also entirely avoids another nearby passage in Amos that treats the same topic—justice and righteousness:

> But you have turned justice into poison
> And the fruit of righteousness into wormwood.
> (Amos 6:12)

By constantly quoting hopeful lines from Amos 5:24 while ignoring other verses, King presents Amos very selectively. To read Amos is to navigate a text that, in chapter after chapter, teems with denunciations of wickedness and oracles of doom, relieved by only a few flecks of hope. The images of judgment that surround Amos 5:24 suggest the overall tone of Amos far more accurately than do the lines that King favors. Consider:

> So I will send a fire upon Judah
> And it shall devour the strongholds of Jerusalem.
> (Amos 2:5)

> Behold, the Lord God was calling for a judgment by fire,
> And it devoured the great deep and was eating up the land.
> (Amos 7:4)

> The end has come upon my people Israel;
> I will never again pass by them.
> The songs of the temple shall become wailings in that day,
> Says the Lord God;
> The dead bodies shall be many;
> In every place they shall be cast out in silence.
> (Amos 8:2-3)

Yet King never quotes these verses or the many other oracles of desolation—and fulminations against abomination—that fill most of Amos.

Further, when quoting Micah, King often prefers

> Every man will sit under his own vine and fig tree
> And none shall be afraid.
> (Micah 4:4)

while continually skirting the utterly shocking metaphors that appear in the preceding chapter of Micah and also in Jeremiah:

> Therefore because of you
> Zion shall be plowed as a field;
> Jerusalem shall become a heap of ruins.
> (Micah 3:12; Jeremiah 26:18)

Like Amos, Micah features many additional reports of iniquity and oracles of devastation, plus numerous examples of what Donald Gowan calls "funeral lament."[42]

In addition, whereas King often plucks

> Nations shall beat their swords into plowshares
> And their spears into pruning hooks.
> Nation shall not lift up sword after nation.
> They will study war no more.
> ([First] Isaiah 2:4; Micah 4:3-4)

from (First) Isaiah and Micah, he eschews the later biblical reversal of this peaceful imagery:

> Beat your plowshares into swords
> And your pruning hooks into spears.
> Let the weak say, "I am a warrior."
> (Joel 3:10)

King regularly neglects all these and many other prophetic statements about destruction and loss. As I mentioned, in "I Have a Dream" and elsewhere, he quotes hopeful lines from (Second) Isaiah 40 that reappear in Luke:

Every valley shall be exalted.
The mountains and hills will be laid low.
The rough places shall be made plain.
The crooked places shall be made straight.
The glory of the Lord shall be revealed
And all flesh shall see it together.

([Second] Isaiah 40:4-5; Luke 3:4-6)

But he never cites the next two, equally well-known verses from (Second) Isaiah 40 that resurface in I Peter:

All flesh is grass....
The grass withereth, the flower fadeth....
Surely the people is grass.

([Second] Isaiah 40:6-7; I Peter 1:24)

Amos, Micah, Joel, and (Second) Isaiah hold no monopoly on biblical evocations of widespread devastation and utter misery. "A pall of death," Gowan declares, "hangs over the entire book" of Jeremiah.[43] Any casual reader of the Hebrew Bible can confirm Gowan's observation: "The theme of lamentation is prominent throughout the prophetic books."[44] Indeed, many of the gloomiest lines in world literature appear in these prophetic texts. Yet King regularly avoids these abundant evocations of colossal loss and unspeakable despair. Consistent with his overall pattern of preferring oracles of hope, King rarely, if ever, preaches on Lamentations, a book packed with unrelieved heartache, grief, and mourning.

King's strong emphasis on prophetic hope does not evince the facile optimism that so often characterizes American sensibilities, optimism that F. Scott Fitzgerald, Arthur Miller, and many African American writers thoroughly debunk. In "I Have a Dream" King signals the reason for mining prophetic material so selectively. He describes "the Negro" as "still sadly crippled by the manacles of segregation and the chains of discrimination" and as "an exile in his own land."[45] He thus defines segregated African Americans as slaves in exile. Unlike the pre-exilic First Isaiah, Second Isaiah writes during the period of Hebrew captivity and exile in Babylon. As Gowan argues, Israelite prophets blast transgressions and sketch a terrifying future during periods of relative prosperity and national independence, not times of destitution and foreign domination. Then, Gowan continues, when the worst has already occurred, that is, when foreigners control Israel and Judah or force Hebrews into captivity and exile, prophets adapt by offering hope to a defeated people.[46] By claiming that African Americans live in captivity and exile and by reiterating an oracle that Second Isaiah originated during the Babylonian exile, King in "I Have a Dream" clearly aligns himself with Second Isaiah. Like Second Isaiah, King attempts to counteract despair and reinvigorate a thoroughly dominated people. As he defines African Americans as captives in exile, King normally quarries the relatively few passages of assurance and harmony from such books as Amos and Micah, instead of their far more numerous cries of outrage and projections of desolation.

In the last two years of his life, however, King shifted his rhetoric as he crusaded against poverty and war while relying more and more on the Bible.[47] King's later emphasis on biblical prophecy and biblical narrative was the greatest rhetorical shift of his entire public career. Drew Hansen emphasizes that after King so memorably announced, "I have a dream," he later repeatedly accused stubborn reactionaries and war-makers of "killing the dream." While continuing to recite his favorite uplifting visions from Hebrew prophecy, he also occasionally evoked the potential for doom—a possibility that he hadn't discussed much prior to 1966. In a late, fiercely antiwar address, "Beyond Vietnam," he details the horrors of the Vietnam War, then oscillates between despair and hope as he announces people's ability "to transform this pending cosmic elegy into a creative psalm of peace."[48] In "Drum Major Instinct," he disturbs his home congregation in Atlanta not only by pondering his own death, but also by mulling the possibility of instantaneous, unimaginable destruction from nuclear war.[49] These passages in "Beyond Vietnam" and "Drum Major Instinct" recall both Hebrew oracles of calamity and the visions of apocalypse projected by Revelation.

Even though King delivered "Our God Is Marching On" in 1965, before his rhetoric grew more radical, this speech broadcasts numerous themes that he extends in "I've Been to the Mountaintop."[50] In each of these orations, he interlinks the themes of Exodus, persecution/redemption, and eschatology. Because the final speech expands, adapts, sharpens, and revises "Our God Is Marching On," understanding his 1965 address is crucial to understanding his last one.

"Our God Is Marching On" caps a demonstration that many view as the apex of the entire civil rights movement. For several years, Selma, Alabama, served as a nexus for protests and speeches aimed at securing the right to vote. In early 1965, on what became known as "Bloody Sunday," white police and posse members grabbed nightsticks and donned gas masks before pummeling and tear-gassing dozens of peaceable marchers. Watching on television as violent police chased nonviolent demonstrators across the Edmund Pettus Bridge, much of the nation recoiled in horror. King then invited sympathizers to fly in and join local activists in marching fifty miles from Selma to Montgomery. After several hundred protestors completed that trek, thousands held a supportive rally on the steps of the capitol. King climaxed the protest by delivering "Our God Is Marching On." Outraged by Bloody Sunday and spurred by the marchers and President Lyndon Johnson, Congress passed the Voting Rights Act. As a result, for the first time, the nation guaranteed that African Americans would be able to vote in the South.[51]

King uses "Our God Is Marching On" to develop his identification of the African American struggle and the Exodus more extensively than he does on any other occasion. Throughout the speech King evokes the Exodus as he generates and elaborates a single metaphor:

Walking = Racial Progress.

He introduces this trope by relating a favorite story from the Montgomery Bus Boycott. As he explains, someone asked an older black woman, Sister Pollard, if she had grown tired of walking day after day across the city while watching buses roll past. King recalls her response: "My feets is tired, but my soul is rested." Then he adds, "And in a real sense this afternoon, we can say that our feet are tired but our souls are rested."[52] In this argument, just as African Americans in Montgomery achieved dignity by walking to integrate buses, current activists achieved dignity by walking to gain the ballot.

King then invokes James Weldon Johnson to argue that black Americans began walking long before recent protests in Montgomery and Selma. Recalling her childhood during the Great Depression, Maya Angelou relates that in her small-town graduation ceremony in Arkansas, her entire eighth-grade class refuted the white supremacist superintendent by belting out Johnson's "Lift Every Voice and Sing." Over a period of decades, Johnson's song became such a favorite in African American schools and churches that it became known as the "Negro National Anthem." King extends his own metaphor,

Walking = Racial Progress,

by quoting Johnson's well-known lyrics:

> We have come over a way
> That with tears has been watered.
> We have come treading our paths
> Through the blood of the slaughtered.
>
> Out of the gloomy past
> Till now we stand at last
> Where the white gleam
> Of our bright star is cast.[53]

Here Johnson clearly refers to slaves walking to the North to escape bondage and also to their children and grandchildren, many of whom also migrated northward to escape sharecropping, lynching, and disfranchisement. In these lines, Johnson represents an abstraction—racial progress—through the following metaphor:

Slaves and Their Descendents Walking = Racial Progress.

With his imagery of tears and blood, however, Johnson complicates his trope. Johnson's trope is not simply

Slaves and Their Descendents Walking = Racial Progress.

Instead, Johnson's trope is

Slaves and Their Descendents Walking and Suffering as Martyrs Fall = Racial Progress.

By citing Johnson's lines, King links the walking of the slaves and their descendents to the walking of bus boycotters in Montgomery and marchers from Selma. King observes that current marching extends these earlier strides, as protestors now seek freedom in the form of voting rights.

King greatly expands this trope by developing a memorable refrain: "We are on the move now.... Yes, we are on the move.... We are on the move now.... We are on the move now.... We are on the move now.... We are moving to the land of freedom."⁵⁴ King follows this refrain with another one that recurs between elaborations, a refrain that equates the literal fifty-mile march from Selma to Montgomery to more abstract racial gains:

> Let us therefore continue our triumphant march to the realization of the American dream. Let us march on segregated housing until every ghetto of social and economic depression dissolves. Let us march on segregated schools.... Let us march on poverty.... March on poverty.... Let us march on poverty.... Let us march on ballot boxes, march on ballot boxes, let us march on ballot boxes.... Let us march on ballot boxes.... Let us march on ballot boxes.... Let us march on ballot boxes.... Let us march on ballot boxes.⁵⁵

After offering this cascading refrain, King portrays the incessant walking of American slaves, their descendents, and contemporary activists as the climax of the entire Exodus narrative—the account in Joshua of the Israelites' arrival in Jericho. Recalling the Hebrews' frustrating years in the wilderness and their long-delayed entrance into the Promised Land, King declares, "The Bible tells us that the mighty men of Joshua merely walked about the walled city of Jericho and the barriers to freedom came tumbling down."⁵⁶ King adds that in an "old Negro spiritual" Joshua yelled, "'The battle am in my hand!'"⁵⁷

Then King enumerates a host of recent civil rights martyrs in Mississippi and Alabama, including Medgar Evers, James Chaney, Michael Schwerner, Andrew Goodman, and four girls slain in an infamous church bombing in Birmingham. Further stretching his expansive metaphor, the civil rights orator directly equates these martyrs with the Hebrews encircling Jericho:

> The pattern of [the martyrs'] feet as they walked through the Jim Crow barriers in the great stride toward freedom is the thunder of the marching men of Joshua. And the world rocks beneath their tread.... The battle is in our hands! *The battle is in our hands in Mississippi and Alabama and all over the United States* [my italics].⁵⁸

By mingling the Exodus narrative and the theme of persecution/salvation, King here explains that the Exodus story guarantees the triumph of racial equality and the eventual, complete defeat of segregation. He notes that each of these martyrs "died in the nonviolent army of our day" and proclaims that current demonstrators can ensure that the martyrs "did not die in vain."[59] He contends that victory for voting rights will, in some sense, redeem the loss of Medgar Evers, the four girls in Birmingham, and all the others recently victimized by racist murderers.

In Johnson's metaphor, slaves and their descendants came "treading . . . paths through the blood of the slaughtered," making progress even as martyrs are falling. Similarly, King maintains, those marching from Selma to Montgomery advance the cause of equality, even as Evers, the four girls, and other martyrs fall around them.

In this argument, current activists lock arms with Joshua's marchers, who, in the biblical narrative, are themselves extending the forty-year slog through the wilderness undertaken by Moses and his followers. According to King, many long decades in the Sinai Desert of slavery and oppression and the deaths of martyrs may not spell defeat, but victory. Those members of his audience who are biblically literate realize that Joshua signals triumph when God splits the Jordan River to allow the long-wandering Hebrews to re-enact the Exodus as they enter the Promised Land. Joshua signals another victory when the Hebrew marchers prompt the walls of Jericho to collapse. By incorporating images of walking that appear in Joshua and in Johnson's lyrics, King indicates that the sojourn from Selma to Montgomery began when Joshua marched around Jericho and continued when slaves deserted the American South. In the world of King's speech, Joshua, American slaves, slaves' descendents, and contemporary protestors all walk the same journey.

King ends "Our God Is Marching On" by quoting a large chunk of Julia Ward Howe's "Battle Hymn of the Republic":

Mine eyes have seen the glory of the coming of the Lord!
He is trampling out the vintage where the grapes of wrath are stored.
He has loosed the fateful lightning of his terrible swift sword.
His truth is marching on!

He has sounded forth the trumpet that shall never call retreat!
He is sifting out the hearts of men before His judgment seat.
O, be swift my soul to answer him!
Be jubilant my feet!
Our God is marching on!
Glory, hallelujah!

Glory, hallelujah!
Glory, hallelujah!
His truth is marching on!⁶⁰

By citing these lines, King indicates that, as current demonstrators and African American slaves alike march together under Joshua's banner, God's truth marches with them. By quoting Howe and two other well-known abolitionist poets—James Russell Lowell and William Cullen Bryant—King in this speech also contends that the civil rights movement extends the nineteenth-century crusade against slavery.

One might sketch King's entire, remarkable argument like this:

Hebrews Walk across the Red Sea and through the Wilderness to Escape Slavery	=	Joshua's Followers Walk around Jericho to Gain the Promised Land	=	American Slaves Walk to Escape Slavery (Martyrs Falling)	=	Postbellum Blacks Walk to Escape Injustice (Martyrs Falling)
Montgomery Bus Boycotters Walk to Integrate Buses	=	Selma-to-Montgomery Protestors Walk to Gain Voting Rights (Martyrs Falling)	=	God's Truth Marches toward the Final Days.		

In "Our God Is Marching On" King expands his biblical hermeneutic by blending his own demands with those articulated in Amos: "The only normalcy that we will settle for is the normalcy that allows justice to run down like waters and righteousness like a mighty stream."⁶¹ King also fuses his vision with one proclaimed in Micah: "Let us march on ballot boxes until we [elect those] who will not fear to do justly, love mercy, and walk humbly with their God."⁶²

Unlike "I've Been to the Mountaintop," which strongly emphasizes parable, "Our God Is Marching On" skips parable altogether. For that reason, "I've Been to the Mountaintop" offers a more comprehensive interpretation of the Bible than does "Our God Is Marching On."

But, together, "Death of Evil on the Seashore," "Birth of a New Nation," "I Have a Dream," and "Our God Is Marching On" explore and develop a rich interpretation of Exodus, prophecy, oppression, persecution/triumph, and eschatology. King clearly re-orchestrates this entire hermeneutic in "I've Been to the Mountaintop."

Of course, Ralph Abernathy, Andrew Young, Jesse Jackson, James Lawson, and some others who heard King's last speech were thoroughly familiar with African American religious rhetoric and with King's own earlier discourse. And many attendees at Mason Temple had soaked for years in African American pulpit oratory; some of them had heard or read at least some of King's earlier discourse. As Abernathy, Young, Jackson, Lawson, and some other members of King's audience had reason to realize, King's final speech extends and brightens a very large and colorful tapestry that African American orators and King himself had been weaving for years.

A work by a stellar novelist or painter frequently rethreads, updates, and re-invigorates a well-known, long-lasting artistic tradition. A later work by such a novelist or painter may also rethread, update, and re-invigorate that same artist's earlier motifs. Similarly, King's last oration rethreads, updates, and re-invigorates familiar biblical and African American traditions. It also extends, reconfigures, and reinterprets King's own earlier motifs.

Readers and listeners encounter the often-reprinted "Letter from Birmingham Jail" and "I Have a Dream" far more frequently than they see or hear King's later addresses. Video journalists and book editors frequently ignore King's later oratory as they endlessly replay and reprint his letter and "I Have a Dream." When they do so, they, in effect, contend that his best-known rhetoric is his best rhetoric. Perhaps they make such judgments automatically, ignoring (and possibly not even reading or hearing) King's later orations. Unfortunately, when editors and popularizers ignore King's later public words, they freeze him in his Birmingham cell or shape him into a marble statue on the steps of the Lincoln Memorial. They erase the last five years of his life as though those years never mattered. But to ignore these years is to seriously diminish King. To discard his later oratory is to overlook his creativity, perseverance, resourcefulness, maturation, and protean capacity to re-imagine his rhetoric and himself. "Our God Is Marching On" provides the most extensive hermeneutic of the Exodus that he ever generated in a single speech or essay. And "I've Been to the Mountaintop" serves as the most complete expression of his entire biblical hermeneutic. Understanding both speeches is crucial to grasping his persuasiveness in 1965 and 1968, persuasiveness that helped lift him to his current iconic status.

CHAPTER 2

A Certain Man Fell among Thieves

King and the Parable of the Good Samaritan

Along with African American preachers, an extensive network of liberal, mainly white homilists and writers supplied King with extensive intellectual and rhetorical resources. Several figures in this network—one in particular—directly shaped an important argument in "I've Been to the Mountaintop." In contrast to slave preachers, who lacked formal education, this leader, George Buttrick, was a well-known scholar and minister who, from 1955 until 1965, held a special position at Harvard.

In this chapter I investigate King's relationship to a group of liberal, largely white Protestant preachers and writers, including Buttrick, and King's tendency to borrow and adjust their sermons and commentaries. I briefly discuss several sermons on the parables that King replayed from Buttrick's *Parables of Jesus*. I also consider a Protestant tradition of interpreting the parables of Jesus and trace Buttrick's and King's use of interpretive commonplaces that date back to 1841. Then I explore King's reuse of Buttrick's material in King's "On Being a Good Neighbor," a sermon about the Parable of the Good Samaritan. Buttrick is important, in part, because King later reused much of Buttrick's text in "I've Been to the Mountaintop."

King's first important contact with a circle of nationally prominent preachers and authors occurred when he met Benjamin Mays, his father's friend, in Atlanta.[1] As an undergraduate, King chose Morehouse College, the school that his grandfather and father attended. There, in chapel services, he often heard Mays, the president of Morehouse, as Mays delivered homilies. Born of illiterate parents, the gifted Mays escaped poverty in

South Carolina to attend Bates College in Maine. Then he earned a PhD at the University of Chicago—a pioneering achievement for an African American. Prior to arriving at Morehouse, he served as dean of the School of Religion at Howard University, where he worked alongside Mordecai Johnson and Howard Thurman. During the 1930s and 1940s, Mays, Johnson, and Thurman envisioned Gandhian nonviolence as a possible solution to what Gunnar Myrdal termed the "American dilemma" of segregation. For that reason, Mays, Johnson, and Thurman made trailblazing journeys way across the globe to India to talk to Mahatma Gandhi himself about solutions to the plight of African Americans.

Encountering Mays at Morehouse undoubtedly helped spur King to depart from the path of his grandfather and father by seeking further education in the North, as Mays had done.[2] King chose Crozer Theological Seminary, near Philadelphia, where he studied the Bible, homiletics, and theology. After graduating from Crozer, he matriculated in a PhD program in religion at Boston University, where Mays's friend, Thurman, served as dean of the chapel. After King delivered "I Have a Dream" at the March on Washington, Mays offered the benediction for the March. King once called Mays "one of the great influences in my life."[3]

Joining prominent white preachers, Mays and Thurman participated in an elaborate system that connected liberal Protestant leaders to masses of people. This network is so forgotten today that it qualifies as a "Lost Continent" of American culture. Before and during King's lifetime, however, it thrived throughout most of the nation, reaching tens of millions of Americans, especially in the Northeast and near the Great Lakes. The network included Crozer and many other seminaries that trained literally thousands of local clergy. It featured huge denominational conventions; a well-established, national pulpit circuit; widely circulating journals (such as *Christian Century*); and popular book publishers (such as Harper). In the first half of the twentieth century, liberal Protestant presses released literally hundreds of books of sermons that related the Bible to everything from factory work to consumer culture, to Victorian poetry, to Freudian psychology, to parenting, to World War II, to Communism and the Cold War. Filling the niche now occupied by self-help books, many of these volumes sold briskly.

Harry Emerson Fosdick did more than anyone else to create a massive audience for liberal Protestant sermons, an audience that made this whole network possible.[4] While teaching at Union Theological Seminary in Manhattan, he served as minister at nearby Riverside Church, which John D.

Rockefeller funded. In addition to commanding the Riverside pulpit on Sunday mornings, Fosdick delivered weekly sermons to a national radio audience over a period of nineteen years. As a teenager and young man in Atlanta, King listened to some of these radio homilies. Fosdick also released a huge stream of books, nineteen of them issued by Harper. While some of these volumes offer pastoral advice or biblical commentary, most are collections of sermons. When Fosdick retired, Robert McCracken assumed his pulpit at Riverside Church and, like his predecessor, authored popular books of homilies. McCracken repeatedly welcomed King to preach at Riverside Church; in 1967, King chose Riverside as the site for a headline-making oration in which he denounced the Vietnam War.

In addition to Fosdick and McCracken, another liberal Protestant luminary was the prolific Halford Luccock, who, for several decades, kept generating books while teaching homiletics at Yale. Beginning in 1948, he wrote a long-standing column for *Christian Century* under the pseudonym of Simeon Stylites. His *In the Minister's Workshop* aided many ministers in their difficult, never-ending challenge of preparing weekly sermons.

Joining Fosdick as a professor at Union Theological Seminary was George Buttrick. Another titan of the Protestant pulpit, Buttrick simultaneously served as minister of Madison Avenue Presbyterian Church and, later, at Harvard as the Plummer Professor of Christian Morals and Preacher to the University. When Thurman worked at Boston University and Buttrick at Harvard, they traded pulpits once a year—an obvious gesture of mutual respect. In addition, during the 1950s, Buttrick coordinated the efforts of Luccock, Thurman, and literally dozens of other contributors for a massive project—twelve sizable volumes of biblical commentary. Titled *The Interpreter's Bible*, these tomes became standard desk references for liberal Protestant ministers. Like many others, King purchased *The Interpreter's Bible* for his library.[5]

This entire network of Mays, Thurman, Fosdick, Luccock, Buttrick, and other Protestant leaders proved absolutely indispensable to King, who constantly used its capacious resources to construct himself as an orator and civil rights leader. Like these other estimable preachers, King often keynoted large denominational conventions and headlined the top venues of the pulpit circuit, such as the Chicago Evening Supper Club and the Detroit Lenten Series. *Christian Century* listed him on its editorial board and published his essays, including the renowned "Letter from Birmingham Jail." And Harper published his five books.

Fosdick, Luccock, Buttrick, and other liberal, white homilists developed a large number of biblical and theological themes that appealed to King. A torchbearer for the Social Gospel, Fosdick maintained that Christianity must address poverty and other social ills. Disillusioned by World War I, he used his national, weekly radio pulpit to renounce war. Similarly appalled by the violence that had ravaged Europe, other highly regarded Protestants also repudiated war. White preachers did not repudiate segregation with the passion of Mays, Thurman, and other African American leaders. But some important white homilists did address racism. As early as 1917, Luccock defended African Americans from racial slurs. Urging respect for diverse peoples and cultures, Buttrick criticized racism in 1928. Fosdick disavowed segregation at least by 1933. Even though J. Wallace Hamilton led a church in Florida, a southern state, by 1946 he joined the ranks of liberal Protestants who opposed Jim Crow.

King almost certainly began reading collections of sermons assiduously during his years in seminary, if not earlier. Throughout his public career, he regularly borrowed and adapted sermonic material from Mays, Thurman, Fosdick, McCracken, Hamilton, Luccock, and Buttrick, plus others. King borrowed not only in the pulpit, but also on the political platform. In 1989 I discovered that King adapted the "Let freedom ring" conclusion of "I Have a Dream" from a speech by Archibald Carey, an African American preacher in Chicago.[6] By borrowing portions of sermons, King followed a common practice shared by many, many preachers, black and white. To cite only one indication of this frequency, King borrowed segments of one sermon from his contemporaries (mainly Hamilton) that can be traced to John Wesley in the early eighteenth century.[7]

King replayed and refashioned sermons for several reasons. Many preachers, in effect, treated sermonic language as congregations treat the lyrics of hymns, that is, as a shared treasure, not private property. Borrowing allowed King to jump constantly onto airplanes for endless rounds of coast-to-coast speaking engagements. His oratorical marathon rivaled that of any earnest presidential candidate, except that it lasted throughout his entire public career. During the heady years from the late 1950s until April 1968, he constantly juggled out-of-state orations, press conferences, visits to the White House, protest marches, jail time, negotiations with city officials, sermons in his home church, and meetings of his civil rights organization—a nearly impossible schedule that left him little time to compose. Borrowing also helped him foolproof his sermons with biblical cornerstones, themes, literary quotations, illustrations, modern applications, and other content that highly regarded preachers had already tested before live audiences and in print.

King chose his sources, one assumes, because he valued other progressives' approach to interpreting scripture and because he embraced their desire to reform a world marred by poverty, segregation, and war.

Like many other liberal ministers, King gravitated to the parables of Jesus and often reiterated and reworked other pastors' explications of those parables. I will examine King's use of sources shortly. But an initial question to ask is, What attracted so many liberal Protestant leaders to the parables in the first place? Unlike many other passages in the Bible, the parables do not directly relate God's mighty acts, broadcast supernatural visions, proclaim Jesus as the Messiah, or predict the apocalypse. Instead, they supply remarkably succinct vignettes, some so succinct that they are barely distinguishable from the aphorisms that Jesus also offers. Because the parables evoke dimensions of ordinary existence, Jesus seems at his most human when he spins them. Filling these pithy stories are common, recognizable characters: prosperous farmers, vineyard workers, home builders, a thief, a merchant, a sickly beggar, wedding guests, and a wastrel. Some of these figures are wise, some foolish; some are generous, others self-absorbed. Usually they appear in recognizable, everyday situations: a woman misplaces a coin, priests take a journey, a shepherd loses a sheep, women pour oil into lamps.

The gospel writers themselves directly indicate the meaning of several parables. Yet, despite this occasional didacticism and despite the apparent simplicity of many parables, interpretations vary greatly. For centuries Augustine, other church fathers, and their heirs explained the parables as allegories. In the late nineteenth century Adolf Julicher rejected parables-as-allegories, and most subsequent commentators joined him. During the twentieth century two influential scholars, C. H. Dodd and Joachim Jeremias, emphasized a relationship between the parables and the arrival of the Kingdom of God. Dazzled by the prospect of uncovering the original, oral setting of the parables, Jeremias and many other modern scholars focus relentlessly on the historicity of the Bible and on technical issues of biblical language. While noting identifiable themes, some critics explain that a chief purpose of many parables is to upend conventional notions without providing a single, exact message that is easily grasped. As Dodd remarks, one goal of such parables is "to tease" the mind "into active thought."[8] Joining the scholarly parade, form critics and structuralists also scrutinize the parables, as do proponents of erudite theories of metaphor and paradox.

In the nineteenth century, such liberal Protestant writers as A. B. Bruce and Marcus Dods approached the parables in a more accessible manner than that favored by Jeremias and other scholars. While Bruce and Dods draw from scholarship, they skirt many of the unending historical and technical issues that fascinate Jeremias and other researchers. For Bruce, Dods, and other popular writers, understanding biblical history is important, not as an end in itself, but as a guide to translating the Bible from crumbling parchment into the present tense. They dive into ancient texts and return with their teeth firmly clamped onto lessons for tomorrow. When expounding those lessons, they refuse to endlessly probe historical enigmas and linguistic paradoxes; they also fail to chase grand theories or promulgate majestic frameworks. Instead, intent on instructing churchgoers about how to live, they characteristically coax spiritual messages from the details of storylines. Celebrating one parable as "a poignant, pleading tale," Buttrick urges his readers to "forget that commentators have tormented themselves and it in their attempt to allegorize and theologize the details."[9] Mays, Hamilton, Luccock, Buttrick, and King all directly participate in this popular interpretive tradition.

During the twentieth century, one of the most notable books in this vein was Buttrick's *The Parables of Jesus*, an explication of forty-four parables that appeared in 1928. After digesting much relevant scholarship about the parables, Buttrick produced sprightly prose aimed at a broad audience of seminary-trained ministers and college-educated laity. Unlike many writers, Buttrick animated his commentary with metaphors that leaped off the pages into his readers' minds. At times sprinkled with excerpts from lofty Victorian poems, Buttrick's prose still seems vivacious and direct. According to his son, David Buttrick (who taught homiletics at Vanderbilt), many ministers bought *The Parables of Jesus*.[10]

In 1960, when King was jailed in Reidsville Prison, he urged his wife, Coretta King, to bring him several of his books, including the Bible, Buttrick's *The Parables of Jesus*, and Hamilton's sermonic collection from 1954, *Horns and Halos in Human Nature*.[11] In various sermons, King relied on this volume by Hamilton, especially Hamilton's analysis of the Parable of the Prodigal Son.[12] But for sermons on the parables, King especially favored Buttrick. For one homily that he delivered more than once, King retooled Buttrick's analysis of the Parable of the Rich Fool.[13] Buttrick and King both emphasize the folly of a wealthy man who builds great barns and chases extravagance at all costs, only to die prematurely and in disfavor with God. For another sermon, King repeated and adapted Buttrick's explication of the Parable of Dives and Lazarus.[14] Both Buttrick and King examine the callous behavior of the finely dressed, well-fed Dives, who ignores Lazarus, a starving beggar who slumps by the gate. In "The Dignity of Labor," his speech in Memphis on March 18, 1968, King explained the Parable of Dives and Lazarus, in part, by replaying and adjusting material from Buttrick.[15] In all these orations about these two parables, King adds racial protest to Buttrick's exegesis, which does not spotlight race.

In "On Being a Good Neighbor," a homily from 1963, King echoed much of Buttrick's treatment of the Parable of the Good Samaritan. After a certain number of years in which he read homilies from papers and notes, King memorized huge chunks of his sermons and reworked them into his extemporaneous oratory. While delivering "The Dignity of Labor" and "I've Been to the Mountaintop" extemporaneously, he repeated portions of his earlier sermons that he had memorized. This repeated material including segments that he had borrowed from Buttrick. *In other words, even though George Buttrick did not realize that his writing in 1928 would appear in a speech in 1968, he definitely composed an important portion of "I've Been to the Mountaintop." He deserves recognition for that contribution, recognition that he has never received before.*

Beginning at least as early as 1841, numerous other writers also produced and repeated motifs and passages that King reiterated in "On Being a Good Neighbor" and "I've Been to the Mountaintop." I explain this process below.

Over a period of many generations, when Protestant scholars and clergy wrote and preached about the Parable of the Good Samaritan, they often repeated each other's views, while adding new twists of interpretation. Beginning at least as early as 1841, Protestant writers generated what became interpretive commonplaces that floated from one book to another and that, one imagines, were preached in many pulpits as well. Consider a description of the setting of the Parable of the Good Samaritan—the road from Jerusalem to Jericho. Between 1841 and 1917, five well-known Protestants vividly evoked this setting by explaining that, during the time of Jesus, robbers attacked and injured so many travelers that this road became known as the "Bloody Way" or the "Bloody Pass."[16] One of these writers was George Murray, in 1916. Another was Halford Luccock, in 1917. Writing eleven years after Luccock, Buttrick became at least the sixth author to characterize this setting for the parable as the "Bloody Way" or the "Bloody Pass." In "On Being a Good Neighbor" and "I've Been to the Mountaintop," King joins this whole string of interpreters who claim that, during the era of Jesus, this road became known as the "Bloody Pass."

In his exegesis of the Parable of the Good Samaritan, Murray recapitulated a number of interpretive commonplaces and described the ancient road from Jerusalem to Jericho as an exceedingly steep highway lined with limestone caves that harbored violent thieves. Defining the geography of the area, Murray also noted that the road joined one city that rose two thousand feet above sea level to a nearby city that lay one thousand feet below sea level. Buttrick presents a very similar account of this road, an account he borrowed from Murray. When Luccock explored the parable, he blended numerous interpretive commonplaces with his own distinctive observations. Buttrick also interlarded his writing with several commonplaces that he borrowed from Luccock.[17]

For his part, in "On Being a Good Neighbor" and "I've Been to the Mountaintop," King directly replayed and adapted Buttrick's text. King almost certainly *only* read Buttrick's explication of the Parable of the Good Samaritan, *not* those of *any* of these other writers.[18] But Buttrick leaned on interpretive commonplaces (such as the nickname "Bloody Way" or "Bloody Pass") that he borrowed from Murray and Luccock. Murray and Luccock were themselves borrowing from a series of nineteenth-century writers before them. So, when King directly echoed lines from Buttrick, he echoed Buttrick's new material while also repeating commonplaces that Murray and Luccock had grabbed from nineteenth-century writers. In other words, nineteenth-century authors generated and circulated interpretive commonplaces that eventually resurfaced in Murray, Luccock, and Buttrick. When King reshaped Buttrick, he was also reshaping the work of this string of writers. *In other words, beginning at least as early as 1841, a whole chain of Protestant writers also helped compose "I've Been to the Mountaintop." Even though they did not realize that they were doing so, they deserve recognition for helping to craft King's final speech, recognition that they have never before received.* Chief among these writers are George Murray and Halford Luccock. (The appendices of this book include all the intertextual material that I mention above, plus other possible sources that offer parallels to portions of "I've Been to the Mountaintop.")

By reiterating liberal Protestant commonplaces, King did not harm himself, but instead *enhanced* his appeal. Northern, liberal, white audiences responded favorably to him and opened their wallets for his cause in part because he mirrored themes that they already liked. Using familiar material enabled King to reassure his audiences by appearing more sympathetic, less strange, and less challenging. That is, borrowing provided him a means to *legitimize* himself to masses of white Protestants and to prod them to support racial equality—a cause that he helped them to embrace as their own. African American audiences, such as the one at Mason Temple, also responded favorably to the commonplaces. During his lifetime, literally no one complained publicly about his habitual practice of repeating chestnuts that he extracted from books of sermons and from biblical commentaries.

For his direct source for "On Being a Good Neighbor" and "I've Been to the Mountaintop," King picked Buttrick partly because Buttrick's writing appeared to stem from many years of deep study and reflection, yet also seemed effortless. Rarely heavy handed, Buttrick seems to revive the ancient lifeworld of the parables while permitting their lessons to unfold of their own accord. That is, he appears to toss aside obstacles and preconceptions and, with minimal interference, to allow the parables to speak to the twentieth century.

An exploration of the Buttrick/King intertext should begin with a brief review of the Parable of the Good Samaritan. It begins when a lawyer converses with Jesus. After a while, the lawyer asks, "Who is my neighbor?" Jesus responds by telling of a man beaten and robbed on the road between Jerusalem and Jericho. In this story, a Jewish priest approaches the man, but strolls right past him. Next a Levite (another kind of Jewish priest) spies the same man, but he also ambles by. A Samaritan then appears, binds the victim's wounds, takes him to an inn, and pays the innkeeper for attending to him. Jesus asks the lawyer, "Who was the neighbor?" The lawyer replies, "The one who helped the victim." Jesus concludes, "Go and do likewise."[19]

In "On Being a Good Neighbor," King credits Fosdick while explaining Fosdick's distinction between enforceable and unenforceable obligations.[20] Failing to acknowledge Buttrick, King borrows a portion of Buttrick's account of the opening dialogue between the attorney and Jesus. King's careful, detailed description of the extremely steep, looping, dangerous road to Jericho also stems directly from Buttrick. Like others before them, both Buttrick and King label the road the "Bloody Pass."

As it appears in the Bible, the parable itself never suggests why the priest and Levite refuse to assist the roadside victim. Instead the parable prods readers to surmise the motives for this failure. Speculating about the behavior of the priest and Levite proved an endlessly enjoyable sport for biblical critics. In 1882 A. B. Bruce explained, "Nothing [is] so easy as to invent excuses for [the priest and Levite]. Every commentator suggests a list of excuses, each one inventing his own list—so plentiful are they."[21] Like others before them, Buttrick and King (in "On Being a Good Neighbor") wonder aloud about the possible motives of the priest and Levite. Both Buttrick and King claim that the priest and Levite might want to cure the persistent problem of roadside ambush by fostering a systematic solution. Noting the hazards of the Jericho Road, Buttrick and King also ponder whether the priest and Levite might neglect the beaten man because they fear being attacked themselves. Further, Buttrick and King note that the Samaritan was a non-Jew, a member of a people with whom Jews refused to interact. Buttrick and King also yank the story into the present by observing that, unlike the generous Samaritan, Americans tend to rigidly classify people as American, black, or Asian.[22]

In "I've Been to the Mountaintop," King reiterates a portion of Buttrick's account of the conversation between the attorney and Jesus, much of Buttrick's description of the Jericho road, and its nickname the "Bloody Pass." King also adjusts Buttrick's speculation about the motives of the priest and Levite and Buttrick's definition of the Samaritan as a foreigner.

While borrowing heavily from Fosdick, Buttrick, and other preachers, King invariably transmutes their material. King's "On Being a Good Neighbor" and "I've Been to the Mountaintop" exemplify such a process. When Buttrick admonishes readers to practice altruism toward those of different races, he obviously spotlights social categories. But he advises readers about their individual attitudes and conduct; he certainly does not advocate massive protest. Indeed, throughout his writings, Buttrick fails to directly espouse organized dissent or large-scale social reform.

Like Buttrick, King uses "On Being a Good Neighbor" to commend one-on-one altruism. But, unlike Buttrick, King uses the Samaritan's principle of "universal altruism" to indict slavery and segregation. Offering an obvious parallel to the roadside victim in the parable, King mentions African American basketball players who were injured in a car wreck. A racist white ambulance driver, he notes, refused to serve them; then, when they eventually reached a hospital, the hospital also turned them aside. They died, he declares, on the way to a more distant hospital designated for African Americans. King observes that this experience is not an anomaly, but merely one of "thousands of inhuman incidents" that occur regularly due to racists' failure to recognize the humanity of all people. King also likens the Samaritan's benevolence to Albert Schweitzer's service in Africa and to Lincoln's decision to sign the Emancipation Proclamation. A serious contemplation of the Samaritan, King contends, would lead Americans to destroy the "evil monster" of segregation.

In his last oration King claims that a serious consideration of the Samaritan would spur authorities in Memphis to recognize justice in the cause of the striking sanitation workers. In both "On Being a Good Neighbor" and "I've Been to the Mountaintop," King's entire argument gains a vastly larger meaning because of his ethos as the most visible leader of a massive, nonviolent campaign to repeal segregation. He is not simply petitioning for that repeal; he and many others are working actively every day to dismantle Jim Crow.

King's whole, detailed exploration and repudiation of racism finds no precedent in Buttrick's *The Parables of Jesus* or in any of Buttrick's other writings. Like Buttrick, Fosdick, Hamilton, and other white commentators and homilists occasionally object to racism but virtually never treat racial protest or racial equality as a central theme for a sermon or a book chapter. When King borrows their sermons, he regularly adds racial protest and constantly treats it as his signature theme. He does that on literally hundreds of occasions. Further, the white pastors never even mention—and certainly never think about leading—a nonviolent movement that could actually dismantle southern apartheid. King invariably alchemizes their sermons in order to envision, justify, promote, and implement exactly such a movement—throughout the nation and currently in Memphis.

CHAPTER 3

I'm Delighted to See Each of You Here Tonight

Pentecostalism and Mason Temple

When the garbage collectors and their supporters parked their rain-slicked cars beside Mason Temple, they did not walk into an ordinary house of worship. Named after Bishop C. H. Mason, Mason Temple served as the national headquarters for the Church of God in Christ (COGIC), a large, African American, Pentecostal denomination. King, a Baptist minister, did not often address congregations of COGIC or other Pentecostal and Holiness churches. But he realized that their members sometimes proved sympathetic to his leadership. In Albany, Georgia, he acknowledged the contributions that members of the COGIC had made to his civil rights campaign there.[1]

Scholars largely ignore Mason, African American Pentecostalism, and COGIC.[2] But Mason, black Pentecostals, and COGIC do not deserve this neglect, partly for the simple reason that they made King's last speech possible in the first place. Without Mason, COGIC, and Mason Temple, King would *never* have given a speech that night at all. *Only* because Mason and COGIC built Mason Temple was it even possible for anyone in Memphis to address two or three thousand African Americans indoors. No other church or hall available to King was close to the size of Mason Temple. As Michael Honey explains, "No other black facility in the South held as many people as Mason Temple."[3] And between 2,500 and 3,000 African Americans assembled there for King's last oration. Recall the huge rainstorm that night and the roaring civil defense sirens. Thinking reasonably, King and Ralph Abernathy expected only a small number to surmount the storm and arrive at Mason Temple. In addition, if King were to address a tiny audience, the press might jump to claim (again) that African Americans would no longer follow him. Further, King was exhausted beyond exhaustion. So King prudently decided *not* to speak that night and dispatched Abernathy to talk in his stead. King *only* left his comfortable room at the Lorraine Motel because Abernathy called to report a surprisingly large, boisterous crowd. If the speech been scheduled anywhere else, a big crowd *could never* have materialized, for no other large indoor facility was available. And, because of the storm, outdoors was obviously impossible. He *only* spoke because Abernathy informed him of a large audience that would vigorously respond, gladly shout, lustily cheer, and blissfully applaud him. And that is *exactly* what Mason Temple—and *only* Mason Temple—made possible. If the rally had been scheduled anywhere else, Abernathy would have never phoned King to interrupt his rest at the motel. Instead, in keeping with their original plan, Abernathy would simply have spoken himself.

As usual when he addressed African American audiences, King relied that night on the call-and-response dynamic that typifies much black preaching. Reacting loudly and exuberantly, many of his listeners repeatedly interjected their vocal encouragement, especially during King's carefully timed pauses. Like many musicians, King often performed at his best before large, enthusiastic crowds. On this night the strong electrical current flowing from King to his large audience and back from his audience to him pushed him toward much greater eloquence than he normally achieved. It is not too much to say that the large, passionate audience spurred King to his extraordinary conclusion that night. And that process was possible *only* because of the close proximity of a large number of fervent listeners to the speaker and because of the wonderful acoustics of Mason Temple. Auditors in the middle and (especially) the rear of a very long, drafty sanctuary (and King sometimes spoke in such sanctuaries) would barely have been able to see him.[4] To them, his voice would have seemed distant, abstract, and/or disembodied, and he would barely have been able to see or hear them at all. Such audiences did not respond so dramatically to King, nor did he respond so dramatically to them. Not only did the unsung architect of Mason Temple make the speech possible by creating a large sanctuary, he also brought speaker and audience close together and thereby contributed mightily to the happy congruence of speaker and listeners.

This chapter examines the Pentecostal bishop who supported the garbage workers' strike and C. H. Mason, the founder of the Pentecostal denomination headquartered at Mason Temple. I also explore the effort to construct Mason Temple during the Great Depression, its stellar architecture, and the surprising presence of a tomb in its vestibule. Finally, this chapter briefly relays Pentecostal ideas and practices that inflected the reception of his final speech by those Pentecostals who heard him.

Evidence strongly suggests that a significant portion of King's listeners were Pentecostals. Rev. James O. Patterson, the bishop of COGIC and minister at Mason Temple, strongly backed the strike. On February 17, 1968, he spoke at Mason Temple to the first large meeting of strikers and their supporters, a meeting in which people donated food and money to assist the union.[5] On February 24, Patterson and other black pastors throughout the city convened in Mason Temple to form a new organization to buttress the strike. On that afternoon Patterson joined James Lawson (among others) at a press conference in which they declared that one hundred ministers had established this organization. Patterson also spoke on live radio to urge support for the garbage workers.[6] And he joined Lawson and King in leading the protest march in downtown Memphis on March 18.[7] Many members of COGIC obviously followed the lead of their bishop, and some strikers themselves belonged to COGIC and were familiar with Mason Temple.[8] Further, King had every reason to believe that members of COGIC were sitting in Mason Temple when he delivered "I've Been to the Mountaintop." In "The Dignity of Labor," his address at Mason Temple on March 18, he directly acknowledged that some of his listeners belonged to COGIC.[9] He would logically have reasoned that some adherents of COGIC would return to their home church to hear "I've Been to the Mountaintop." He also definitely understood that he was speaking in a Pentecostal setting. But even if, somehow, he did not understand where he was speaking, he absolutely did deliver his address at the national headquarters of the largest African American Pentecostal denomination. And members of his audience definitely comprehended that setting, even those who were not Pentecostals themselves. Again, although King was never a Pentecostal, distinctive elements of Pentecostalism inflected the meaning and reception of the speech, especially among the Pentecostals who attended.

In order to understand African American Pentecostalism, its hub at Mason Temple, and its impact on King's oration, one starts with C. H. Mason, who began his life modestly but who lived to spur a large religious movement. The son of newly freed slaves, Mason was born into poverty near Memphis in 1866, immediately after the dissolution of bondage.[10] In 1879 and 1880, he contracted yellow fever, nearly died, and viewed his recovery as a miracle from God.[11] After drifting to Arkansas, he became a Baptist minister in 1893. Dissatisfied with Baptist religion, he gravitated toward the Holiness movement and co-founded COGIC. In 1907, he learned about a religious awakening, and, in his words, "'was led by the Spirit to go to Los Angeles, California.'"[12] There, in a ramshackle neighborhood, he located William Joseph Seymour, an African American with little formal education, who preached enthusiastically night after night to black and white listeners alike. Holding forth in a tiny, modest room, Seymour galvanized an ever-growing band of janitors, maids, and day laborers during the Azusa Street Revival.[13] The fervor on Azusa Street was so intense that Seymour and his followers sensed that they were re-living a biblical episode from Acts known as the Pentecost. According to Acts, the Holy Spirit visited a group of early Christians, granted them "tongues of fire," and bid them to talk in unintelligible languages—a phenomenon that came to be known as "speaking in tongues."[14] At the Azusa Street Revival, Seymour and others sensed "tongues of fire" descending directly from the Holy Spirit, and they began speaking in tongues. Seymour also delivered highly intelligible, articulate messages that captivated many. Years later, Mason remembered hearing Seymour's "wonderful sermon" that consisted of "sweet and powerful" words.[15]

Sparked initially by Seymour and the now legendary Azusa Street Revival, the Pentecostal and Holiness movement has grown so phenomenally across the nation and that planet that, today, a staggering one billion people worldwide worship at Pentecostal and Holiness churches.[16]

Upon C. H. Mason's return to the Mid-South, he delivered sermons that proved, in the words of an associate, "soul-stirring, convincing, and irresistible."[17] Deeming Mason "a virtuoso of slave religion," Robert Franklin explains, "By stridently reintroducing drums, spontaneous song celebrations, call-and-response preaching, dancing, and emotionally liberating worship, Mason sought to re-Africanize black churches."[18] He certainly fueled African American Pentecostalism. For over fifty years—from 1907 until his death in 1961—Mason presided over the growth of COGIC into a robust national institution with a reported one million members.[19] Although the denomination denied women the right to become ordained as ministers, Mason cooperated with a strong band of female leaders who, according to Anthea Butler, "formed the backbone" of COGIC.[20] COGIC loyalists concentrated on promoting the virtues of Victorian family life while fostering

African American pride and dignity. As they nurtured their denomination, COGIC officials generally eschewed political agitation. Even though this strategy did not appeal to the likes of W. E. B. Du Bois, it did offer some advantages. By developing their own thriving institution, these African Americans combated white stereotypes and exerted leadership roles that were entirely unavailable to them in the dominant culture.

When the Japanese bombed Pearl Harbor in 1941, attitudes in COGIC began to shift and the denomination gradually eased its way toward greater civic engagement. As Butler explains, "The entrance of the United States into World War II blew away the walls separating [COGIC] from the modern world."[21] One female leader of COGIC developed a strong friendship and close working relationship with Mary McLeod Bethune, an extremely important African American figure who joined a different branch of the Holiness movement.[22] In 1955 another member of COGIC, Mamie Till-Mobley, actively publicized white supremacists' murder of her teenage son, Emmett Till—a slaying that helped trigger the entire civil rights movement. In 1957 C. H. Mason moved into a house in a white neighborhood of Memphis; unhappy with his decision to integrate the community, white racists burned a cross on his front yard.[23]

Shortly before 1940, C. H. Mason, Elizabeth "Lizzie" Robinson, and other captains of COGIC began to wonder about a sanctuary in Memphis large enough to host a yearly, national convocation. Such an ambitious project was conceivable precisely because COGIC officials had devoted so many decades to watering and nurturing COGIC. Yet chronic poverty among African Americans loomed as a gigantic obstacle to fundraising, especially during a time of the Great Depression and the strain of World War II. Through remarkable perseverance, Mason, Robinson, and other church stalwarts proved able to amass the astonishing sum of $275,000 to construct their national hub.[24] A close associate of Mason emphasizes the great challenge of building this church, Mason Temple, and members' considerable pride upon its completion.[25] As one COGIC document explains, the previously tireless, now aging and frail Robinson was "greatly interested in building our National Headquarters and, with her very efficient daughter as her secretary, She kept her national drives functioning until she knew [that Mason Temple] was ready for dedication."[26] In 1945, during the long-awaited first convocation that christened Mason Temple, the eighty-five-year-old Robinson died. On the last day of that otherwise joyful gathering, COGIC officials conducted her funeral at their new facility, which one person described as "'the largest convention hall owned by any Negro church group in America.'"[27]

When a taxi dropped me at Mason Temple, I expected what a number of writers and scholars describe as a coldly impersonal, "cavernous" auditorium—that is, something akin to a gigantic warehouse or an airplane hangar.[28] Glancing around and feeling puzzled, I immediately asked the driver if he had the correct address. Yes, he did. After walking inside, I decided that the prominent writers and researchers were wrong. Far from impersonal and cavernous, Mason Temple is large, yet paradoxically compact. Along with its size, its extraordinarily fine architecture accounts for African Americans' decision to select it as the site for the great singer Paul Robeson to present a concert in 1948 and as the location for speeches by Walter White, Medgar Evers, and (as I mentioned earlier) Roy Wilkins, and Bayard Rustin.[29]

By neglecting or misrepresenting Mason Temple, many who write about King obscure its exceedingly talented architect. Historians of American architecture also bypass this figure, lending him further obscurity. Because he served as an elder in Mason's church, he was almost certainly an African American. But almost nothing else is known about him. His full name is lost. Even his abbreviated name is a mystery. One can confidently say that he is either H. Taylor or W. H. Taylor, but no one knows which.[30]

Yet, instead of vanishing from history, Taylor merits acclaim. In the early 1940s, very few architects in the South were black. For Taylor or any other Southern black at that time, simply becoming an architect would constitute a major accomplishment. But Taylor is not merely an architect and Mason Temple is not merely a building. Instead, Mason Temple is an extraordinary achievement and a splendid species of American design. Taylor performed his architectural wonder by ingeniously and meticulously faceting the geometry of its sanctuary in order to reconcile opposing architectural goals—to create a space that was decidedly compact, yet large enough to comfortably hold a sizable congregation. He did so by conceiving a balcony, painstakingly tape-measuring the balcony, and ingeniously distributing every wall. He also shrewdly avoided any eye-popping, radically modernist design that would distract from worship. And he outright rejected church architects' common decision to create extra room by simply elongating the back of the worship space—a practice that distances latecomers from the proceedings in front and that often muffles the sound. Instead, with rigorous exactitude, he shifted the pulpit and the entire chancel forward a few dozen feet, far enough to wrap seats around and behind them, but not far enough to create the peculiarity of a circular sanctuary.

Further, Taylor realized that, in traditional church pews, people often fail to sit shoulder-to-shoulder and instead put space in between themselves. So he boldly rejected pews in favor of bolted auditorium seats that offer reasonable comfort while forcing congregants to sit closer together, shoulder-to-shoulder. By choosing auditorium seats instead of pews, he seated many more people than pews normally accommodate and thereby made maximum use of the available space in the sanctuary.

In sum, while crafting Mason Temple, Taylor juggled four aims, some of which appear irreconcilable: first, the sanctuary would approximate a traditional worship space; second, it would feature uniformly superb acoustics; third, it would accommodate 3,734 people, a very large number; fourth, all those people would sit comfortably; and, fifth, despite its size, the sanctuary would feel cozy and intimate. The able Taylor achieved each of these goals.

By envisioning and constructing Mason Temple, Mason, Robinson, and other COGIC leaders created, for the first time, the possibility that sizable African American audiences in Memphis could assemble indoors. Decades after Mason Temple was built, this decision made King's last speech possible. By finessing an exceedingly astute design for Mason Temple, the almost unknown, but gifted Taylor contributed greatly to the union between speaker and audience on the night of King's final address. His talent helps account for the eloquence of "I've Been to the Mountaintop."

After C. H. Mason died in 1961, COGIC officials remembered and honored him in several ways. On the night that King delivered "I've Been to the Mountaintop," the rafters held one huge, very visible white banner hung high and to King's right, plus a second, equally huge, equally visible, white banner hung high and to his left. In very large, bright red letters, these identical banners proclaimed:

FOUNDERS DAY

Both banners celebrated Mason's importance, and almost anyone watching King deliver his oration could easily read them.[31]

Upon Mason's death, Taylor's building received a more unusual touch. COGIC leaders made the extremely rare gesture of placing Mason's elegant, marble tomb inside the vestibule of Mason Temple, entirely above ground and close to the front doors.³² Dodging the rain, King's listeners entered the front doors of Mason Temple and stood briefly in its vestibule, shaking water off their umbrellas. Then they filed directly past Mason's tomb and into the sanctuary. A considerable number of them were quite familiar with the building because they annually attended Mason Temple. Inasmuch as Mason died only seven years earlier, some of them almost certainly heard his sermons and knew him personally. For that reason, they did not experience the "shock" that struck Abernathy when he stumbled onto the tomb while searching for a phone to call King.³³ Of course, many attendees were not Pentecostals. Yet most of them would definitely have heard about Mason and the phenomenal success of COGIC—a success evidenced by the impressive structure of Mason Temple itself. For his part, King apparently entered the front doors of the temple and walked past Mason's tomb into the sanctuary.³⁴

For anyone who noticed the tomb, it served as a bold reminder both of the proximity of American slavery and of the potential for black accomplishment. Certainly the tomb could easily prompt some to reflect on death. The themes of slavery, triumph, and death figure prominently in King's last oration. The achievements of Bishop Mason—and the location of his tomb—lent those themes a special resonance to some who heard "I've Been to the Mountaintop."

As everyone knew, King was a lifelong Baptist, not a Pentecostal. He definitely never contemplated speaking in tongues; nor did he engage in other distinctively Pentecostal practices. Neither did his closest associates. Neither did his wife, his parents, Benjamin Mays, his professors, or members of his churches in Montgomery and Atlanta. But elements of Pentecostalism inflected some listeners' reception of "I've Been to the Mountaintop."

Those elements mainly relate to the human body. Pentecostalism appealed to Mason and others, in part, because it emphasizes the body as a site of fervent religious activity. COGIC worship services fostered (and fosters) devout prayer, earnest hymn singing, chanting, shouting, and dancing. Sometimes termed a Sanctified Church, COGIC aimed (and aims) to facilitate a certain spiritual quest or process known as sanctification. Along with other practices, sanctification can involve the rigorous physical experience of fasting. One expression or index of sanctification, speaking in tongues, is also, of course, a physical activity. After a churchgoer has reached a certain point in the steps toward sanctification, that process can proceed through an extremely intense physical experience known as "tarrying." As James Tinney explains, tarrying can occur when a congregant approaches the altar and begins to pray loudly, sweat profusely, shout, and toss his or her body about. This "seeker," Tinney notes, will strive to reach "a state of possession, if it takes hours upon hours of struggling. Hair will become matted, clothes will become dirtied, the flesh will become sick and feint until 'the power comes' from the Holy Spirit."[35]

Tinney observes that the experience of tarrying can be so extraordinary as to represent what he calls "a break with rational thought and language."[36] He also claims that the rituals of tarrying and speaking in tongues represent, in his words, "a total rejection of American mainstream values."[37] Somewhat similarly, Cheryl Sanders argues that African American Pentecostals "institutionalize dissociative religious experience" that separates them from the dominant, white, religious culture.[38]

Tinney, Sanders, and other church historians maintain that Mason and his spiritual allies sought to reclaim and preserve slave religion while stoutly resisting efforts to convert ex-slaves and their children to the prevailing culture.[39] As one scholar explains, "Holiness advocates recalled the experiential dimension of slave religion and defended [its] particular liturgical practices. ... Mason upheld the sacred canopy of slave religion buttressed by those practices."[40] This researcher links the ritual of tarrying to that of the ring shout enacted by slaves.[41]

Again, King absolutely never spoke in tongues; nor did he ever advocate or practice fasting or tarrying. But, as I will explain, King manages, in "I've Been to the Mountaintop," to provoke his listeners' minds while constantly affirming the religious significance of the human body. While sitting in the national headquarters of their denomination, Pentecostals in his audience would have been especially alert and sensitive to this emphasis.

CHAPTER 4

Across the Red Sea

The Exodus Continues

As King walked to the microphone at Mason Temple, he badly needed to reinvent the garbage workers' strike and the city of Memphis. He also needed to resurrect the civil rights movement. So much had happened; so much had changed. And the change came very quickly.

In 1947 Jackie Robinson integrated major league baseball, raising the hopes of African Americans. Despite Robinson's heroics on the diamond, almost no one anticipated that in 1954 the Supreme Court would inspire more hope by mandating the racial integration of all public schools in the United States. The wanton murder of a teenage boy, Emmett Till, in Mississippi prompted greater awareness of the perils of white supremacy. Starting in 1955, the yearlong Montgomery Bus Boycott vaulted King into the national spotlight, and the Supreme Court vindicated the boycotters by ruling against segregation on public buses. All these events helped trigger the largest mass struggle for human rights in American history. Newspapers and television screens relayed chapter after chapter of the nonviolent movement: first Montgomery, then Little Rock, then Lunch Counter Sit-Ins, Freedom Rides, James Meredith at Ole Miss, Birmingham, Freedom Summer, Atlantic City, and Selma. At the March on Washington in 1963, King cemented his reputation as the leader of the movement when he delivered "I Have a Dream" from the steps of the Lincoln Memorial. Ignored for decades, race and poverty emerged as the only domestic issues that mattered. The stunning victories for the movement included the Civil Rights Act of 1964 and the Voting Rights Act of 1965—legislation that no one in the United States predicted ten years earlier.

But in 1968, only three years after Selma, events had shattered much of the hope and idealism that fueled the movement. Medgar Evers, the most prominent civil rights leader in Mississippi, had been assassinated in his driveway. Shortly after King delivered "I Have a Dream," white racists murdered four innocent girls at their church one Sunday in Birmingham. A few weeks later, a sniper assassinated a young president in Dallas. During the following summer, white supremacists murdered three civil rights volunteers in Mississippi. Meanwhile Malcolm X castigated King, James Farmer, and other nonviolent leaders while advancing the Nation of Islam and advocating Black Nationalism. Then Malcolm X, too, was murdered.

Disillusioned by the failure of the federal government to protect the lives of nonviolent organizers in the South, many exasperated activists shifted their orientation. Stokely Carmichael and others in the Student Nonviolent Coordinating Committee dropped the goal of racial integration in favor of Black Nationalism. Even though King had officiated at the wedding ceremony of Cleveland Sellers, Sellers joined Carmichael in abandoning nonviolence and espousing Black Power.[1]

In addition, international events often generated fear and confusion. While the Cold War divided Berlin and sparked the Cuban Missile Crisis, it also propelled anti-Communism at home. President Kennedy and President Johnson shipped thousands of Americans to Vietnam, but a quick victory proved elusive and thousands died. The length, expense, and deadliness of the war splintered the nation. And, in a number of mostly northern big cities, rioters seized the spotlight that had shone on King and the entire southern movement. Many now viewed King as irrelevant and doubted that a nonviolent movement was still possible.

King's need to reimagine the strike, Memphis, and his movement seems clear when, in "I've Been to the Mountaintop," he admonishes, "We don't need any bricks and bottles. We don't need any Molotov cocktails." As his audience realized, Molotov cocktails are bottles filled with gasoline and stuffed with rags that, when lit and hurled, dramatically shatter, explode, and blaze. Locked into ghettoes, some inner-city blacks seethed over the sometimes hostile, often racist treatment from largely white police, an alien power occupying their communities. In 1965 impoverished residents of the Watts section of Los Angeles rebelled against police and the National Guard. The disturbance consumed thirty-four lives.[2] A riot unnerved Chicago the following summer. In 1967, less than a year before the strike in Memphis, no fewer than 164 disorders rattled American cities and towns, including sizable disturbances that left people shuddering in Nashville, Tampa, Cincinnati, and Newark.³ Attracted to violence, the national news media eagerly and repeatedly splashed dramatic images and accounts of riots onto television screens and front pages.

The worst disorder of 1967 rocked Detroit. Fires slashed the night, first silhouetting, then devouring a cityscape. Atop and inside tall buildings, snipers poured gunfire on police, state troopers, and the National Guard, who, hiding behind armored personnel carriers, peppered upper stories with bullets. In a dispatch headlined "Guerilla War Rips 12th," a journalist observed, "A machine gun roared in 30-second bursts, sweeping a roof, building, or alley" on the "riot-blackened streets."⁴ At least one reporter and one participant compared the "house-to-house war" to Korea and Vietnam.⁵ Forty-three people died.⁶

Appointed by President Lyndon Johnson, the Kerner Commission investigated the unrest and recorded that Molotov cocktails had ignited fires in Harlem, Bedford-Stuyvesant, Watts, Cincinnati, Newark, Detroit, and elsewhere.⁷ A police officer in Detroit related: "My uniform was torn, my pants were shredded on one side, shirt was torn, and I was just covered with soot because we were in the middle of fire for six or eight hours straight."⁸ By the time Motor City calmed, a whopping 1,397 fires had ravaged an area of 140 blocks.⁹ Instead of a huge urban vista, one reporter lamented, "All you see is rubble."¹⁰

When King admonishes listeners to avoid bricks, bottles, and Molotov cocktails, he summons bleak memories of this recent violence. He warns about Molotov cocktails because exasperated people in Watts, Newark, Detroit, and elsewhere *had* flung the explosive, homemade devices. Many feared that another Watts or another Detroit—or even worse—would erupt *somewhere* when "riot season" would arrive in the summer, a few weeks after King's speech.

In order to reframe the strike, King needed to allay such fears. Such a task was formidable because local newspapers and city officials persistently confused nonviolent protest with communist subversion. In the eyes of many whites, laborers on strike were assisting Moscow, and ministers who marched peacefully equaled rioters who burned Detroit. Certainly, Mayor Loeb strongly supported segregation and brooked no dissent from African Americans.

The civil rights preacher also faced a huge challenge in wrestling with the national news media. Following their seemingly inviolable dictum—"If it bleeds, it leads"—the national press generally ignored the trash collectors' strike until violence erupted. On television sets from coast to coast, Memphis only popped up when King defiled his image by leading a nonviolent march that went awry. Ignored were the intolerable conditions that prompted the march. Ignored was the unity of the strikers. Ignored were their attempts to communicate with Mayor Loeb. Also ignored was Loeb's intransigence. Whites around the nation remained highly uninformed about the city—a situation that shoved King into a corner. His entire, final speech is an effort to escape that corner. In order to succeed, he needed to drastically redefine the strike and Memphis. He also needed to revive hope.

In this chapter I analyze King's ability to escape his rhetorical corner by framing the Exodus as a model for later, liberatory events in African American lives, including the strike in Memphis. As I explain, King's discussion of the Exodus alludes to the biblical account of the creation of the world and to the Passover; the Sinai Covenant; the Ten Commandments; and the entire, multifaceted life of Moses. I note that King also summons the pattern of loss and redemption that often occurs in later biblical narratives and in African American orations as well. And I explicate King's adaptation of the Exodus narrative to reconceive the garbage carriers' walkout.

King begins "I've Been to the Mountaintop" by thanking Ralph Abernathy and by saluting the crowd for ignoring the downpour to drive to Mason Temple.

Immediately after lauding Abernathy and his listeners, King makes his initial move to escape his rhetorical dilemma. He asks God to transport him out of Memphis. Not only does he request to fly across the ocean, he also asks to glide into the ancient past. By fantasizing travel as far from Memphis as possible—both in time and space—King deserts Memphis for the purpose of radically reinventing it.

Zooming through time enables King to shed white supremacist frames for viewing Memphis and to begin the process of refashioning and redefining it. He projects the city onto a stage and casts himself, his listeners, the trash collectors, the mayor, and the press as actors in a play. King imagines that the play began centuries ago and that its audience is huge. Despite the gross inattention of national journalists, people around the world are watching the strike, King insists, and future generations will witness it, too.

Stepping into his time machine, King flies far beyond the landscape of American history. He asks to witness the Exodus: "I would take my mental flight by Egypt, and I would watch God's children in their magnificent trek from the dark dungeons of Egypt ... across the Red Sea, through the wilderness, on toward the Promised Land." King declares, "And in spite of its magnificence, I wouldn't stop there."

Instead, he asks God to escort him to ancient Greece, specifically to the Parthenon, where he could hear Socrates, Plato, Aristotle, Sophocles, and Euripides debate "the great and eternal issues of reality." This destination on the time machine, however, would also fail to satisfy him. He asserts, "But I wouldn't stop there!" He next wishes to see "the great heyday of the Roman Empire" and "developments around there, through various emperors and leaders." After that visit, however, he again states that he wants to travel more.

For his next destination in his time machine, he chooses the Italian Renaissance—a time when Leonardo da Vinci, Michelangelo, and Raphael created stunning works of art. Yet again, he insists, "But I wouldn't stop there!" Instead, he wants to witness Martin Luther hammer ninety-five theses onto the door of a German church, thus propelling the Protestant Reformation. Even after mentioning that Martin Luther is his namesake, he again reiterates, "But I wouldn't stop there!"

Then he asks to cruise back across the ocean to visit American history. He wants to venture to the White House, where he could see, "a vacillating president by the name of Abraham Lincoln finally come to the conclusion that he had to sign the Emancipation Proclamation." By now the next line has become a refrain: "But I wouldn't stop there!" He also wishes to hear President Franklin Roosevelt use the radio to calm a nation facing the perils of the Great Depression. And, again, he replays the refrain, "But I wouldn't stop there!"

On King's tour through history, he creates, for each spot on his itinerary, a pivotal scene in a great pageant: the Exodus, classical Athens, classical Rome, the Italian Renaissance, the Protestant Reformation, the Emancipation Proclamation, and the New Deal.[11] For King and his listeners, each of these developments elevated humanity.

Some—or all—of these seven stops of King's time machine resonate with each other. The Exodus obviously chimes with the Emancipation Proclamation. Both the Exodus and Lincoln's edict overcame a massive and seemingly invincible institution—slavery—while initiating freedom for huge numbers of people. In both cases, the arrival of freedom engendered uninhibited joy. In both cases, that joy preceded a time of struggle: the Exodus introduced the Hebrews to forty years of wandering the Sinai desert; American emancipation introduced the tortuous years of Reconstruction. And, in both cases, the great leader associated with emancipation died dramatically: Moses succumbed on Mount Pisgah just before the Hebrews could reach the Promised Land; Lincoln was murdered immediately after the end of the Civil War. Further, abolitionists sometimes claimed that, like the Exodus, the defeat of American bondage fulfilled the divine will.

For King's liberal Protestant listeners, the Protestant Reformation and the New Deal, two other destinations for King's time machine, also paralleled the Exodus. History seemed to shift in all three of these moments, uplifting large numbers of people. John Wycliffe, Martin Luther, and other dissidents shook the Catholic Church while instituting Protestantism, thereby affecting generations of believers (including African American Protestants, like King). According to King and many others, Franklin Roosevelt's policies eventually raised millions from poverty. King implies that, like the Emancipation Proclamation, the Reformation and the New Deal resemble the Exodus inasmuch as all these events spelled massive social upheaval that replaced oppression with hope and opportunity.

Even though the cultural achievements of fifth-century Greece, classical Rome, and the Italian Renaissance did not include an escape from Pharaoh or any other social revolt, one can also view those accomplishments metaphorically as forms of Exodus. Athenian and Roman civilizations created inestimable breakthroughs in rhetoric, law, philosophy, drama, poetry, sculpture, pottery, architecture, engineering, and government. Cresting in the work of Leonardo da Vinci and Michelangelo, the Renaissance replaced late medieval religion with an expansive Christian humanism and a new sense of human possibility.

Despite witnessing glorious moments from his time machine, King explains that seeing any one of these events would not fulfill his life. Actually, he claims that witnessing *all* these breakthroughs *combined* would leave him dissatisfied. One could easily wonder: What would be wrong with observing sublime moments of liberation, thought, and creativity? Recognizing that his dissatisfaction might seem peculiar, he explains: "Strangely enough, I would turn to the Almighty and say, 'If you allow me to live just a few years in the second half of the twentieth century, I will be happy.'" He immediately admits that this choice is odd: "Now that's a strange statement to make." The assertion indeed seems puzzling. It appears even more perplexing when he admits: "The world is all messed up. The nation is sick. Trouble is in the land. Confusion all around." Choosing to live in the present seems not merely puzzling, but bewildering. Current circumstances are not simply unprepossessing or ambiguous; they are, rather, stark, dismal, and threatening.

Yet, despite—or perhaps because of—this bleak situation, King explains, God is now actively working for change: "Something is happening in our world." What? "Masses of people are rising up!" King cites South Africa, Kenya, Ghana, New York City, Atlanta, Jackson, and Memphis as places where, he exclaims, "The cry is always the same: 'We want to be free!'" King here links the nonviolent African American revolt in the United States to grassroots rebellions in Africa nations, seventeen of which had overthrown European colonialist rule and established their independence in a single year—1960—joining eight other liberated African colonies.[12] All these movements undermined white domination.

Not only does King connect African anti-colonialism to American civil rights, he also aligns these popular struggles with the Exodus, Reformation, and Emancipation Proclamation. These uprisings are so significant, he argues, that their importance relates to—and possibly rivals—that of American emancipation, the birth of Protestantism, and even the Exodus. All are moments, he claims, when oppressed masses claim a measure of freedom, freedom that has yet to be fully achieved. Only one reason would spur King to desert the pinnacles of history—the parted Red Sea, the Parthenon, classical Rome, the Italian Renaissance, Luther's church door, Lincoln's White House, and Roosevelt's microphone—to visit the present. The one reason is that the present moment, albeit still in process, has the potential to become another historical watershed. Only a moment of potentially equivalent greatness could summon any sane person from landmark historical events to the troubled present.

With this reference to the Exodus, King begins his biblical narrative and biblical hermeneutic. He starts by simply mentioning his desire to witness "God's children in their magnificent trek from the dark dungeons of Egypt ... across the Red Sea, through the wilderness, on toward the Promised Land." These sentences present the bare bones of a theological narrative that four books of the Pentateuch (Exodus, Leviticus, Numbers, and Deuteronomy) relate at great length. Because the story is exceedingly grand and extremely familiar to devout Jews and Christians, King's evocation of the Exodus is huge, especially for the ministers and the many other regular churchgoers and Bible readers among his audience.

When King mentions Egyptian slavery and the triumphant crossing of the Red Sea, he summons the larger Exodus narrative and the narrative theology that the authors of the Pentateuch generated. While the Bible includes many literary genres, most biblical writers and editors primarily present their theology not via philosophical propositions but, rather, through story. Andre LaCocque notes that one of the authors of the Pentateuch, the Yahwist, assumed "that there is no better vehicle for theology than narration." LaCocque explains that the Yahwist viewed "ever-changing history itself" as "a carrier of revelation, a revelation whose continuity was dialectically qualified by unpredictable versatility."[13] Most of the Pentateuch, including portions not written by the Yahwist, reflects these assumptions.

Obviously, in any narrative, authors and editors assert their themes, in part, through the way they sequence chapters and events. The Pentateuch begins, of course, with Genesis and its explanation of the creation of the universe and the fall of Adam and Eve. The second book of the Bible, Exodus, resonates in important ways with the story of Genesis. When King mentions the movement of the Hebrews "across the Red Sea," he summons the familiar image of the waters separating from the land—the mighty act that enabled the Hebrews to overcome Pharaoh and escape Egyptian slavery. In Genesis, God generates order from chaos in part by dividing the waters from the land.[14] In Exodus, the image of God splitting the waters from the land reverberates with the earlier imagery of creation.[15] Noting the consonance between creation and the miracle at the Red Sea, Terence Fretheim suggests that the Exodus narrative presents a "theology of creation" and notes the "cosmic freight of God's victory" against the pharaoh.[16] On several occasions (Second) Isaiah also drapes the miracle at the Red Sea in what Bernhard Anderson terms "the mythopoetic colors of creation."[17] (Second) Isaiah does so by explicitly and strongly likening God's division of waters and land during creation with God's parting of the Red Sea during the Exodus.[18] Psalms offers the same equation—a congruence that obviously underscores the theological importance of the Exodus.[19] As Anderson explains, "[God's] redemptive acts are acts of creation; and his creative acts are acts of history."[20] Few other events echo the creation of the world. When King and other ministers mention the Exodus, they inescapably allude to what Michael Fishbane calls "foundational cosmic patterns from a prehistorical period."[21]

By summarizing the Exodus narrative, King also recalls a narrative of hope and salvation that contrasts to the distressing tale of loss that precedes it in Genesis. There, the human story begins with a sad manifestation of evil: Adam and Eve face temptation, commit sin, and are expelled from Paradise. For centuries Christians interpreted this exit as a fall from grace and defined the Fall as an essential Christian doctrine. Of course, falling from grace strongly implies the need for redemption, and Exodus narrates the first biblical story of redemption. Its promise of new land and favor from God counteracts the account of sin and expulsion from the Garden of Eden. Through its narrative Exodus explains that God is not only the agent who punishes Adam and Eve for their misdeeds, but also the agent who rescues an entire people from a hopeless situation.[22]

By defining ancient Egypt as a set of "dark dungeons" to be overcome, King re-articulates the theme of emancipation and redemption. He alludes to the biblical account of long-suffering Hebrew slaves who groan under the excesses of Pharaoh, their tyrannical, egotistical, and stupid ruler. King is claiming that Pharaoh so grossly and repeatedly misused his power that he transformed his nation into a prison. In a number of orations, including "I've Been to the Mountaintop," King treats Egyptian slavery as incontestably an arrangement of severe economic exploitation and domination—an arrangement that God overcomes decisively. In King's account, no one circumvents or surpasses Pharaoh's oppression by negotiating individual salvation or by achieving a mystical union with God. Rather, in an event of massive social dislocation, God overcomes Pharaoh's power by leading the *entire* Hebrew people on what King terms a "magnificent trek" from the Egyptian prison house to freedom.

Unlike secular historians writing about, say, the Civil War, King explains Egyptian slavery by postulating the utter inevitability of the outcome. In his view, no matter how gloomy seem the slaves' prospects, no matter how prosperous and mighty Pharaoh appears, God shapes history; further, by defying God, Pharaoh dooms slavery. King's interpretation of inevitable victory mirrors the view articulated in the Pentateuch.

Of course, Moses is such a prominent figure in the Exodus that King's summary of the Exodus necessarily alludes to Moses. His spectacular leadership implicitly serves as the precedent and prototype for King's other landmark examples of leadership—Luther guiding the Reformation, Lincoln issuing the Emancipation Proclamation, Roosevelt crafting the New Deal, and anti-colonialist and civil rights leaders now demanding equality in Africa and the United States.

A long account of Moses is, of course, familiar to virtually anyone who reads the Bible or merely attends church. Moses first appears as a baby hidden in a basket that floats on the Nile River until Pharaoh's daughter discovers him and raises him. As a young man, exasperated by the exploitation of the Hebrews, he angrily kills an Egyptian who is beating a slave. He flees to Midian and marries Zipporah, a Midianite who saved his life and bears their two children. He then climbs a mountain, sees God in the form of a burning bush, and learns the name of God ("I am who I am"). Selected by God to challenge Pharaoh, he reluctantly accepts this duty. But Pharaoh rebuffs him and orders taskmasters to increase the slaves' workload by forcing them to make bricks without straw. With God's help, Moses and Aaron perform marvels and outduel Pharaoh's magicians. After Moses and Aaron plead with Pharaoh to relent, the oblivious ruler again refuses. God then uses Moses and Aaron to initiate a series of frightful plagues—of frogs, gnats, flies, cattle, boils, hail, locusts, and darkness—each of which fails to jolt Pharaoh. Finally God strikes dead the firstborn child in each Egyptian household while sparing the Israelites through the Passover.

After Moses directs the Hebrews to the bank of the Red Sea, he lifts his rod and God miraculously separates the waters from the land. When the Hebrews walk safely across the dry seabed, Pharaoh's army pursues them; but tumultuous waters crash upon the soldiers, drowning them. Moses's sister Miriam celebrates the escape in a poem. He then guides the former slaves across the Sinai desert, where God supplies water, bread, and quail and then provides a covenant and the Ten Commandments. After Aaron leads the Israelites in an act of ungrateful apostasy—the worship of a golden calf—God rages at an entire, unfaithful people until Moses convinces him to curb the fury. Moses later serves as a judge and creates an entire judicial system. In addition he supervises the construction of an extremely magnificent tabernacle. At the end of the Israelites' forty-year sojourn in the wilderness, he climbs Mount Pisgah and, from there, gazes at their destination—Canaan, the Promised Land. Immediately after glimpsing Canaan, he dies. Joshua, the book following the Pentateuch, relates that shortly thereafter Joshua leads the Hebrews into the Promised Land.

Moses looms prominently in Judeo-Christianity because, as Norman Gottwald aptly explains, he performs a dazzling spectrum of crucial functions:

> negotiator with Pharaoh, miracle worker by a magical wand, logistics expert in leading the exodus and wilderness trek, covenant mediator between

Yahweh and Israel, lawgiver to the community, military commander in chief against Amalek and Midian, appointer and installer of priests, judge of disputes among the people, and prophet—indeed more than a prophet—in the directness of his communication with God.[23]

To this list Gottwald forgot to add that for centuries Jews and Christians believed not only that Moses performed in these capacities, but also that he wrote the entire Pentateuch. The greatly beloved King James Version of the Bible—the most famous of all English translations and one that King cites frequently—lists Genesis as the First Book of Moses and Exodus as the Second Book of Moses, and so forth. These titles indicate not only that Moses is a character in the Pentateuch, but also the belief that he authored them. The point is not that Moses actually wrote the Pentateuch—scholars deny any such possibility—but that for centuries many faithful believed that he did, an ascription that invests even greater importance in Moses.

When King refers to the Exodus, he suggests all the myriad facets of Mosaic leadership even as he emphasizes the most important role of Moses in liberating an oppressed people—a crucial theme throughout African American religion, beginning with slavery. By initiating the jaw-dropping wonder of the Exodus, Moses contrasts sharply with King David and King Solomon, the greatest monarchs of the Israelites, whose reign began long after the Hebrews entered the Promised Land. Unlike Moses, who directed an enslaved, then nomadic people, King David and King Solomon ruled a large city, commanded standing armies, administered a complex system of taxation, and governed a small empire. Solomon constructed a splendid temple with costly and lavish ornamentation. He also supervised a sizable bureaucracy, oversaw international trade, garnered impressive wealth, conscripted laborers, and assembled a large harem. Both David and Solomon embody impressive authority; their rule exemplifies what Walter Brueggemann terms "royal consciousness" and "urban imperial consciousness," which he contrasts to the "liberation consciousness of the Mosaic tradition."[24] Tilting toward Mosaic justice, the Hebrew Bible clearly indicates that Moses was closer to God than was anyone else, including David and Solomon. Significantly, King rarely, if ever, preached on either David or Solomon and, throughout his final address, decidedly emphasized the liberation consciousness of the Mosaic tradition.

King's comment about the Exodus also evokes other, familiar events in the narrative that are crucial to the entire formation of Judaism and Christianity. One is the Passover. As Exodus records, God instructs the Hebrews to slaughter lambs, smear the lambs' blood on doorposts, and hold a special meal—all in anticipation of their escape from Pharaoh.[25] Numbers, Deuteronomy, and Ezekiel instruct the Hebrews to observe the Passover as an annual celebration of their emancipation from slavery.[26] Throughout the biblical era and afterward, the observance of Passover became a quintessential commemoration of the Jewish faith. Passover also symbolizes freedom itself. Jews have celebrated Passover for literally thousands of years, up through King's lifetime and ours. The Christian Bible and Christian tradition also seize the imagery of Passover and transform it in their treatment of the Last Supper.

King's remarks about the Exodus also recall the dispensation of the Sinai Covenant—a defining element of Judaism. Even though God grants a covenant to Abraham and another to Noah, God establishes the more significant covenant with Moses on Mount Sinai, following the Israelites' escape from slavery and near the middle of the entire Exodus narrative. Many biblical writers repeatedly cite the Sinai Covenant as *the* defining moment in the life of the Israelites and the indisputable cornerstone of God's relation with them. While the meaning of the Sinai Covenant is theological, the covenant occurs inside a story. God dispenses the covenant at a specific moment in the plotline of the Exodus, a moment that did not happen and could not have happened during slavery in Egypt.

King's account of the Exodus evokes believers' memory of yet another hugely significant event—the reception of the Ten Commandments. Although the Decalogue might appear to be a timeless and universal foundation for Jewish and Christian morality, biblical writers and editors carefully place the revelation of the Ten Commandments after the granting of the Sinai Covenant. Before dispensing the Ten Commandments, God first needed to liberate the Hebrews from Egypt, then to establish the Sinai Covenant. As James Sanders explains, "The basic structure of the Pentateuch is not that of a law code but rather that of a narrative."[27] Paul Ricoeur concurs: biblical "law," he explains, "is not atemporal." Rather, authors and editors of the Pentateuch locate the Ten Commandments within a grand narrative frame of emancipation and thereby enact what Ricoeur calls a "narrativization of ethics and ethicization of the narratives."[28] Throughout "I've Been to the Mountaintop," King similarly narrativizes ethics and ethicizes narratives.

Further, King's discussion of the Exodus recalls the grand theme and pattern of promise/failure/fulfillment that occurs repeatedly in the Bible. Note these examples: God creates a flood to destroy sinful humanity but saves the righteous Noah and his family. A young, helpless David, armed with a mere slingshot, defeats the oversized warrior Goliath. God decides to bring his Word to Nineveh; a whale swallows God's reluctant messenger Jonah, who miraculously survives to preach the Word. An imprisoned Samson loses his hair—the source of his strength—but eventually kills a large number of evil Philistines. Sinful Hebrews ignore God's will and are dragooned from their homeland into captivity in Babylon, where they are reduced to dry bones; acting through Cyrus, a Persian, God mercifully leads them back to the Promised Land. The faithful Daniel enters a den of hungry lions, but God clamps the lions' jaws. King Nebuchadnezzar of Babylon tosses the saintly Shadrach, Meshach, and Abednego into a fiery furnace; God spares their lives. Jesus arrives as the Savior, is crucified by the Romans, and rises from the dead. Paul and other early Christians are persecuted, yet Christianity flourishes.

The pattern of promise/failure/fulfillment underlies the Exodus narrative and serves a prototype or parallel for other biblical narratives of promise, failure, and fulfillment. When King invokes the Exodus in "I've Been to the Mountaintop," he summons this entire biblical structure and theme. When he arranges "I've Been to the Mountaintop" according to the same pattern and theme, his speech further resonates with the Exodus and many other biblical narratives.

King's celebratory citation of the Exodus recalls biblical authors' and editors' treatment of the Exodus as a linchpin of Hebrew religion. Many, many biblical texts supply many, many citations of the Exodus, the Passover, the Sinai Covenant, the Ten Commandments, and the Promised Land. Such passages occur many times in Numbers, Deuteronomy, Joshua, I Samuel, Ezra, Nehemiah, Psalms, Isaiah, Jeremiah, Ezekiel, Daniel, Hosea, Amos, and Micah. For the writers of these texts, no other benchmarks are more important than the Exodus, the Passover, the Sinai Covenant, the Decalogue, and the Promised Land.

King's mention of the Exodus also recalls repeated references to it in the Christian scripture, for writers of the Christian Bible often cite and reinterpret the identical Mosaic events and signposts noted by the authors of sacred Hebrew literature. The authors of Matthew, Mark, Luke, John, Acts, Romans, I Corinthians, II Corinthians, Hebrews, and Revelation all reflect on the same Mosaic touchstones.

Although Matthew traces the genealogy of Jesus back to David, rather than Moses, the Christian Bible repeatedly links Moses to Jesus. Luke notes that Jesus undergoes the transfiguration when Moses and Elijah miraculously appear on a mountain with him. Matthew, Mark, Luke, and John all directly associate the Lord's Supper with the Passover.[29] Acts and Hebrews present fairly long biographies of Moses.[30] I Corinthians, II Corinthians, and Hebrews characterize the leader of the Exodus as a precursor to Christ.[31] While proclaiming that Christ's covenant replaces the old Mosaic covenant, Hebrews relates that Moses possessed foreknowledge as he reflected on the "abuse" that he "suffered for the Christ."[32] By reinterpreting the Mosaic tradition, Paul in I Corinthians and II Corinthians, the author of Luke and Acts, and the writer of Hebrews all venerate and wrestle with the heritage of Moses, the Exodus, and the Mosaic Covenant.

When King refers to the Exodus, he calls the Hebrews "God's children." Christian scripture uses this phrase to designate both Israelites and Christians. A bit later King articulates the aspirations that underlie the trash collectors' strike:

> We are determined to gain our rightful place in God's world. And that's all this whole thing is about. We aren't engaged in any negative protest and in any negative arguments with anybody. We are saying we are determined to be men. We are determined to be people.... We are saying that we are God's children. And if we are God's children, we don't have to live like we are forced to live.

Here King's phrase "God's children" designates the striking sanitation workers and, by extension, the entire African American community in Memphis. By deploying the same biblical phrase—"God's children"—to designate the biblical Hebrews and African Americans in Memphis, King telescopes two groups of people who lived thousands of years and a large ocean apart.

Beginning with his next sentence, King elaborates this equation:

> Now what does all of this mean in this great period of history? It means that we've got to stay together. We've got to stay together and maintain unity. You know, whenever Pharaoh wanted to prolong the period of slavery in Egypt, he had a favorite, favorite formula for doing it. What was that? He kept the slaves fighting among themselves. But whenever the slaves get together, something happens in Pharaoh's court, and he cannot hold the slaves

in slavery. When the slaves get together, that's the beginning of getting out of slavery. Now let us maintain unity.

Weigh the last lines: "When the slaves get together, that's the beginning of getting out of slavery. Now let us maintain unity." When King says "us," who are the "us"? The "us" are the slaves in Pharaoh's court. The "us" are also the garbage workers in Memphis. King explicitly uses the pronoun "us" to identify the enslaved Hebrews in Egypt with the exploited strikers in Memphis. By arguing that the trash collectors are, to use Kenneth Burke's term, "consubstantial" with ancient Israelite slaves in Egypt, King implies that Mayor Henry Loeb, who refuses to recognize the workers' union, is Pharaoh.[33] Reinforcing this implication, King soon exclaims, "Mayor Loeb is in dire need of a doctor!" Here King clearly uses the Exodus to reframe Memphis.

Not everyone adjusts the centuries-old Exodus narrative to reconceive a new dispute. In his recent book, *The Ethics of Memory*, Avishai Margalit contends that the memory of Exodus is historical, final, and immutable. Margalit defines "closed memory" as a shared, valorized recollection of a signal event, a recollection so reified within a culture that it cannot be interrogated, overturned, transmuted, or reinterpreted. In his words, "the Exodus memory . . . is a *closed memory* of the event: the only line of memory leading to this event is the one authorized by the tradition of the community as its canonical line of memory."[34] Margalit has a point. Whereas most pious Jews and Christians quarry the Bible for guidance about personal behavior, many synagogues and churches codify sacred Hebrew narratives into sets of iconic stories trapped in amber that clergy and parents hand to generations of admiring schoolchildren. During King's lifetime, churchgoers often froze the stories because they assumed that they lived in a "Christian nation" that had already achieved freedom, justice, and godliness. They regarded their mayors as democratically elected officials and as fellow Christians, not Pharaohs. Yet, to petrify the Exodus narrative is to create a species of what Burke deems "bureaucratized imagination," which forces readers to walk a "cow-path . . . in pious obedience to . . . the authority of custom."[35] Such a closed memory or bureaucratized imagination is exactly what King shatters in "I've Been to the Mountaintop."

For biblically literate members of King's immediate and later audiences, his expansion of the Exodus to encompass contemporary strikers in Memphis represents a further extension of biblical writers' numerous recapitulations of the Exodus. After Moses dies and Joshua assumes his position of leadership, Joshua explicitly announces that God dries the Jordan River to facilitate the Hebrews' entry into Canaan—an unmistakable re-enactment of the earlier crossing of the Red Sea.[36] Psalms also equates the parting of the Red Sea to the entrance into the land of milk and honey.[37] Later, reflecting on the period of Assyrian domination of Judah and Israel, (First) Isaiah, Micah, and Hosea prophesy a new Exodus from Assyrian vassalage.[38]

In 587 BCE the Babylonians seized the Hebrews in their remaining, southern kingdom of Judah, hauling them into captivity in Babylon. For several biblical writers, the Exodus serves as a lens for interpreting this catastrophe and the ensuing misery. Ezekiel blames the Babylonian subjugation on the Hebrews' unfaithfulness during the original Exodus.[39] Zephaniah and Ezra define the return from Babylonian exile as a new Exodus; Ezra states that the Hebrews departing from Babylon will receive silver and gold, just as they did when they followed Moses out of Egypt.[40] All three major books of Hebrew prophecy—Isaiah, Jeremiah, and Ezekiel—provide not only oracles of doom, but also oracles of hope, specifically hope for a return from Babylonian exile to Israel. Jeremiah explains that the glory of the new Exodus from Babylon will *surpass* that of the original Exodus from Egypt.[41]

(Second) Isaiah repeatedly marshals the imagery of Exodus when prophesying the return from Babylonian captivity. As Bernhard Anderson notes, reimagining the Exodus is one of the "dominant themes" in (Second) Isaiah.[42] Walther Eichrodt insists that (Second) Isaiah "gives full force" to this project, returning to it "again and again."[43] In chapters 41, 42, 43, 48, 49, 51, 52, and 55, (Second) Isaiah presents the Exodus as a cosmic drama that continues to engulf human life, rejoicing that the Israelites in Babylon—and all exploited peoples—will recapitulate the Hebrews' earlier experience of escaping Egypt. Far more extensively than any other writer of Hebrew scripture, Second Isaiah envisions that to live faithfully in any oppressive Babylon is to abide in Pharaoh's Egypt while awaiting a planetary and human (re-)creation and (re-)emancipation. Significantly, King in "I Have a Dream" quotes one of the most important, Exodus-related passages in (Second) Isaiah.

Other writers of Hebrew scripture also expand the Exodus beyond the Israelites. Amos mentions that the Philistines and Syrians *already* experienced their Exodus.[44] (First) Isaiah prophesies that *even the Egyptians* will undergo an Exodus.[45] Walter Brueggemann emphasizes that, when Amos declares that the Philistines and Syrians have undertaken an Exodus, Amos implies that Exodus is a drama that repeatedly liberates oppressed people.[46] (Second) Isaiah makes the same point directly. As these writers reiterate and reconfigure the narrative of the Exodus, they generate what Fishbane calls the "dynamic interaction, dynamic interpenetration, and dynamic interdependence" that characterizes much Hebrew scripture.[47]

In short, biblical authors and editors often stretch, interrogate, reconfigure, and relocate the Exodus. They do so because, as Brueggemann suggests, "the Exodus grammar ... saturates the imagination of Israel."[48] While the circumstances of each Exodus vary, the grand, underlying plot continues unimpeded.

More simply, all these typological plotlines impose pattern and definition on what Kenneth Burke calls "the Scramble, the Wrangle of the Market Place, the flurries and flare-ups of the Human Barnyard."[49] These dust-ups might otherwise defy comprehension. Fishbane insists that biblical typologies serve "as the means whereby the deeper dimensions perceived to be latent in historical events are rendered manifest and explicit to the cultural imagination."[50]

Burke is especially helpful for understanding the energetic intertextual relations that often prevail in the Bible. He departs from Russian formalists and other structuralist critics by defining literary structure not according to any set of formal patterns that can be identified in a text. Instead, he contends that literary form lies in writers' attention to the "psychology of the audience." He insists that form "is the creation of an appetite" and the "satisfying of that appetite."[51] He continues, "Form in literature is an arousing and fulfillment of desires. A work has form in so far as one part of it leads a reader to anticipate another part, to be gratified by the sequence."[52] He employs the term "entelechy" to designate literary form as a process that functions, in his words, as a "goad" to flesh out "implications" or as a "temporizing of essence."[53] He holds that someone interested in entelechy "would locate the 'principles' of a form not in temporarily past moments that a form develops *from*, but in possibilities of perfection which reside in the form as such and *toward* which all sorts of stories might gravitate."[54]

Biblical authors and editors interpret the Exodus narrative in an entelechial fashion, that is, as entelechy or process toward which other stories might gravitate. Whereas one might think that Joshua's arrival in Canaan would satisfy readers' desire for a wondrous conclusion to the whole Exodus saga, much Hebrew scripture—especially (Second) Isaiah—treats the entrance into the Promised Land instead as an incident that arouses desires among biblical readers. The authors of (Second) Isaiah and other sacred texts emphasize that the entrance into the Promised Land described in Joshua is not simply a past moment whose meaning is known and exhausted, but instead an indicator of possibilities of perfection that reside in the form of the Exodus narrative and toward which a variety of stories might gravitate. Those stories include the narrative of the Hebrews' return from Babylonian exile and narratives of the Syrians, Philistines, and Egyptians as well. Many writers of Christian scripture treat the Exodus in an entelechial manner as well, in their case as an indicator for a story of the perfection made possible by Jesus, the Messiah.

Although Malcolm X offers salient criticism of King and other mainstream civil rights leaders, King here implicitly answers a rebuke from Malcolm X.[55] Urging African Americans to separate from whites, Malcolm X lambastes King by arguing that, whereas Moses led slaves *away* from Pharaoh, King urged people to integrate with Pharaoh.[56] By implying that the Exodus must mean separating geographically from Pharaoh, Malcolm X interprets the Exodus literally and claims that King should interpret it literally, too. But, like many biblical writers, King explains the Exodus imaginatively, not literally. (First) Isaiah anticipates a new Exodus for the Egyptians but does not expect that that new Exodus will necessarily lead the Egyptians out of Egypt. Similarly, King views the Exodus as a narrative of liberation that might or might not involve geographical separation.

By equating Hebrew slaves to oppressed garbage workers in Memphis, King reignites numerous biblical writers' own entelechial hermeneutic of the Exodus as an ongoing process of emancipation. Like these writers, King construes the Exodus not as a frozen event that affected a single generation of Hebrews, but as a great, transformative drama that shapes human history.

King also shatters the dominant frames for comprehending Memphis. Exiting Memphis in his time machine enables him to reverse local whites' view of themselves as guardians of American democracy and order. He defines them instead as Egyptian slave-owners whose leader, the mayor, is the pharaoh. He also rejects national reporters' view of the Memphis strike as beneath their notice. Quite to the contrary, he defines the strike as the latest act in the liberatory drama of the Exodus. In King's argument, this drama will eventually offer deliverance to the strikers in Memphis and to all oppressed people.

CHAPTER 5

Fire on the Streets and in the Bones

King Revives Hebrew Prophecy

When King finishes his journey through time, he makes another huge move in his project of reimagining Memphis. Throughout his career, he failed to preach on the ethics of charity articulated in Proverbs. Instead, he embraced the more demanding ethics of justice announced in the Pentateuch and reiterated by the Hebrew prophets. Indeed, many people compared him to a Hebrew prophet; others, such as Rev. C. T. Vivian, a fellow activist, deemed him an actual prophet.[1] In "I've Been to the Mountaintop," King definitely presents or constructs himself as a prophet.

He begins by connecting distress in Memphis to broader disturbances. In his words, "The world is all messed up. The nation is sick. Trouble is in the land. Confusion all around." Note that he fails to qualify his judgment. Singapore is not a mess. Argentina is not mess. Rather, the *entire globe* is a mess. Also, Vermont is not ill. Wyoming is not ill. Rather, the *entire nation* is sick, troubled, and confused. These lines announce that a monstrous crisis engulfs not only Memphis, but the whole United States and the whole planet. The crisis is so severe, he maintains, that "if something isn't done and done in a hurry to bring the colored peoples of the world out of their long years of poverty, their long years of hurt and neglect, the whole world is doomed." Not only do Hebrew prophets decry moral sickness, pervasive trouble, and widespread confusion, they also warn of impending doom.

Through this passage, King only begins his process of invoking prophecy. Throughout much of "I've Been to the Mountaintop," he suggests, adjusts, explains, approximates, and resuscitates many of the elements, contours, and dynamics of Hebrew oracles. By approximating, reconfiguring, and reconstituting these oracles, King reshapes and reconstitutes Memphis. Below I analyze King's adaptation of many of the rhetorical dynamics of Hebrew prophecy. Then I examine how this rhetorical move enables him to resituate Memphis.

Before investigating King, however, I hazard a summary of the dynamics of prophecy as they appear in the Hebrew Bible itself. This summary matters, in part, because, even though many journalists, historians, and church leaders have identified King as a prophet, they have simply assumed that this claim is self-validating. But anyone who would call King a prophet needs to analyze prophecy and to supply reasons, evidence, and elaboration for considering King a prophet.

What exactly is a prophet? In an attempt to answer that question, Hebrew scripture features three exceedingly long, major books of prophecy—Isaiah, Jeremiah, and Ezekiel—and twelve minor books as well. In addition to the fifteen prophets who animate these books, other prophets surface elsewhere in the Hebrew Bible. Each of them is complex. For its part, the Christian Bible incorporates, yet notably refashions, Hebrew prophecy. If biblical writers and editors had been able to encapsulate prophecy briefly, they would have done so. Instead, they define prophecy as complicated and multilayered, deeply situated in historical circumstance, yet somehow germane for succeeding generations. Comprehending Hebrew prophecy is no simple task. And comprehending any attempt at *modern* biblical prophecy proves no simple task either. Although no summary of scriptural prophecy could ever prove entirely satisfactory, any interpretation of King-as-prophet must begin with such a summary. Understanding the richly variegated complexity of prophecy proves crucial to understanding King's invocation of prophecy and his refashioning of Memphis.

In my account of prophecy below, I concentrate especially on Jeremiah and Amos—two texts that King directly quotes in "I've Been to the Mountaintop."

The narrators of Jeremiah, Amos, and other prophetic books sometimes project doom as inevitable. As Donald Gowan explains, "Jeremiah's oracles put less emphasis on predicting the end of the kingdom of Judah and more emphasis on lamenting its desecration and desolation."[2]

At other times, prophets trumpet devastation as possible, but avoidable.

Walter Brueggemann remarks, "On occasion . . . the prophetic rhetorical strategy is not to announce disaster as a foregone conclusion, but to warn Israel that it is late . . . but not too late. . . . Israel can turn and repent . . . and so avert disaster."[3] At times the narrator of Amos wonders about desolation that is likely, but not certain:

> Shall not the day of the Lord be darkness and not light?
> Even very dark and no brightness in it?
> (Amos 5:20)

As prophets point toward impending or potential calamity, they repeatedly pinpoint moments of great danger. Never imagining the possibility of a humdrum future, these seers, Brueggemann declares,

> characteristically perceive their time and place as a circumstance of crisis, a context in which dangers are great and life-or-death decisions must be made. Or perhaps it is better to say that the appearance and utterance of the prophets *evokes* a crisis circumstance where none had been perceived previously. That is, the prophets not only respond to crisis, but by their abrupt utterance, they generate crisis.[4]

Instead of qualifying their announcements of crisis, prophets intensify their proclamations by insisting that they speak directly for God. In Brueggemann's words, "The prophets . . . are compelled by an inexplicable force that is taken to be the summons of Yahweh."[5] The narrator of Amos asks simply,

> When the Lord speaks, who can but prophesy?
> (Amos 3:8)

The narrator of Jeremiah also declares that God demands speech:

> I am full of the wrath of the Lord.
> I am weary of holding it in.
> (Jeremiah 6:11)

> If I say, "I will not make mention of [the Lord], nor speak any more in his name,"

> There is in my heart a burning fire shut up in my bones,
> And I am weary with holding it in,
> And I cannot.
>
> (Jeremiah 20:09)

Similarly, other prophetic texts announce God's direct choice of a special person to prophesy. Still other books imply such a claim when a prophet asserts, "Thus says the Lord" or "Hear the Word of the Lord." Such phrases appear so frequently in Hebrew prophetic literature that they amount to what scholars call "a messenger formula."[6]

A divine call, however, does not necessitate prophecy. Two major Israelite prophets, Isaiah and Jeremiah, hesitate to accept their sacred roles before eventually fulfilling them.[7] So does Gideon.[8] The entire plotline of Jonah hinges on one man's effort to shirk God's order to prophesy in Nineveh. Seeking to elude God's attention, Jonah jumps aboard a ship headed away from Nineveh. When a tempest threatens to engulf the vessel, the other sailors toss Jonah overboard; and a whale swallows him. Yet he miraculously survives and finally obeys God's demand to testify.

Perhaps these figures sometimes resist their commissions because their roles are unenviable and their witness often unrelenting and harsh. Jeremiah asserts that those who deliver happy messages are false witnesses whom God never summoned.[9] Instead of flattering anyone, in each of the fifteen prophetic books—and elsewhere in Hebrew scripture as well—prophets characteristically speak like extraordinarily aggressive courtroom prosecutors. They pile charge upon charge in the process of cataloguing a shocking inventory of faithlessness and transgressions. In 1962 Abraham Heschel, King's friend, observed, "God is raging in the prophet's words," which express "breathless impatience with injustice" in a world that "reels in confusion" while people manifest blockheaded "indifference" that requires "ceaseless shattering."[10]

Undeterred by worldly authority, prophets repeatedly heap opprobrium on powerful sovereigns who, the prophets maintain, spawn one disaster after another. Few noteworthy rulers elude scorn. David, the greatest monarch of Israel, definitely is not spared. II Samuel explains that David desires the lovely Bathsheba so much that he places her husband in the frontline of a battle, hoping that he will be killed. After this hapless man dies in combat, Nathan, a prophet, boldly confronts David and directly accuses him of murder.[11]

Not content to censure rulers, prophets also indict high-ranking priests who sanction an unjust social order. In Amos, God, speaking through the prophet, declares:

> I despise your feasts and your solemn assemblies.
> Even though you offer me your burnt offerings and grain offerings,
> I will not accept them....
> Take away from me the noise of your songs;
> To the melody of your harps I will not listen.
> But let justice roll down like waters
> And righteousness like a mighty stream.
> (Amos 5:21-24)

Through such statements, Amos and other prophetic texts unequivocally decry empty, formal worship performed by religious leaders who ignore poverty and injustice. Amos does so by directly contrasting the artificiality of insincere worship to the natural force of rushing water.[12]

As if exposing the apostasy of sovereigns and priests were not enough, prophets repeatedly excoriate the entire Hebrew people for grossly unethical behavior. The narrator of Amos angrily rails at those who

> sell the righteous for silver
> and the needy for a pair of shoes—
> they that trample the head of the poor
> into the dust of the earth
> and turn aside the way of the afflicted.
> (Amos 2:6-7)

When conduct lamented by the prophets becomes pervasive within the dominant culture, they do not reconsider their rhetoric. Quite the contrary: the very popularity of transgressions spurs prophets to express greater and greater heartache, disillusionment, and fury. They often castigate masses of ordinary Jews for worshipping false gods instead of—or in addition to—Yahweh. For prophets, the commonplace, syncretic practice of blending the worship of God with reverence toward another deity does not render syncretism more acceptable but, instead, more appalling.

Alongside their denunciations, prophets incessantly plead for rightful daily conduct. Like Moses, who demands justice for Pharaoh's slaves, prophets insist on justice for the downtrodden. They champion fairness and kindness toward aliens, the poor, widows, and children.

For the authors of prophetic literature, marginalized people count because the entire Hebrew people matter. In prophetic discourse, as in the Pentateuch, no one achieves a form of individual salvation. Rather, as in the Pentateuch, the entire Israelite community seesaws between oppression and redemption. Indeed, with a few exceptions (such as Job and Ecclesiastes), the Hebrew Bible concentrates primarily on the spiritual and ethical (and sometimes geographical) direction of all Israelites.

Of course, as the prophets—and Judaism as a whole—suggest, God helps shape this destiny, even as the Hebrews' political situation teeters, first one way, then another. Like the Pentateuch, the prophetic books propound a narrative theology tied to large historic events, such as the Israelites' experience of vassalage to Assyria or exile in Babylon. Again like the Pentateuch, prophetic literature meshes broad theological and ethical concerns with a keen recognition of specific, current circumstances that Hebrews face.

Although bitter fulminations and doom-laden oracles dominate much of Jeremiah, Amos, and numerous other prophetic texts, those works also supply the potential for repentance and renovated innocence. Prophets (or their editors) sometimes spotlighted and sometimes minimized the drastically shifting historical scene that provoked their changing emphases from definite or possible cataclysm to attainable glory. Partly for those reasons, Isaiah, Jeremiah, Ezekiel, Amos, and other prophetic texts juxtapose vivid oracles of colossal suffering against equally vivid oracles of hope and bliss. In the rhetorical universe of the prophets, ordinary existence was unimaginable. Instead, hovering just beyond the brink of the most excruciating crisis, both devastation and redemption seem—or are—paradoxically possible or even imminent.

Even though the sequence of promise, then loss, then redemption repeats itself frequently in much Hebrew scripture, biblical writers never present that pattern as an inexorable, mythical cycle of eternal return. Rather, they assert that, over the centuries, Israelites freely and repeatedly choose behavior so abominable that it portends or triggers calamity.

Just as prophetic language is often extreme, so, sometimes, are prophets' actions. Consider bizarre behavior in Isaiah, Jeremiah, and Ezekiel. For three years, a naked Isaiah ambles around Jerusalem. Offering another curious sight, Jeremiah strides through Jerusalem with an ox yoke fastened onto his neck. Ezekiel sleeps on one side for 40 days and on the other side for

150 days. He also swallows a scroll. Biblical texts portray these and other seers as extraordinary figures who often inhabit and speak from a dimension quite apart from their more conventional peers, a dimension inspired, yet troubled, filled with both ecstatic dreams and bitter visions. Their often disturbing, sometimes utopian rhetoric frequently appears to spin from trance-like or supranormal states. Ezekiel experiences trances that seem related to the sometimes phantasmagorical imagery of the book that bears his name.

As one might imagine, in the prophetic literature, royal figures and their loyal priests often despise those who dramatically hurl so many denunciations their way. Various biblical narratives portray prophets who face neglect or outright persecution: Ezekiel is disregarded; Isaiah spat on; Jeremiah threatened with murder and dragooned into Egypt; Amos banished; and Zechariah stoned to death.[13] Jeremiah reports that another prophet was also slain.[14] I Kings and Nehemiah unhappily conclude: Hebrews kill their prophets.[15] Prophets' inability to win approval from their immediate listeners might help explain their rage and their sometimes bizarre behavior, both of which can be seen, in part, as attempts to smash complacency. Hosea deems a "prophet" to be a "fool" and describes the "man of spirit" as one who became "mad" because of the Hebrews' "great iniquity and great hatred."[16]

Many of the dynamics and contours of prophecy begin with Moses. In Exodus, before exercising leadership, he encounters a burning bush and receives a sacred commission that he tries to refuse. After he reverses himself and accepts his call, he proclaims a crisis—slavery—and spawns further crises by summoning plagues that engulf Egypt. He also severely challenges political and military authority, accusing Pharaoh of ghastly misdeeds and claiming that God is more righteous and more powerful than any human ruler. In Pharaoh's court, Moses and Aaron expose the weakness of Egyptian religion by performing wonders that outdo those of Pharaoh's priests. Moses repudiates everyday political and economic culture in Egypt, which is based on slavery, and demands freedom for those who groan in chains. His claim that God is much greater than Pharaoh is so at odds with the dominant Egyptian worldview that Pharaoh cannot begin to understand him, even after calamitous plagues envelope Egypt. Then, while brandishing a promise of freedom, Moses witnesses an inestimable national catastrophe when Pharaoh's intractability triggers the deaths of the Egyptians' firstborn sons.

As if this were not enough, Moses anticipates the behavior of subsequent prophets when he directs the Hebrews during their forty years in the wilderness. He spotlights a crisis—the worship of a homemade Golden Calf—and, enraged, assails the Israelites for crafting a metallic idol while rejecting the Sinai Covenant. Later, again furious at the Hebrews' transgressions, he breaks the tablets containing the Ten Commandments, which he had just received on Mount Sinai. But he eventually presents the Decalogue to the Hebrews and continues to lead them across the wilderness toward the Promised Land.

Not only does the Pentateuch present Moses as one who repeatedly embodies the dynamics of prophecy, but Hosea flat-out states that Moses was a prophet.[17] Going further, Numbers and Deuteronomy insist that Moses, the first prophet, surpasses every later prophet. Of all the prophets, Numbers explains, *only* Moses received God's word "mouth to mouth"; Deuteronomy notes that *only* Moses sees God "face to face."[18]

Deuteronomy insists that Israelite kings should govern within the framework of the Sinai Covenant and announces that God will appoint prophets to correct any waywardness from it. On dozens of occasions, Psalms, Amos, Jeremiah, Ezekiel, Micah, (First) Isaiah, (Second) Isaiah, (Third) Isaiah, and other sacred Hebrew books all repeatedly allude to the Exodus narrative and the Sinai Covenant as the cornerstone of Hebrew religion and Hebrew identity.[19] As Gowan explains, Amos explicitly summons the Hebrews "back to the law of Sinai."[20] James Sanders elaborates:

> When [Amos] levels indictments against Israel . . . he accuses them, first, of maltreating the poor and needy. . . . And then just after these summary indictments he proceeds to cite . . . the Torah story . . . which is his authority. . . . And the point he makes is unmistakable: the story describes the way of pharaoh in making the early Israelites slaves, and the way of Yahweh in freeing them from slavery. And then when Israel came into her own nationhood . . . she imitated Pharaoh by "tramp[ling] . . . the poor into the dust of the earth and turn[ing] aside from the way of humility."[21]

Gerhard von Rad asserts, "Jeremiah stands and acts upon the Exodus-Sinai tradition."[22] Going farther, Marvin Sweeney observes that Jeremiah appears as a "second Moses."[23] In Brueggemann's words, prophets frequently "replicated the constitutive word of Moses" while exemplifying "the liberation consciousness of the Mosaic tradition." Biblical editors, Brueggemann adds, "channeled" the "rich, wild, and imaginative utterances of the prophets" into "Mosaic categories."²⁴

The continual process of re-interpreting the Exodus-Sinai tradition exemplifies what Michael Fishbane calls the "dynamic interaction, dynamic interpenetration, and dynamic interdependence" that characterizes sacred Hebrew books.²⁵

In "I've Been to the Mountaintop" King approximates or re-animates each of the rhetorical dynamics of Hebrew prophecy that I discuss above. King begins to do so by following the sequence of biblical editors: he hails the wonder of the Exodus before quoting Jeremiah and Amos. In doing so, King, like the biblical writers and editors, suggests that Jeremiah and Amos extend the Exodus-Sinai tradition.

Near the middle of "I've Been to the Mountaintop," King adapts and compresses Jeremiah's metaphor of "fire in the bones": "Who is it that is supposed to articulate the longings and aspirations of the people more than the preacher? Somehow the preacher must have a kind of fire shut up in his bones, and whenever injustice is around he must tell it." Then King immediately quotes Amos: "The preacher must say with Amos, 'When the Lord speaks, who can but prophesy?'"²⁶ He then recites memorable metaphors from Amos: "Again, along with Amos, the preacher must cry, 'Let justice roll down like waters and righteousness like a mighty stream.'"²⁷

Significantly, King explicitly adjusts the prophetic commissions from Jeremiah and Amos to maintain not only that biblical prophecy extends into the present, but also that *every* contemporary preacher should function as a prophet. This contention is roughly consistent with biblical accounts of the many prophets in Israel and with the Hebrew prophets' condemnation of courtly priests who fawn over rulers while failing to prophesy.²⁸ King's evocation of scriptural calls to prophecy is the cornerstone of his definition of preaching or, possibly, *is* his definition of preaching—a message especially salient for the numerous homilists listening at Mason Temple.

Given King's status as the best-known preacher in the nation, he also implicitly, but obviously, affirms that he, too, is chosen to prophesy, just as Jeremiah, Amos, and all other prophets were tapped. Further, by repeating the divine commissions found in Jeremiah and Amos, King signals that he is prophesying *right now*, in this oration.

When King mentions "window breaking . . . [and] a little violence," he briefly refers to the disorderly march that he led in Memphis on March 28. Later in the speech, he notes his return from Atlanta to Memphis on April 3, the day that he delivers "I've Been to the Mountaintop." But why did he retreat to placid Atlanta immediately after the disturbance in Memphis? And why did he mention that retreat—hardly his most heroic moment—in his address? King sometimes complained privately that he wished to shed his public role.[29] One can view King's comment about his withdrawal from Memphis as an admission of his resistance to his prophetic call. His return to Memphis would then evince his renewed acceptance of the same prophetic commission.

Like a Hebrew prophet recoiling at the sight of corrosive evil, King repeatedly excoriates the powerful in Memphis, portraying officials as unworthy and their authority as fraudulent. He hurls invective at Mayor Henry Loeb, implicitly labeling him a pharaoh and directly calling him a sick man who requires a doctor. Through these accusations, King implies that most members of the city council, who strongly support the mayor, are assisting the pharaoh and abetting evil.

Continuing to denounce officeholders, King rails at Judge Bailey Brown of US District Court, who had issued an injunction to prohibit King's next demonstration. This federal order, King insists, is bogus: "We have an injunction and we're going into court tomorrow morning to fight this illegal, unconstitutional injunction." The judge's decision, King charges, is something that one would expect "in China or even Russia or any totalitarian country" but not in the United States, which dedicates itself to "First Amendment privileges." Obviously, judges sometimes err. But why does King call Judge Brown's injunction "illegal" and even "unconstitutional"? Why doesn't he speak more respectfully and simply say that Brown made a mistake? Wouldn't that make it easier to get the injunction overturned, which, King explains, he is trying to accomplish the following day?

By labeling the judge's edict "illegal, unconstitutional," King accuses a federal judge of failing to comprehend even the rudiments of democracy. He continues to jab sarcastically at the federal bench: "But somewhere I read of the freedom of assembly. Somewhere I read of the freedom of speech. Somewhere I read of the freedom of the press. Somewhere I read that the greatness of America is the right to protest for right." He obviously read about freedom of assembly, freedom of speech, and freedom of the press in the US Constitution, specifically in its Bill of Rights. Although he alludes to "First Amendment privileges," he never directly mentions that the Constitution and the Bill of Rights contain the First Amendment that guarantees all these freedoms. No, he never directly mentions the Constitution or the Bill of Rights at all. Instead, by declaring four times that he read about these liberties "somewhere," he flatters his listeners. He doesn't need to explain where "somewhere" is or where the "First Amendment" is because, he implies, everyone in Mason Temple already understands what document contains the First Amendment. He implies that *all* his listeners—many of whom had little formal education—grasp the meaning of the Bill of Rights. At the same instant, by reiterating "somewhere," he directly mocks the federal judge, who, he implies, apparently knows nothing about the freedom of assembly, freedom of speech, and freedom of the press. Unlike African Americans assembled in Mason Temple, he asserts, this white judge, a privileged and well-educated practitioner of jurisprudence, grossly fails to comprehend the Constitution.

Here King's words completely overturn and reverse the white supremacist social order of Memphis. In his rhetorical universe, supposedly ignorant and inferior African Americans comprehend American democracy and don't need to be reminded of which foundational document guarantees their rights. In this same rhetorical universe, the supposedly expert federal judge displays an utter failure to grasp the most elementary principles of American law. By supplying an injunction against innocent, nonviolent protestors, King contends, the federal judiciary violates the Constitution while promulgating white supremacy and reinforcing black poverty. The Constitution is the true authority, King maintains, not the judge who flouts it and whose authority, therefore, is spurious.

King then declares: "We aren't going to let any mace stop us!" This defiant comment condemns local law enforcement. Inasmuch as police never used mace against protestors in any of King's previous campaigns, King here specifically refers to Memphis police, who maced black clergy and other peaceful demonstrators. But, instead of using the past tense—"We didn't let mace stop us!"—King tells what will happen in the future: "We aren't going to let any mace stop us!" He thereby implies that the police macing was not an accident and that the strikers should prepare for more ferocity by police for the "crime" of seeking racial equality and decent wages.

Lauding the ministers who support the union, King hails James Lawson, Ralph Jackson, and Billy Kyles by name while noting that "time will not permit" him to list any other supportive pastors by name. Lawson and Jackson were two of the clergy that the Memphis police assaulted with mace a few weeks earlier. In an emotional voice, Jackson vigorously protested the macing on black radio station WDIA.[30] Clearly, many in the African American community, including many of King's listeners in Mason Temple, realize that Lawson and Jackson had been maced. By singling out for praise *only* these three clergy—two of whom were assaulted by police—King intensifies his indictment of the Memphis police and their city.

By assailing Mayor Loeb, the city council, Judge Brown, and the police, King decries virtually every governing authority in Memphis. He could hardly have offered a more thorough or a more searing indictment of officialdom.

In addition King remonstrates against mainstream pastors, contrasting them to their activist colleagues: "But I want to thank all of [the clergy who support the strike] because so often preachers aren't concerned about anything but themselves." Here he accuses many clergy of utter egotism and selfishness.

King's praise of Lawson, Jackson, and Kyles and his invocation of Jeremiah and Amos implicitly rebuke a group of well-known clergy in Memphis, including Rabbi James Wax, who refused to confront civic authority. In various meetings with the mayor, the city council, and union officials, Wax and other moderate white clergy sought to promote "good will" while remaining neutral in the labor dispute.

King strongly implies that, by eschewing their responsibility to prophesy, these religious leaders expressed vacuous sentiments that failed to aid the exploited trash carriers or anyone else. He further implies that such clergy—like those he had calmly and reasonably, but forcefully, attacked in his "Letter from Birmingham Jail" of 1963—repudiated their divine missions by refusing to promote racial justice.[31] He elaborates this critique by thanking Lawson, Jackson, and Kyles for demanding fairness for city employees. Unlike Wax and many other comfortable moderates, King implies, Lawson and Jackson were willing to suffer a police attack in their pursuit of racial justice. Thereby, King indicates, Lawson and Jackson proved themselves worthy of the tradition of biblical prophets, who unequivocally advocated justice and resolutely refused to compromise with inequities.

King also directly challenges ministers to expand their theology:

> It's all right to talk about "long white robes over yonder," in all of its symbolism, but ultimately people want some suits and dresses and shoes to wear down here. It's all right to talk about streets flowing with milk and honey, but

God has commanded us to be concerned about the slums down here and his children who can't eat three square meals a day. It's all right to talk about the New Jerusalem, but one day God's preacher must talk about the new New York, the new Atlanta, the new Philadelphia, the new Los Angeles, and the new Memphis, Tennessee.

Here he adapts images about heaven familiar in many folk sermons—"long white robes" and "streets flowing with milk and honey"—by linking them to bodily concerns: suits, dresses, shoes, hunger. He also mentions the New Jerusalem, an eschatological image from Revelation of a divine city that descends from heaven to earth.³² Instead of focusing simply on the New Jerusalem, he insists, preachers must also concentrate on American cities that require wholesale transformation in order to become "the new New York," "the new Atlanta," and "the new Memphis, Tennessee." Throughout this passage he intertwines the themes of otherworldly deliverance and this-worldly salvation, claiming that ministers are half-right in emphasizing the afterlife. Preachers should, he argues, continue to guide people toward heaven, but they also must alleviate hunger and deprivation. In King's argument, physical needs are spiritual needs, for the physical is spiritual. This theme is articulated and reiterated throughout much of the Hebrew Bible, including Exodus, Jeremiah, and Amos.

King also lambastes the most prominent voices of the local white community—its main newspapers, the *Memphis Press-Scimitar* and *Commercial Appeal*. Referring to the demonstration of March 28, he declares:

You know what happened the other day and the press dealt only with the window breaking. I read the articles. They very seldom got around to mentioning the fact that thirteen hundred sanitation workers are on strike and that Memphis is not being fair to them and that Mayor Loeb is in dire need of a doctor! They didn't get around to that.

By concentrating on one march gone haywire while ignoring the gross oppression of African Americans decade after decade in Memphis, the *Memphis Press-Scimitar* and *Commercial Appeal*, he claims, sanctioned and buttressed white supremacy. He coolly observes that reporters "very seldom got around to mentioning" unjust working conditions and the strike; he critiques them through a devastating understatement. He reinforces this powerful, ironic comment by calmly reiterating, "They didn't get around to that."

When King decries the press, he indicts not only local reporters and editors, but also the national news media. His observation signals his auditors' awareness that, before one march turned sour, local and national reporters generally presented little substantive reporting about racial conditions in Memphis, systematically omitting the conditions that garbage workers faced, the dignity of their nonviolent marches, and the recalcitrance of Mayor Loeb.[33]

Around the nation, King implies, millions had little choice but to assume that life in Memphis was serene. King implicitly claims that, when slumbering journalists on the East Coast awoke to relay accounts of a single inglorious march, the press was implicitly but strongly suggesting that its turmoil came from nowhere.

King's listeners were not surprised by his indictment of the press. As Laurie Green explains, the *Memphis Press-Scimitar* and *Commercial Appeal* systematically refused to report racial exploitation and surging civil rights protests in Memphis during the early 1960s. She observes, "The perception of Memphis as a place of racial harmony ... had been reinforced during the early 1960s" when the media minimized or ignored black grievances and activism, especially from students. She adds that the firm refusal of the white newspapers to report extensive civil rights protests and arrests in Memphis left the white public unprepared when the trash carriers idled their city trucks. In her words, "The contrast between the intensity of the [garbage workers'] movement and the myth of the city's racial harmony caught thousands of white Memphians by surprise in 1968."[34]

Further, as King's audience thoroughly understood, not only did Memphis newspapers fail to discuss racism, those newspapers constantly perpetuated it. Neither paper employed any African American reporters. Further, the *Commercial Appeal* featured an ugly, disgusting, daily cartoon that showcased a racist caricature of an impoverished, but humble and harmless, African American dubbed "Hambone," who deferentially referred to whites as "boss man" and "missuz."[35] Earlier in his speech, King reminded some of his auditors of "Hambone" when he dismissed African American subservience—of the kind epitomized in "Hambone"—as utterly outmoded and spent: "I can remember when Negroes were just going around, as Ralph [Abernathy] has said so often, scratching where they didn't itch and laughing when they weren't tickled. But that day is all over."

Not content with such fulminations, King tosses sulfurous accusations at several big companies, which, he argues, continually prey on African

Americans. While indicting these corporations, he simultaneously explains how his supporters in Memphis—and across the nation—can begin to demand and implement justice throughout their daily lives: "We just need to go around to these stores and to these massive industries in our country and say, 'God sent us by here to say to you that you're not treating his children right. And we've come by here to ask you to make the first item on your agenda fair treatment where God's children are concerned.'" Continuing, King pinpoints companies whose behavior, he attests, is so outrageous and despicable that they merit no more customers:

> "Now if you're not prepared to do that, we do have an agenda that we must follow. And our agenda calls for withdrawing economic support from you." And so, as a result of this, we are asking you tonight to go out and tell your neighbors not to buy Coca-Cola in Memphis. Go by and tell them not to buy Sealtest Milk. Tell them not to buy—what is the other bread?—Wonder Bread. And what is the other bread company, Jesse? Tell them not to buy Hart's Bread.

While explaining the logic of boycotts, he also illuminates the interlocking relationships among the business and political elites in Memphis. He observes that Coca-Cola and Sealtest Milk can reverse their tacit allegiance with the mayor and help the strikers win a victory:

> As Jesse Jackson has said, up to now, only the garbage men have been feeling pain. Now we must kind of redistribute the pain. We are choosing these companies because they haven't been fair in their hiring policies, and we are choosing them because they can begin the process of saying they are going to support the needs and the rights of these men who are on strike. And then they can move on downtown and tell Mayor Loeb to do what is right.

Elaborating his call to enact justice in everyday affairs, King urges listeners to shun white banks and to deposit their money instead in an African American bank: "I call upon you to take your money out of the banks downtown and deposit your money in the Tri-State Bank. We want a 'bank-in' movement in Memphis." He notes that his own organization, the Southern Christian Leadership Conference, had done just that. Through this entreaty, he joins other regional and national civil rights leaders in endorsing the Tri-State Bank of Memphis and Nashville, which African

Americans had operated successfully for years.[36] Urging further support for local African American businesses, he urges his audience to patronize "six or seven black insurance companies here in the city of Memphis." Although he admits that millions of individual African Americans "are poor" he explains that, on the whole, they are wealthy. In his words, "Never stop and forget that collectively ... we are richer than all the nations of the world, with the exception of nine. Did you ever think about that? ... That's power right there. If we know how to pool it."[37] Because of this wealth, he contends, boycotts orchestrated by united, well-disciplined communities will succeed.

King's mention of Coca-Cola, the largest national company that he fingers for a boycott, is particularly striking, given that Coca-Cola placed its headquarters in Atlanta, King's hometown. By championing a boycott of Coca-Cola, the civil rights preacher demands justice even at the cost of alienating a political ally—Robert Woodruff, the CEO of Coca-Cola. After King won the Nobel Peace Prize in 1964, Woodruff insisted that the business leaders in Atlanta join him in celebrating King's award by attending a lavish banquet in honor of their hometown hero. Woodruff's invitees thoroughly understood the importance of Coca-Cola, one of the largest and most prestigious companies in the United States. Many of the invitees surrendered any misgivings they may have had and accepted Woodruff's invitation to congratulate the controversial King.[38] King, Ralph Abernathy, Andrew Young, Jesse Jackson, James Lawson, and possibly others in Mason Temple understood that boycotting the beverage company would mean cutting ties not only with Woodruff, but also with other, economically powerful supporters, especially in Atlanta. By advocating a boycott of Coca-Cola, King insists that injustice needed to be tackled, even if one angers one's own moderate allies.

Earlier King argued that every preacher should act as a prophet. By proposing consumer boycotts of large corporations, he implies that every listener in Mason Temple—and every other supporter in Memphis—can receive divine inspiration to demand justice from the wealthy and powerful.

By now, King has explicitly castigated Mayor Loeb, Judge Brown, police, moderate clergy, large banks, insurance companies, local news outlets, the national press, Coca-Cola, Sealtest Milk, Wonder Bread, Hart's Bread—basically, every pillar of civic and economic authority in Memphis, plus some national institutions as well. His treatment of the mayor and the federal judge is so acidic and his indictment of the city so thorough that one could easily wonder what else he could possibly add. Yet he manages to simultaneously broaden and intensify his denunciation by reiterating his earlier call for nothing less than a general strike throughout the city: "And when we have our march, you need to be there. If it means leaving work, if it means leaving school, be there. Be concerned about your brother." Of course, given the large African American population in Memphis, a general African American walkout on the day of King's proposed march would directly impact the entire town and would shock white complacency. Further, perhaps a one-day strike would lead to lengthier protests and boycotts, in the manner of the Montgomery Bus Boycott, which began as a mere one-day affair.

For King, urging the halt of normal functions of businesses and schools means stigmatizing the *complete* social status quo as illegitimate. He implicitly upbraids the entire mainstream community of Memphis—the society that elects mayors, pays police, reads newspapers, patronizes banks, purchases insurance, quaffs Coca-Cola, chomps Wonder Bread, munches Hart's Bread, and undergirds the complete, local establishment.

Rejecting the facile individualism that underlies much of American culture, King underscores the importance of the entire community. When advocating support for the garbage workers, he insists, "either we go up together or we go down together." In this appeal, those who gather the trash should not try to lift themselves above other blue-collar workers by attending college. Nor should the middle class seek riches by navigating the stock market. Rather, everyone should work to elevate *every* African American in their city by demanding fair treatment and good wages and by boycotting Coca-Cola and other companies that practice racism.

King grounds his demand for justice by narrating the garbage workers' strike as a new Exodus and by quoting Amos: "Let justice roll down like waters and righteousness like a mighty stream." By attending to the particularities of the strike, he follows the prophets' common practice of blending larger themes with a recognition of specific, current circumstances.

Early in "I've Been to the Mountaintop" King weighs nothing less than the future of the world:

> Men for years now have been talking about war and peace. But now no longer can they just talk about it. It is no longer a choice between violence and nonviolence in this world. It's nonviolence or nonexistence.

That is where we are today. And also, in the human rights revolution, if something isn't done and done in a hurry to bring the colored peoples of the world out of their long years of poverty, their long years of hurt and neglect, the whole world is doomed.

Adding his hopeful quotation from Amos to his earlier doomsday warning, King, like the Hebrew prophets, offers the choice between the prospect of peace and equanimity and that of utter desolation. Redemption, he maintains, stems from nonviolence: "We don't have to curse and go around acting bad with our words. We don't need any bricks and bottles; we don't need any Molotov cocktails." As he often explained throughout his career, instead of seeking to destroy their fervent political enemies, nonviolent activists strive to convert them. By embracing nonviolence, he, in effect, asks Mayor Loeb, the police, and other opponents to repent. He also implicitly requests that, following such repentance, the sanitation workers forgive the mayor and police in an act of reconciliation and renewal. He implies that seriously exploited, but peaceable African Americans in Memphis can succeed only if the white power structure can examine itself, repent, and receive forgiveness.

For some among King's audience, his strategy of connecting the Exodus to the prophets recalls the insistence in Deuteronomy that Israelite kings should observe the Sinai Covenant while also recalling the Deuteronomic announcement that God's prophets will continue to uphold the supreme importance of that covenant. King's quotations from Amos and Jeremiah remind some that Amos, Jeremiah, and other prophetic texts repeatedly define the Exodus narrative and the Sinai Covenant as the basis for Judaism.

Near the end of his last speech, King manifests another dynamic of Hebrew prophecy by explaining that he has already survived one assassination attempt and expects that someone will murder him. He implicitly argues that attempts to stifle his demands for justice parallel ancient efforts to silence and murder the Hebrew prophets.

As King reached his conclusion, he manifested—or at least approached—one final, dimension of Israelite prophecy: to move beyond normal experience.

One could argue that the purpose of many African American sermons is to transport churchgoers beyond their ordinary consciousness. Certain elements of "I've Been to the Mountaintop" resemble practices common among African American preachers who pursue such a goal. Many start their sermons very slowly, almost sleepily. Like jazz trumpet players whose notes begin half-heartedly but begin to bounce and glow in the middle of a tune, their voices gain rhythm and clarity as their sermons progress. As they begin to resolve their themes in a conclusion, their cadences grow ever more pronounced and their voices more insistent and louder, commanding greater and greater attention. As preachers approach their endings, some congregants (especially in the Amen Corner) may clap, jump, stomp, and shout. King seldom, if ever, engaged in the full-scale "whooping" typical of folk preachers.[39] But, when he addressed African American audiences, his voice often started slowly, almost as though he were engaged in a routine conversation. Then his phrases would gradually become more rhythmical and his voice grew more confident and more emphatic.

Recall that, on the night of King's final address, civil defense sirens warned lukewarm people to stay dry at home. Recall the rain hammering cars on the wet streets as wholehearted union supporters ignored the storm for a chance to hear King. Recall the large number of ministers who attended in a display of unity. On this night the passion of the listeners and the architecture of Mason Temple transformed the entire sanctuary into the Amen Corner.

As with "I Have a Dream" and many other orations, King started slowly. When his voice became stronger, some listened in awe while others, including Ralph Jackson, interjected, "Tell it!" "That's right!" and "Go on ahead!"[40] Not only did shouts punctuate the speech, so did thunder, lightning, and cascading rain. One listener, Jesse Epps, declared: "I'm not a religious fanatic. But at some high points where there should have been applause, there was a real severe flash of lightning and a real loud clap of thunder that sort of hushed the crowd."[41]

Well into the oration, Rev. Harold Middlebrook began wondering to himself, "'Where can the man go next to climax this thing? . . . When he got to a point where he could have climaxed, he didn't."[42] Middlebrook worried that King was endangering his entire speech. This concern was reasonable: many African American preachers aim for the right conclusion, what King and others called the "landing strip."[43] For King and others, to miss the landing strip would jeopardize the whole oration.

When King finally reached his landing strip, the crowd cheered and shouted in near pandemonium. Even the television crew stood and applauded.[44] By many accounts, a sense of catharsis, renewal, and exaltation permeated the whole sanctuary. Billy Kyles recalls, "I saw ministers who ordinarily would keep their composure just break down."[45] One pastor released a keening wail.[46] Jesse Jackson remembers that King "was lifted up and had some mysterious aura around him."[47] James Lawson felt "a great sense of oneness" and adds, "I was basking in this feeling... of kinship and warmth and the struggle."[48] Abernathy, who had listened to King on scores of occasions, recounts, "I had heard him hit high notes before, but never any higher."[49] Another clergy notes, "When Dr. King spoke that night, we knew that we were going to win [the strike]."[50] Around midnight that night, Maxine Smith, who missed the speech, attended a strategy session in which, she states, several people "'remarked how unusual" the oration was.[51]

As King was finishing the speech, one listener observed, "He had a strange look on his face."[52] The video recording of "I've Been to the Mountaintop" suggests that, during his conclusion, his facial expression is indeed unusual and hard to pinpoint with words. Perhaps at this moment he is dazed, even stunned; or possibly he is locked in deep concentration. He stands visibly in the pulpit of Mason Temple, covered in one of his interchangeable, very proper suits, yet perhaps he also seems transported. Perhaps at that moment he reconciles opposites: a quintessentially rabble-rousing labor leader who is also, simultaneously, a Christian mystic. He appears there and not there.

A moment later, when King turned from the microphone, with the same facial expression, aides noticed sweat glistening on his forehead and tears streaming from his eyes.[53] King did not cry after "I Have a Dream." Rarely, if ever, did he weep after his hundreds of orations. Further, despite the lateness of the hour and the deep fatigue that almost stymied his appearance at Mason Temple, he abandoned his standard practice of departing an arena immediately after speaking. Instead, he eagerly lingered, smiling, shaking hands, exchanging joyous words with listeners who filed to the platform—he and they together prolonging their shared sense of elevation.

Possibly one could describe King, at the end of this speech, as entering a trance-like state. If so, he exemplifies a prophetic tendency of entering a supranormal state far removed from ordinary existence.

By donning the mantle of prophecy, King extends biblical narrative and stretches the prophets' devotion to Mosaic tradition. While contending that contemporary America still needs Mosaic justice, he also provokes ministers with his remarkable claim that God calls not some, but all Christian clergy to prophesy.

King also suggests that each agitator crusading in Birmingham five years earlier—and, by extension, each activist in Memphis—fulfills a prophetic call. In Birmingham, demonstrators spilled from Sixteenth Street Baptist Church to face police and fire fighters directed by "Bull" Connor, commissioner of public safety. A notorious racist, Connor sometimes dispatched sharp-toothed German shepherds against the marchers and, on other occasions, ordered fire fighters to wash them down the street with water flying from large hoses. King relates:

> We would move out of the Sixteenth Street Baptist Church day after day. By the hundreds we would move out, and Bull Connor would tell them to send the dogs forth, and they did come. But we just went before the dogs, singing, "Ain't gonna let nobody turn me around." Bull Connor next would say, "Turn the fire hoses on." . . . Bull Connor didn't know history. He knew a kind of physics that somehow didn't relate to the transphysics that we knew about. And that was the fact that there was a certain kind of fire that no water would put out. . . .
>
> And we won our struggle in Birmingham.

King asserts that the "transphysics" of Birmingham involved "a certain kind of fire that no water would put out." This holy fire within the body, he claims, defeated Bull Connor and created an inestimable victory for Birmingham and the entire nation. Not long after these statements, King adjusts Jeremiah's words by saying: "Somehow the preacher must have a kind of fire shut up in his bones." In part, King quotes the image of fire in Jeremiah's bones to clarify the earlier image of "a certain kind of fire that no water would put out." King argues that a sacred fire animated Jeremiah's prophecy and that a similar sacred fire enlivened protests in Birmingham. Repeating and adapting this trope, he, in effect, maintains that the fire within activists in Birmingham—inexhaustible fire that defies the laws of physics—is the same hallowed flame that flickered within Jeremiah's bones. In this argument-by-metaphor, an identical, irresistible, sanctified impulse propelled both Jeremiah's prophecy and a nonviolent revolution in Birmingham.

For many in King's audience, his account of an unquenchable fire in Birmingham recalled many other instances of the common biblical symbol of fire as the embodiment of holiness. In various sacred Hebrew narratives, a fire on the altar of the tabernacle indicates sacredness. Ezekiel presents visions of fire, lightning, and burning coals next to cherubim.[54] More obviously, given King's earlier references to the Exodus, his repetition of Jeremiah's image of holy fire alludes to an account in Numbers of a cloud of fire that hangs above the tabernacle in the wilderness.[55] King also suggests an image in Exodus of a pillar of fire that guides the Hebrews through the wilderness toward the Promised Land.[56] Even more obviously, as Susannah Heschel notes, King's image of "fire that no water would put out" recalls Moses's first encounter with God, who appears in the form of a burning bush. It defies the laws of physics by blazing continuously without extinguishing itself.[57]

In Exodus the images of the sacred cloud of fire and the sacred pillar of fire resonate with the earlier image of the burning bush. In the biblical hermeneutic of "I've Been to the Mountaintop," the imagery of fire in Jeremiah's bones resonates with the imagery of fire in the Exodus narrative, especially with the burning bush. King's use of metaphors of fire indicates that Jeremiah's prophecy continues the process of Exodus and that both Exodus and prophecy extend into Birmingham and Memphis.

When King assumes the mantle of Hebrew prophecy, he builds upon his earlier Mosaic narrative. In this plot, the trash collectors are not simply one side of a labor dispute ignored by the national press. Rather, they are enslaved by a mayoral pharaoh while police, newspaper editors, television reporters, a federal judge, downtown bankers, insurance mangers, and business executives all enforce a variation of Egyptian bondage. According to King, the city workers are agents promoting the justice announced in Exodus and demanded by the prophets. As King narrates, the sacred fire of prophecy began with the burning bush, continued in Jeremiah's bones, and now flames within activist clergy and other racial agitators in Birmingham and Memphis. In King's discourse, the prophetic tradition that damned iniquity in Jerusalem reaches across the centuries to condemn wrongdoing in Alabama and Tennessee. Further, the Mosaic justice that prophets demanded from rulers, priests, and commoners in ancient Israel is the same justice that King demands from authorities in Memphis.

King's decision to fashion himself into a prophet empowers him to knit civic employees and other blacks in Memphis into a single body. By reigniting biblical narrative and prophecy, he stretches this ecumenical community to encompass sympathetic Jews and Christians from across Memphis. His rhetoric also enlists for this community those who triumphantly protested five years earlier in Birmingham while participating in a similar biblical drama.

Through his powerful, imaginative rhetoric, King enrolls not only residents of Birmingham and Memphis into his religious community, but also many generations of justice-loving religious ancestors, stretching from the ancient Israelites depicted in the Bible to many, many succeeding generations of devout believers who view their own lives through biblical lenses. These faithful people include whole generations of African American Christians, including slaves who, through sermon and song, struggled alongside Moses and Joshua. Into his community, King also encompasses several later generations of devoted African Americans, including such obviously well remembered leaders as Bishop C. H. Mason.

In other words, King's act of reconfiguring biblical rhetoric enables him to construe many devout and ethical Jews and Christians, both living and dead, as (to use Kenneth Burke's term) "consubstantial" with the striking garbage collectors. By inscribing Birmingham and the sanitation strike within a biblical narrative, King crafts for his hearers a means of grasping and enacting an identity that seems knowable, reliable, and praiseworthy.

King could thread such a community together because he built into his rhetoric an assumption shared by certain biblical authors and many believers, namely, that the Bible contains, in John Barton's words, "not only the history of the world," but also "all that is still to take place."[58] According to this assumption, the Bible is, as Brevard Childs explains, "stable in the sense of having an established structure and content and adaptable in addressing the community in each generation."[59] King treats the established biblical narrative as authoritative and sturdy, yet also flexible, sufficiently flexible to bind together blue-collar strikers in Memphis, their supporters, and whole generations of Jews and Christians who are capable of heeding the call in Amos for Mosaic justice. As King rhetorically constructs a biblical community that is old, yet also new, he forms his listeners and many others into a united whole while prompting them to succeed in winning victory for the union.

CHAPTER 6

If I Do Not Stop, What Will Happen to Them?

King's Rhetoric of the Body

While extending the Exodus and Hebrew prophecy in "I've Been to the Mountaintop," King also interprets the Christian Bible. In doing so, he carefully knits together Jewish and Christian themes. Early in this chapter I explain this process by analyzing his use of passages that resonate in the Hebrew Bible and in two books of the Christian Bible—Luke and Acts. Then I explicate his interpretation of the Parable of the Good Samaritan. Next I investigate his implicit, but firm argument that Judaism forms the inescapable foundation for Christianity, an argument that radically reconceives a centuries-old tradition of dominant Christian attitudes toward Judaism. I conclude the chapter by examining his construction of a biblical narrative that strongly emphasizes the body as a site of spiritual struggle and triumph.

Consider King's use of quotations that illustrate the reliance of the Christian Bible on the Hebrew Bible. When King shoves Hebrew prophecy into Memphis, he adds another commission to those from Jeremiah and Amos:

> Somehow the preacher must have a kind of fire shut up in his bones and, whenever injustice is around, he must tell it. Somehow the preacher must be an Amos, who said, "When God speaks, who can but prophesy?" Again with Amos, "Let justice roll down like waters and righteousness like a mighty stream." Somehow the preacher must say with Jesus: "The Spirit of the Lord is upon me because He's anointed me to deal with the problems of the poor."

King's proclamation, "Somehow the preacher must say with Jesus: 'The Spirit of the Lord is upon me because He's anointed me to deal with the problems of the poor,'" encapsulates a sacred call that appears in (Third) Isaiah:

> The Spirit of the Lord God is upon me,
> Because the Lord has anointed me
>   To bring good tidings to the afflicted;
> He has sent me
>   To bind up the brokenhearted,
>   To proclaim liberty to the captives
>   And the opening of the prison
>   To those who are bound,
>   To proclaim the year of the Lord's favor.
>   ([Third] Isaiah 61:1–2)

As many of King's listeners realized, in a key passage in the Christian Bible, Jesus quotes these lines. Luke relates:

> And Jesus came to Nazareth ... and he went to the synagogue ... on the Sabbath day. And He stood up to read; and there was given to Him the book of the prophet Isaiah. He opened the book and found the place where it was written:
> The Spirit of the Lord is upon me
> Because He has anointed me
>   To preach good news to the poor.
> He has sent me
>   To proclaim release to the captives
>   and recovering sight to the blind,
>   To set at liberty those who are oppressed,
>   To proclaim the acceptable year of the Lord.
> ... And he began to say to them,
> This day is this scripture fulfilled in your ears.
>   (Luke 4:16–19)

In this passage, Luke presents Jesus seizing a portion of (Third) Isaiah for the purpose of announcing and enacting, for the first time, his role of prophet and Messiah. Obviously, these lines are extremely important to anyone who wishes to grasp the message of the Christian Bible. The great significance of this passage ensured that it would become very familiar to Christians.

When King offers this refrain,

> Somehow the preacher must have a kind of fire shut up in his bones. . . . Somehow the preacher must be an Amos who said: "When God speaks, who can but prophesy?"

and again with Amos,

> "Let justice roll down like waters and righteousness like a mighty stream." Somehow the preacher must say with Jesus: "The Spirit of the Lord is upon me because He's anointed me to deal with the problems of the poor,"

he aligns the commission statements of Jeremiah, Amos, Third Isaiah, and Jesus, thereby strongly tying the three prophets to each other and to Jesus.

King reminds biblically minded listeners that the Jesus of Luke refashions the dynamic lexicon of prophecy that animates (Third) Isaiah, the same lexicon that enlivens Jeremiah and Amos. By choosing a passage from (Third) Isaiah that Luke reconfigures, King notes that, for biblical writers, God's calling of a prophet does not end prophecy, nor does God's fulfillment of an oracle exhaust that oracle. Rather, the fulfillment of Third Isaiah's call to prophecy suggests that, hundreds of years later, the call can be reconfigured and refulfilled by Jesus. As Michael Fishbane explains, the process of reconfiguring and refulfilling earlier texts is a means by which biblical writers establish "a sure link between memory and hope."[1] King's citation of this biblical double passage highlights what Paul Ricoeur terms the "network of intersignification" that underlies biblical texts and the "interpretive dynamism" that propels them.[2]

And just as the author of Luke reimagines a segment of (Third) Isaiah, King reimagines the same passage in Luke in order to explain contemporary preachers' commission to prophesy. King directly cites the project in Luke of refashioning (Third) Isaiah as the basis for King's own project, which is to rework the dynamic lexicon of prophecy yet again, this time in Memphis. He undertakes this project when he insists that preachers in Memphis must now re-engage the mission of Jeremiah, Amos, Third Isaiah, and Jesus.

For some listeners, King's emphasis on the similarities of these commission announcements summons other scriptural passages that also strongly tie the prophets to Jesus. The author of Luke also wrote Acts. Acts features a speech in which Stephen quotes Amos and criticizes Israelites for rejecting Moses, for rejecting the prophets, and for rejecting Jesus.[3] For the author of Acts, accepting Moses and accepting the prophets aligns with accepting Jesus. According to Acts, interpenetrating themes connect the Exodus narrative, the prophetic books, and Jesus.

King's use of "fire in the bones" and "fire no water could put out" relies on a basic metaphor:

Holiness = Fire.

Variations of this metaphor appear in various biblical books. One instance is the "burning bush" through which God speaks to Moses in Exodus.[4] Another is the "pillar of fire" that helped lead the Israelites through the wilderness during the Exodus.[5] A subset of this biblical metaphor is:

Holiness = Fire within the Human Body.

One example of this subset is the "fire in the bones" that impels Jeremiah to speak for God. Another example is the "tongues of fire" that Acts associates with the arrival of the Holy Ghost during the Pentecost.

Of course, the phrase "tongues of fire" also serves as the crucial metaphor for the intense religious experience of the Azusa Street Revival. In explaining his epiphany on Azusa Street, C. H. Mason invokes this image from Acts: "'I was led by the Spirit . . . to go to Los Angeles, California, where the great fire of the latter reign of the Holy Ghost had fallen on many.'" He adds, "'A flame touched my tongue which ran down in me. My language changed and no word could I speak in my own tongue. Oh, I was filled with the glory of the Lord.'"[6] By the time of King's last speech, several hundred thousand Pentecostals throughout the United States had, like Mason, experienced the key Pentecostal phenomenon of "tongues of fire."

Remarkable is the similarity of these three metaphors:
Fire in the bones (in Jeremiah and King's speech),
Fire within protestors that no water could put out (in King's speech),
Tongues of fire (in Acts and Mason's rhetoric).

Each of the three metaphors is a variant of this metaphor:

Holiness = Fire within the Human Body.

All three tropes uphold and reinforce the general emphasis that Holiness and Pentecostal churches place on the fusion of holiness and physicality. As one scholar explains, Holiness and Pentecostal Christianity "insists . . . on the individual human body as the dwelling space of the Spirit of God, the true Temple of the Holy Spirit."[7] For Pentecostals at Mason Temple, King's direct use of two images of holy fire within the human body would sound reminiscent of Pentecostal preaching and Pentecostal worship. King certainly does not duplicate Pentecostal themes, but parts of his oration *rhyme* with the Pentecostal emphasis on the indwelling of the Holy Spirit within the body.

Further, for King's biblically literate listeners, his use of "fire in the bones" from Jeremiah connects both backwards from Jeremiah's time to the earlier burning bush in Exodus and forward from Jeremiah to the later "tongues of fire" in Acts.

King elaborates his interpretation of the Christian scripture when, in considerable detail, he recounts another passage in Luke—the Parable of the Good Samaritan.

Only Luke depicts Jesus reading his commission from a scroll with the words of (Third) Isaiah; similarly, only Luke features Jesus telling what became his most famous story.[8] Does it matter that, among the four gospels, only Luke presents both the passage from (Third) Isaiah and this parable? Yes. As Luke and King indicate, Jesus accepts a mission:

> The Spirit of the Lord is upon me
> Because He has anointed me
>   To preach good news to the poor.
> He has sent me
>   To proclaim release to the captives
>   and recovering sight to the blind,
>   To set at liberty those who are oppressed.

Luke portrays Jesus fulfilling this mission in various ways, including his decision to narrate the Parable of the Good Samaritan.[9] The badly injured—half dead—victim of the parable certainly exemplifies a person who is poor, captive, blind, and/or oppressed.

After King quotes (Third) Isaiah/Luke, "Somehow the preacher must say with Jesus: 'The Spirit of the Lord is upon me because he's anointed me to deal with the problems of the poor,'" King addresses and, if you will, fulfills this commission in his speech in part by summarizing and interpreting the renowned parable. He emphasizes its importance by devoting not five or six sentences to his exegesis, but instead thirty-nine sentences, most of which follow:

> One day a man came to Jesus and he wanted to raise some questions about some vital matters of life. At points he wanted to trick Jesus and show him that he knew a little more than Jesus knew and throw him off base. He asked Jesus, "And who is my neighbor?" Now that question could easily have ended up in a philosophical and theological debate. But Jesus immediately pulled that question from midair and placed it on a dangerous curve between Jerusalem and Jericho. And he talked about a certain man who fell among thieves. You remember that a Levite and a priest passed by the other side; they didn't stop to help him. Finally, a man of another race came by. He got down from his beast, decided not to be compassionate by proxy. But he got down with him, administered first aid, and helped the man in need. Jesus ended up saying this was the good man, this was the great man because he had the capacity to project the "I" into the "Thou" and to be concerned about his brother.
>
> Now, you know, we use our imagination a great deal to try to determine why the Priest and the Levite didn't stop.... But I'm going to tell you what my imagination tells me. It's possible that those men were afraid. You see, the Jericho Road is a dangerous road.... In the days of Jesus it came to be known as the "Bloody Pass." And you know, it's possible that the Priest and the Levite looked over that man on the ground and wondered if the robbers were still around.... And so the first question that the Priest asked, the first question that the Levite asked was, "If I stop to help this man, what will happen to me?"
>
> But the Good Samaritan came by, and he reversed the question: "If I do *not* stop to help this man, what will happen to him?"
>
> That's the question before you tonight. Not, "If I stop to help the sanitation workers, what will happen to my job?" Not, "If I stop to help the sanitation workers, what will happen to all of the hours that I usually spend in my office every day and every week as a pastor?" The question is not, "If I stop to help this man in need, what will happen to me?" The question is, "If I do

not stop to help the sanitation workers, what will happen to them?" That's the question.

Although most of King's entire analysis here stems directly from George Buttrick and from Protestant commonplaces, King completes his discussion by inserting the garbage carriers of Memphis into the parable—a move that dramatically changes the interpretation provided by his sources. Through this move, King explains the entire parable as a scriptural imperative to support the strikers. King argues that just as, in the parable, the Good Samaritan braved the dangerous Jericho Road to rescue the roadside victim, so should people of good will aid the wounded and bleeding sanitation workers. King constructs this equation:

$$\frac{\text{Good Samaritan}}{\text{Roadside Victim}} = \frac{\text{Strike Supporters}}{\text{Striking Sanitation Workers.}}$$

But, as King explains, the bloodied traveler and the Samaritan are not alone in the parable: two leading religious officials, the priest and Levite, amble straight past the wounded victim, leaving him bleeding and helpless in the ditch.

King clearly invites his audience to ask, If the victim and the Samaritan have their counterparts in Memphis, then what about the other players in the drama? Do the callous and self-absorbed priest and Levite appear in some form in Memphis? Who is blithely strolling past the garbage workers, the roadside victims? King's audience, of course, realizes that a few minutes earlier he criticized many contemporary clergy in Memphis: "so often preachers aren't concerned about anything but themselves." King obviously suggests a parallel between the moderate clergy of Memphis and the self-important priest and Levite who ignore the bloodied traveler. King strongly implies that clergy who seek political neutrality in Memphis are contemporary priests and Levites. While pretending to be leaders, he suggests, they refuse to risk the security of their jobs—or even to leave the comforts of their offices—thus failing to help innocent people who are robbed and beaten. Here is his equation:

$$\frac{\text{Priest and Levite}}{\text{Roadside Victim}} = \frac{\text{Moderate Clergy}}{\text{Striking Sanitation Workers.}}$$

Yet another actor appears in the parable—the thief. If the trash collectors are twentieth-century equivalents of the stricken man in the parable, then someone must be beating and robbing them. Who? In King's appeal, the answer is obvious: the boss of Memphis, who continues to oppress city workers while stubbornly refusing to negotiate. In this argument, the mayor's intransigence is the reason that the laborers are hurting and need to strike. King implies that Mayor Loeb is a new bandit who springs on hapless sojourners:

$$\frac{\text{Robber}}{\text{Roadside Victim}} = \frac{\text{Mayor Loeb}}{\text{Sanitation Workers.}}$$

Earlier in the speech King identified Mayor Loeb as Pharaoh and the laborers as Egyptian slaves:

$$\frac{\text{Pharaoh}}{\text{Egyptian Slaves}} = \frac{\text{Mayor Loeb}}{\text{Sanitation Workers.}}$$

By using the same speech to imply that Mayor Loeb is both the pharaoh in Egypt and the violent thief in the parable, King implicitly asks listeners to combine these equations:

$$\frac{\text{Pharaoh}}{\text{Egyptian Slaves}} = \frac{\text{Mayor Loeb}}{\text{Striking Sanitation Workers.}} = \frac{\text{Robber}}{\text{Roadside Victim}}$$

One could easily object that the resemblances don't work. Loeb, who guides a medium-sized city from a swivel chair alongside his wooden desk, is definitely not a mighty, dictatorial ruler of a large nation who, one supposes, comes outfitted in elaborate finery and reclines on a huge, golden throne. One could also object that, operating in city hall, Mayor Loeb is not precisely a roadside outlaw who engages in assault and armed robbery. One could further object that Mayor Loeb cannot be *both* Pharaoh *and* a highway thief because such figures are inherently dissimilar: one is royalty, the other lowlife. But these objections all rely on a literal interpretation of the Bible—an interpretation that King emphatically rejects. Tossing aside any biblical literalism, King presents an intricate logic that holds that—notwithstanding outer appearances—Pharaoh, the robber in the parable, and Mayor Loeb exemplify the same oppressive *form* of biblical evil.

In this argumentative system, if Pharaoh resembles the robber, then there must be a role for Moses. By equating Pharaoh with the robber, King implies that Moses resembles the Good Samaritan:

$$\frac{\text{Moses}}{\text{Egyptian Slaves}} = \frac{\text{Good Samaritan}}{\text{Roadside Victim.}}$$

Because King explicitly claims that

$$\frac{\text{Good Samaritan}}{\text{Roadside Victim}} = \frac{\text{Strike Supporters}}{\text{Sanitation Workers.}}$$

attentive listeners will infer that, in this argumentative system, supporters of the union resemble both Moses and the Good Samaritan:

$$\frac{\text{Moses}}{\text{Egyptian Slaves}} = \frac{\text{Good Samaritan}}{\text{Roadside Victim}} = \frac{\text{Strike Supporters}}{\text{Sanitation Workers}}$$

By linking Pharaoh to the robber and Moses to the Good Samaritan, King joins authors of the Christian Bible in reworking what Walter Brueggemann calls the "grammar of the Exodus" from the Hebrew scripture. King does so by creating strong typological links between the Hebrew Bible and the Christian Bible and by creating equally strong typological links between both sets of scripture and the strike in Memphis.

This orator extends this process by explaining that the Good Samaritan achieved greatness because, in King's words, "Jesus ended up saying this [Samaritan] was the good man; this was the great man because he had the capacity to project the 'I' into the 'Thou' and to be concerned about his brother." King thereby adapts the language of twentieth-century Jewish theologian Martin Buber, whom King mentions by name in "Letter from Birmingham Jail." Buber's book *I and Thou* had endeared itself to religious liberals and had become a widely read classic. Here King uses a Jewish theologian's conception of I-Thou relationship to help explain the meaning of the Parable of the Good Samaritan. In doing so, King offers a remarkable assertion of the crucial relation between Judaism and Christianity. In King's rhetoric, a modern Jewish thinker helps illuminate the message of Jesus.

Earlier in the speech King announced, "Either we go up together or we go down together." Albeit not explicitly biblical, this sentiment reiterates an extremely important theme in the Exodus narrative and the prophetic texts. Through this statement King expresses his concern for the entire African American people and the entire American people—a theme buttressed by Exodus and by the texts of Hebrew prophecy that King cites.

Through his use of Buber and his affirmations about Moses, Hebrew prophets, and Jesus, King strongly counters two popular Christian interpretations of the Bible—developmentalism and supersessionism. As James Barr (in 1966) and Brevard Childs (in 1979) observed, many Protestants scarcely noticed the Hebrew Bible at all. For many Christians, the doctrines of developmentalism and supersessionism dictated this inattention. Developmentalists (including Harry Emerson Fosdick) propose that the Bible presents a "progressive revelation" about God.[10] According to this view, biblical texts initially present a crude, primitive portrait of a wrathful, destructive God before eventually stumbling toward a more admirable portrait of a loving and nurturing God. Developmentalists insist that Christ emerges as the apex of this long, progressive revelation. For their part, Christian supersessionists have, for centuries, claimed that the revelation of Christ decidedly surpasses literally everything in the Hebrew Bible. For supersessionists, Moses and the prophets mainly serve as a hazy backdrop to the birth of Jesus. Of the entire body of Hebrew scripture, supersessionists treasure the small number of lines that, they believe, directly forecast the eventual arrival of Christ. In the view of developmentalists and supersessionists alike, the sublimity of Christ greatly eclipses everyone and everything that preceded him, and that eclipse is the whole point of Christianity.

The doctrine of supersessionism undergirded the overriding theme of personal sin and personal salvation that issued from many American pulpits before, during, and after King's lifetime. Many white evangelicals (such as Billy Graham) and some African American ministers (including some Baptists and Pentecostals) continually emphasized this theme. Many of them still do.

In "I Have a Dream," "I've Been to the Mountaintop," and elsewhere, King repudiates developmentalism and supersessionism. He implicitly, but clearly, maintains that one does *not* achieve redemption by simply bypassing Judaism on route to accepting Christ as Savior. Instead of contending that Jesus represents a radical break in the history of Judaism, King explains Jesus as a continuation, extension, and fulfillment of the revelation that preceded him. King implicitly, but strongly, argues that one approaches Jesus by taking three steps *in order*. First, one approaches and grasps Egyptian slavery, Moses, the Exodus, and the Sinai Covenant. Second, one approaches and grasps prophetic testimony, which extends, elaborates, and adjusts the Exodus tradition. Third, one can *then* encounter Jesus, who realizes the legacy of Moses and prophecy. Insisting on the significance of Moses and the Israelite seers helps King assert that Christianity offers more than a heavenly afterlife of "long white robes over yonder" and "streets flowing with milk and honey." Affirming the crucial role of Hebrew scripture—especially the Exodus narrative and prophecy—enables King to counter developmentalism and supersessionism and the related emphasis on individual salvation. Such an emphasis, King strongly implies, may diminish or even preclude the possibility of enacting social justice.

Touting the function of the Christian Bible as an interpretation of the Hebrew Bible, King clearly explains that both Testaments present a dynamic of exploitation and redemption that are both individual and social. And, just as King explicates the Exodus as a drama now re-emerging in Memphis, he treats the prophets' demand for justice for the poor as a demand that resurfaces when Jesus cites lines from (Third) Isaiah. King thereby declares that the need to prophesy for justice did not change in the centuries that separate Moses, Amos, Jeremiah, and Third Isaiah from each other and from Jesus. King further contends that the need to prophesy for justice has not changed in the almost two thousand years that separate the lifetime of Jesus from the present. For King and his listeners, Hebrew prophecy—specifically, a passage in (Third) Isaiah—re-emerges centuries later in Christian scripture and again in Memphis.

For King, explicating the Parable of the Good Samaritan serves other important purposes as well. As King announces, the parable begins when a lawyer asks Jesus, "Who is my neighbor?" As King indicates, this lawyer's question is philosophical, and it obviously calls for a philosophical answer, specifically for a formal definition of "neighbor." Offering such definitions was a common practice in ancient Greco-Roman rhetoric and, I assume, in ancient rabbinic circles as well. Yet, King notes, Jesus did not respond with a definition or with any other type of philosophical answer. Jesus obviously ducked the lawyer's philosophical inquiry, preferring to tell a story instead. Why? On its face, the lawyer's question sounds perfectly reasonable. Don't many people, like the lawyer, wonder exactly how far their ethical obligations extend? Gigantic numbers of people populate the earth, and many of them are hurt and in need. How many of them can I possibly help? How many of them can you possibly help? How many of them can any one of us possibly help? "Who is my neighbor?" sounds like a fair question. But King claims that, far from posing a fair query, the lawyer "wanted to trick Jesus" and "throw him off base." King adds, "Now that question could have easily ended up in a philosophical and theological debate." Yes, it certainly could have. Such a debate, King expressly indicates, is exactly what Jesus deliberately skirted. But, again, why?

King implies a larger point: Jesus did not talk like a formal philosopher, either in responding to the lawyer's question or on other occasions. King implies that Jesus was not a formal theologian and never attempted to create a systematic philosophy or a systematic theology. King emphasizes that Jesus instead narrated stories that could jar listeners' sensibilities and spur them toward spiritual awareness and compassionate behavior. Many scholars have attempted to portray King as a theologian, a theologian whose ideas, they claim, stemmed from the formal theology that he studied in graduate school.[11] But, significantly, throughout his public career, King *never* once offered formal, abstract theology. Not in any speech. Not in any essay. He never came close. Here, in his last speech, he explains that Jesus *explicitly rejected* a clear, open invitation to proffer abstract philosophy or theology. Instead, King indicates, Jesus delivered his theology via parable, via narrative. King notes that Jesus supplied a type of narrative theology, if you will, and that he—King—uses "I've Been to the Mountaintop" in an effort to extend biblical narrative and prophecy into the present. King *does* assert biblical concepts in his final speech. But he plainly refuses to present them simply as abstract propositions. Instead, he carefully situates them within the biblical narrative and prophecy that he locates in Memphis. He implicitly justifies his extension of biblical narrative and prophecy by emphasizing that Jesus directly rejected an opportunity to speak philosophically and instead chose to narrate.

Recounting the Parable of the Good Samaritan enables King to articulate an interpretation of the Bible that is not only conceptual, but also profoundly physical. King's biblical interpretation is decidedly an interpretation of *embodiment*. Of course, all Christians believe that Jesus was God incarnate, God become flesh, God entering human form. The gospels indicate that Jesus began his life in a barn, changed water into wine, healed the sick, created the miracle of the loaves and fishes, rode a donkey into

Jerusalem, and died a tortuous death while nailed to a cross. In King's discussion, the Parable of the Good Samaritan provides the memorable image of a victimized body—a bloody pulp tossed along the roadway.

Significantly, King immediately follows his account of the parable with one of the most memorable passages in his entire oratory—his narration of a frightening experience in 1958:

> Several years ago I was in New York City autographing the first book that I had written. And while sitting there autographing books, a demented black woman came up....
>
> The next minute I felt something beating on my chest.... I had been stabbed by this demented woman. I was rushed to Harlem Hospital.... And that blade had gone through and the X-rays revealed that the tip of the blade was on the edge of my aorta, the main artery. And once that's punctured you're drowned in your own blood; that's the end of you.
>
> It came out in the *New York Times* the next morning that, if I had merely sneezed, I would have died. Well, about four days later, they allowed me, after the operation... to move around in the wheelchair in the hospital. They allowed me to read some of the mail that came in, and from all over the states and the world kind letters came in.... I had received one from the President and the Vice President. I've forgotten what those telegrams said. I received a visit and a letter from the Governor of New York, but I've forgotten what that letter said. But there was another letter that came from a little girl....
>
> And I looked at that letter and I'll never forget it. It said simply, "Dear Dr. King: I am a ninth-grade student at the White Plains High School.... While it should not matter, I would like to mention that I'm a white girl. I read in the paper of your misfortune and of your suffering. And I read that, if you had sneezed, you would have died. And I'm simply writing to say that I'm so happy that you didn't sneeze."
>
> And I want to say tonight... that I, too, am happy that I didn't sneeze. Because, if I had sneezed, I wouldn't have been around here in 1960, when students all over the South started sitting-in at lunch counters. And I knew that, as they were sitting in, they were really standing up for the best in the American dream. And taking the whole nation back to those great wells of democracy dug deep by the founding fathers in the Declaration of Independence and the Constitution. If I had sneezed, I wouldn't have been around here in 1961, when we decided to take a ride for freedom and ended segregation in interstate travel. If I had sneezed, I wouldn't have been around here

in 1962, when Negroes in Albany, Georgia, decided to straighten their backs up. And, whenever men and women straighten their backs up, they are going somewhere because a man can't ride your back unless it is bent. If I had sneezed, I wouldn't have been here in 1963 when the black people of Birmingham, Alabama, aroused the conscience of this nation and brought into being the Civil Rights Bill. If I had sneezed, I wouldn't have had a chance later that year to try to tell America about a dream that I had had. If I had sneezed, I wouldn't have been down in Selma, Alabama, to see the great movement there. If I had sneezed, I wouldn't have been in Memphis to see a community rally around those brothers and sisters who are suffering. I'm so happy that I didn't sneeze.[12]

In King's recounting of the parable, a violent attacker bloodies an innocent man who, after lingering close to death, eventually recovers from his injury. In King's recounting of his stabbing in Harlem, a violent attacker bloodies an innocent man (King) who, after lingering close to death, eventually recovers from his injury. King does not equate himself with the mugged traveler in the parable. But King's decision to juxtapose these roughly similar images of violence and victimage strengthens his system of biblical interpretation as an ongoing drama of embodiment.

King presents both stories—the parable and the Harlem stabbing—as spiritual narratives of the body. The parable directly contrasts the Priest and the Levite, who are spiritually empty, to the magnificently compassionate Samaritan. In his narration of the Harlem stabbing and its aftermath, King implies that God intervened, touched King, and saved his life. This intervention, King implies, allowed him to participate in spiritual milestones of the African American struggle. He enumerates and describes each of them: Lunch-Counter Sit-Ins, Freedom Rides, Albany movement, Birmingham crusade, March on Washington, Selma-to-Montgomery March, and Memphis strike. Each of these episodes, he suggests, serves as a pivotal freedom moment that recapitulates the meaning that he had celebrated earlier in his speech, namely, the meaning of the Exodus, the Reformation, and the Emancipation Proclamation. He strongly implies that, in each civil rights campaign that he enumerates—from Exodus to Memphis—God works through history to overcome evil.

Note that King explains many of these triumphs with images that blend the body with abstract ideals. As students "started sitting-in at lunch counters" he notes, "they were really standing up for what is best in the American dream." Here he equates opposites—sitting with standing. In his word play, the physical act of sitting at lunch counters embodies the abstraction of standing for the principle of racial equality. The Freedom Riders, he declares, "decided to take a ride for freedom and ended segregation in interstate travel." Here the dissidents' physical ride on a bus achieved the abstract ideal of freedom. Blacks in Albany, Georgia, he continues, "decided to straighten their backs up. And whenever men and women straighten their backs up, they are going somewhere because a man can't ride your back unless it is bent." Accustomed to bending their backs all day while picking cotton, sharecroppers in rural Georgia could both literally and figuratively straighten their backs as an act of defiance against white supremacy.

These metaphors of the body—sitting down, standing up, riding a bus, bending backs, and straightening backs—add to a whole panoply of bodily tropes that King assembles in the spiritual narrative that he builds throughout the speech. He begins by evoking a massive migration: "the magnificent trek" of the Israelites walking "across the Red Sea, through the wilderness, on toward the Promised Land." Next he explains, "We aren't going to let any mace stop us." Then he describes the attack dogs and water cannons that police leveled at demonstrators' bodies in Birmingham before jamming those bodies into paddy wagons:

> And we just went on before the dogs and we would look at them, and we'd go on before the water hoses.... And we'd just go on singing, "Over my head, I see freedom in the air." And then we would be thrown into paddy wagons, and sometimes we were stacked in there like sardines.... And we would just go on in the paddy wagons singing "We Shall Overcome." And every now and then we'd get in jail, and we'd see the jailers looking through the windows, being moved by our prayers and being moved by our words and our songs.

Then he invokes the fire in Jeremiah's bones. He also criticizes preachers for overemphasizing "long white robes over yonder" and "streets flowing with milk and honey," explaining that they also need to clothe bodies in Memphis with "suits and dresses and shoes" and noting the physical need for "three square meals a day." He denies the need for disaffected people to retaliate by injuring the bodies of police: "We don't need any bricks and bottles. We don't need any Molotov cocktails." He also instructs listeners "not to buy"—or drink—Coca-Cola or Sealtest Milk and "not to buy"—or chew—Wonder Bread or Hart's Bread. Finally, he implores his audience to abandon their offices and school desks as they enact a general strike that would completely shut down Memphis.

All these bodily images precede King's rendering of the bloody victim in the Parable of the Good Samaritan and his account of his nearly fatal knifing in Harlem. As if this were not enough, King then mentions his pilot's fear that the plane of that same morning would be blown up simply because King was a passenger. As if even this were not enough, he concludes by implying unmistakably his expectation that he will soon be killed, thus "fulfilling" the goal of the Harlem assailant ten years earlier.

In the very extensive narrative of the body that King generates throughout this address, the body is thoroughly spiritual and the spiritual thoroughly embodied. The embodiment of spirituality and holiness is not limited to the incarnation of Jesus. Rather, in King's biblical hermeneutic, *every movement toward freedom in every human body is thoroughly spiritual.*

King calls his listeners not to spend their lives either creating or contemplating abstract philosophical and theological propositions, but rather to exemplify and embody loving, Christian relationships. For him, the problem Jews and Christians face is not to reach theologians' usual goal of producing a rigorously consistent and well-nuanced set of abstract theological propositions. Instead, for King, the problem is to spur people to manifest religious concern in concrete ways every day, to care for every victimized traveler, even at the risk of death.

King explains that Jesus spurned the opportunity to speak in philosophical and theological abstractions in favor of offering a narrative of a body bloodied then rescued.

Explaining this decision enables King to support his hermeneutic of the Bible as a narrative of the body and spirit, a narrative that encompasses the story in Luke of the beating and recuperation of the roadside victim and his account of his own stabbing and recuperation in Harlem. By spiritualizing physicality, King's final oration provides a sermonic alternative to the systematic and abstract philosophy and theology that he studied in graduate school. These works of philosophy and theology presented few reflections on the human body. By contrast, in passage after passage after passage, King's last speech very strongly emphasizes the body. King intensifies this message by delivering it at the national headquarters of a denomination that lionizes the image of "tongues of fire," an image of sacredness within the body. And King cites Jesus as his authority for using narrative to spiritualize the body. For King and his listeners, the authority of Jesus, clearly articulated in the Christian Bible, carries infinitely more weight than the authority of any and all theologians. And the genre that Jesus uses in his parables is narrative—a genre that King imaginatively extends in "I've Been to the Mountaintop."

CHAPTER 7

Mine Eyes Have Seen the Glory

Julia Ward Howe, the Bible, and Memphis

Nearing the end of final speech, King approaches his "landing strip" as he describes his near-assassination in Harlem in 1958. Then, in his electrifying conclusion, he explains his visit to the mountaintop, his sight of the Promised Land, his prediction of his own possible death, and his vision of the Second Coming of Christ:

> Well, I don't know what will happen now. We've got some difficult days ahead. But it really doesn't matter with me now. Because I've been to the mountaintop! And I don't mind. Like anybody, I would like to live a long life: Longevity has its place. But I'm not concerned about that now. I just want to do God's will. And He's allowed me to go up to the mountain. And I've looked over and I've seen the Promised Land! I may not get there with you. But I want you to know tonight that we, as a people, will get to the Promised Land! And so I'm happy tonight; I'm not worried about anything; I'm not fearing any man. Mine eyes have seen the glory of the coming of the Lord!

Despite its popularity as an isolated segment, this climax makes little sense by itself and can only be understood in relation to the themes that King has developed throughout his entire speech. He completes his biblical theme of persecution preceding triumph by discussing the near tragic episode in Harlem. Then he brings that theme and his Exodus narrative to fruition while also proclaiming the Second Coming of Christ.

In this chapter I examine King's account of his stabbing in Harlem and its relation to two key litanies in the speech. I also explore his discussion of his own possible death and its relation to his narration of African American progress, Moses, the Exodus, the Promised Land, and the Second Coming. I also investigate the complex meaning of his final sentence: "Mine eyes have seen the glory of the coming of the Lord!" As I remark in this chapter, this line is an quotation from Julia Ward Howe's "Battle Hymn of the Republic," an anthem that she penned during the Civil War using imagery that she gleaned and abstracted from the Bible. I analyze Howe's (sometimes misconstrued) lyrics and show how King intertwines his narration of the Memphis strike with imagery from Howe and from the Bible, especially its final book, Revelation, which announces the Second Coming.

When King recalls his near-assassination in Harlem ten years earlier, he chooses not to discuss his decision to autograph books at Blumstein's Department Store (which normally did not sell books) while bypassing the nearby National Memorial African Bookstore and its controversial owner. Nor does King mention the ongoing, tight race for governor of New York at that time, which pitted Averill Harriman against Nelson Rockefeller. Nor does he mention the inexcusable, life-threatening delay at Harlem Hospital before doctors performed the surgery that saved his life.[1]

Instead of noting any of these events, King retells the stabbing incident while extending the theme of persecution leading to triumph that he implied in the earlier, time-travel portion of the speech. In that earlier sequence, the persecution of Hebrews in Egypt precedes the triumph of the Exodus, the persecution of Luther precedes the triumph of the Reformation, the crucible of the Civil War precedes the triumph of the Emancipation Proclamation, and the suffering during the Great Depression precedes widespread prosperity. Later in the speech King extends that sequence by arguing that his nearly fatal persecution in the knifing episode precedes seven great events of the civil rights movement—the Lunch Counter Sit-Ins, Freedom Rides, Albany campaign, Birmingham crusade, March on Washington, Selma-to-Montgomery March, and Memphis strike.

When King repeats this refrain-like form

Because if I had sneezed...
If I had sneezed...
If I had sneezed...
If I had sneezed...
If I had sneezed...

> If I had sneezed...
> If I had sneezed...

seven times, he loops back to the only other refrain in the entire oration, which he also repeats seven times:

> I wouldn't stop there!...
> But I wouldn't stop there!...
> But I wouldn't stop there!...
> But I wouldn't stop there!...
> But I wouldn't stop there!...
> But I wouldn't stop there!...
> But I wouldn't stop there!

That earlier refrain occurs at the end of each episode in his time machine. King declares that he wishes to visit the Exodus before insisting, "I wouldn't stop there!" He announces his desire to witness other glorious moments, including the Protestant Reformation and the emancipation of American slaves. After each of them, he again insists, "I wouldn't stop there!" He "wouldn't stop" at the Exodus, the Reformation, the Emancipation Proclamation, or the New Deal because he longs to live in the second half of the twentieth-century, where the centuries-old, noble struggle for freedom continues. Hailing racial protests in Africa and the United States, he declares, "The cry is always the same, 'We want to be free!'"

Near the end of the oration, the "If I had sneezed" litany now *fulfills* his riff about traveling through time. In the "If I had sneezed" segment, he specifies several of the recent moments when "the cry is always the same, 'We want to be free!'" Those moments include the Lunch Counter Sit-Ins, Freedom Rides, Albany campaign, Birmingham movement, March on Washington, Selma-to-Montgomery March, and Memphis strike. Each of those episodes, he implies, provides a reason he "wouldn't stop" at the earlier landmark events. Each of those episodes, he implies, is a contemporary variation of the Exodus.

Through the "If I had sneezed" refrain, King also asserts that the persecution inflicted during Egyptian slavery, the Reformation, and American slavery reverberates today in segregated America. Through the same litany, King contends that the Lunch Counter Sit-Ins and the other 1960s protests serve as exemplary triumphs that push the nation closer toward racial equality. In this argument, just as persecution yielded to the Exodus, the Reformation, and the Emancipation Proclamation, persecution will certainly yield in Memphis. In this argument, even though Memphis has not yet produced success (because the strike is ongoing), the just demands of the garbage workers will eventually dissolve the intransigence of the mayor. Victory in Memphis is inevitable, he attests, because biblical logic shapes all history as persecution ushers in triumph and oppression surrenders to freedom.

In the "If I had sneezed" refrain, King obviously emphasizes that only his miraculous recovery from the hands of a would-be killer in Harlem enables him to lead or witness liberatory moments in the South. Wrapping the theme of Exodus with that of persecution/triumph, he strongly implies that God chose to spare his life during the Harlem incident so that he might participate in great events.

Two sentences after the "If I had sneezed" segment, King re-emphasizes the possibility of his own death:

> I left Atlanta this morning, and as we got started on the plane . . . the pilot said over the public address system: "We are sorry for the delay, but we have Dr. Martin Luther King on the plane. And to be sure that all of the bags were checked, and to be sure that nothing would be wrong on the plane, we had to check out everything carefully. And we've had the plane protected and guarded all night.

He continues: "And then I got into Memphis. And some began to say the threats, or talk about the threats that were out or what would happen to me from some of our sick white brothers."

Reaching his "landing strip," King brilliantly interweaves and completes his themes of Exodus and persecution/triumph while simultaneously evoking the final Mosaic vision and introducing eschatology:

> But it really doesn't matter with me now because I've been to the mountaintop! And I don't mind. Like anybody I would like to live a long life: Longevity has its place. But I'm not concerned about that now. I just want to do God's will. And He's allowed me to go up to the mountain. And I've looked over and I've seen the Promised Land! I may not get there with you. But I want you to know tonight that we, as a people, will get to the Promised Land! And so I'm happy tonight; I'm not worried about anything; I'm not fearing any man. Mine eyes have seen the glory of the coming of the Lord!

Here he meshes the themes of Exodus and persecution/triumph, indicating that he may not reach the Promised Land himself because of the possibility—rather, the likelihood—that he will be murdered.

When King mentions the mountaintop, he does not invent a novel location, but instead enlists familiar biblical associations. Even though Judaism does not deify mountains, biblical writers regularly designate them as sites of holy experience. Perhaps mountains present a more likely opportunity for revelation because their geographical remoteness and relative inaccessibility render them distant from the corruption of human settlements in more habitable valleys. Genesis, Exodus, Deuteronomy, Joshua, II Kings, (First) Isaiah, and Ezekiel all associate mountains with sacredness.[2] Psalms, (First) Isaiah, Joel, and Micah specify Mount Zion as a site and symbol of God's presence and majesty.[3] I Kings explains how, on Mount Carmel, the prophet Elijah vanquishes the many prophets of Baal.[4]

King obviously compares himself to an elderly Moses on Mount Pisgah, whom God allows to view the Promised Land just before he dies. Through this comparison, King summons for listeners not only an association with Moses on Mount Pisgah, but also an entire sequence of associations in which Moses meets God. According to Exodus, Moses receives his divine call when he encounters a burning bush on Mount Sinai. Later, again on Mount Sinai, God dispenses the Sinai Covenant to Moses. Still later, with thunder and lightning, God revisits Mount Sinai and grants the Ten Commandments to Moses. Soon afterward, Moses returns to Mount Sinai yet again to hear God explain that Aaron is leading the Hebrews to worship a Golden Calf. Moses descends, breaks the tablets engraved with the Ten Commandments, denounces the Hebrews' transgression, and burns the metallic idol. Once again the Israelite leader returns to Mount Sinai, where God renews the Sinai Covenant and promises that the Israelites will arrive at the Promised Land. Finally, Deuteronomy relates, after the Hebrews spend forty years trudging through the wilderness, God allows Moses, now an old man, to ascend Mount Pisgah and glimpse the Promised Land.[5]

In the Pentateuchal narrative, Moses's experience on Mount Pisgah culminates his series of holy experiences on mountains. Exodus and Deuteronomy present the Moses-on-the-mountain sequence in part to affirm that Moses, unlike Aaron, consistently maintained his role as God's devoted servant—from his mountaintop calling until his mountaintop death. Further, by connecting the death of the biblical patriarch to the Hebrews' arrival in the Promised Land, the episode on Mount Pisgah invites readers to anticipate the resolution of the entire Mosaic/Exodus plotline—Moses as a baby,

Moses encountering the burning bush, Moses in Pharaoh's court, Moses summoning the plagues, Moses at the Passover, Moses parting the Red Sea, Miriam celebrating this miracle, Moses receiving the Sinai Covenant, Moses accepting the Ten Commandments, Moses furious about the Golden Calf, Moses leading the trek through the wilderness, and Joshua directing the Hebrews into the Promised Land. When the author of Deuteronomy records the final epiphany of Moses on Mount Pisgah and relates his death there, that author concludes the long plotline of Moses while simultaneously completing Deuteronomy and the entire Pentateuch. This account of Moses's last epiphany and death also generates momentum for Joshua, the book that immediately follows Deuteronomy. By narrating Joshua's leadership of the Israelites across the Jordan River and into the Promised Land, the book of Joshua culminates the entire saga of the Mosaic Exodus.

For Christians, the significance of peaks does not end there, for gospel writers also associate mountains with sacred experience. Not by accident, the most famous homily that Jesus delivers is the Sermon on the Mount.[6] Mark and Luke explain that Jesus visits the Mount of Olives before entering Jerusalem.[7] Luke and Acts state that, after the resurrection, Jesus returns to the Mount of Olives and from there ascends to heaven.[8] In Mark, after Jesus leads his disciples Peter, James, and John onto a mountain, Jesus undergoes the transfiguration—an experience in which Moses and Elijah appear and speak.[9] As part of the constellation of signifiers that shine through King's evocation of Mount Pisgah, the transfiguration of Christ on the mountain is particularly important. The transfiguration emphasizes the narrative and thematic continuity of the Exodus (Moses), Hebrew prophecy (Elijah), and Jesus. King, of course, argues for a similar continuity throughout "I've Been to the Mountaintop."

But King does not conclude his oratorical tapestry simply by reconsidering Moses. Defying the wisdom of speech teachers, who routinely tell students not to conclude an address with new material, King does exactly that. His final sentence, "Mine eyes have seen the glory of the coming of the Lord!" directs his listeners beyond the Exodus, Hebrew prophecy, Christian prophecy, and Christian parable by adding the spectacular element of eschatology. Despite its newness, the eschatological dimension proceeds logically from King's preceding themes and serves to illuminate the entire speech.

When King announces,

And He's allowed me to go up to the mountain. And I've looked over and I've seen the Promised Land! I may not get there with you, but I want you to know tonight that we, as a people, will get to the Promised Land!

he says nothing at all about what the Promised Land looks like. He simply states that God allowed him to behold it. Then he ends his speech: "And so I'm happy tonight! I'm not worried about anything! I'm not fearing any man! Mine eyes have seen the glory of the coming of the Lord!" His final sentence, "Mine eyes have seen the glory of the coming of the Lord!" states that he visualizes the glory of the Second Coming of Christ. He explains that this vision accounts for his happiness and fearlessness even as he anticipates his impending death. He feels his fate in what he cannot fear. He remains calm, avoiding sadness and anxiety, because he realizes that the Second Coming will resolve every evil, vanquish every injustice, and vindicate every righteous person.

In this passage he closely juxtaposes three distinct visions. In a few lines, "And He's allowed me to go up to the mountain. And I've looked over and I've seen the Promised Land! I may not get there with you, but I want you to know tonight that we, as a people, will get to the Promised Land!" he relates the death of Moses; his own possible, impending death; and African Americans' entrance to the Promised Land. Then he quickly adds, "Mine eyes have seen the glory of the coming of the Lord!" In these few words, "I've seen the Promised Land! ... Mine eyes have seen the glory of the coming of the Lord!" he presses together Moses's vision of the Promised Land, his own vision of African American freedom, and a glimpse of the Second Coming of Christ. He uses the same verb "have seen" to express both his view of the Promised Land and his view of the Second Coming. By using the same verb to express both epiphanies, he strongly suggests that the view of the Second Coming extends, exemplifies, and overlaps the earlier view of the Promised Land.

King's logic is biblical. Salvation oracles in (Second) Isaiah, Jeremiah, and Ezekiel blend the salvation history of the original Exodus with a promise of escape from Babylonian exile and return to the Promised Land. In Christian scripture, salvation history (from Egypt and Babylon) and salvation prophecies receive their later realization in Jesus Christ. Of course, a basic tenet of Christian texts and doctrine is that Jesus will return during the Second Coming to enact the Final Judgment and Final Redemption.

Building on the salvation history and salvation prophecies of sanctified Hebrew texts, the Christian Bible provides a strong, imaginative precedent for King's decision to merge visions of the Promised Land and the Second Coming.

Earlier in the speech King alluded to the Second Coming by mentioning the New Jerusalem. In a passage in Revelation, the final book of the Christian Bible, the narrator stands on a mountain and envisions the Final Salvation and the New Jerusalem. This narrator explains that an angel

> carried me away to a great high mountain
> and showed me the holy city Jerusalem
> coming down out of heaven from God.
>   (Revelation 21:10)

By the time readers of the Bible peruse this verse, they are, of course, quite familiar with narrators experiencing holy visions on mountains. When the book of Revelation presents a narrator on a mountain glimpsing a holy vision, that book re-fulfills the earlier biblical imagery of Moses on Mount Pisgah viewing the Promised Land and Christ on the Mount of Olives ascending to heaven. At the end of his oration, King, like the narrator of Revelation, gazes at the wonders that await the faithful at the Second Coming. Both the narrator of Revelation and King stand on a hallowed mountain as they glimpse the Final Redemption. King thus *simultaneously* merges his own vision from a mountaintop with the vision of Moses from Mount Pisgah *and* the vision of the narrator of Revelation from a mountain. In King's single (yet multiple) image, Moses on a mountain views the Promised Land, the narrator of Revelation views the New Jerusalem and the Second Coming, King views African Americans' arrival in the Promised Land, and King also views the Second Coming:

Moses Views Promised Land	=	Narrator of Revelation Views New Jerusalem and Second Coming	=	King Views Arrival at Promised Land	=	King Views Second Coming

In King's imaginative universe, Moses, the narrator of Revelation, and King become one.

Of course, when King announces, "Mine eyes have seen the glory of the coming of the Lord!" he also quotes the first line of Julia Ward Howe's well-known "Battle Hymn of the Republic." The relationship of King's speech to Howe's anthem is extremely important. Why does he use her lyrics when discussing his own epiphany, that is, what his eyes have seen? And how does this last sentence finalize the biblical narrative and biblical hermeneutic that he has used to reimagine Memphis throughout his oration?

Although King only quotes Howe's first line, he clearly implies other lines from "Battle Hymn of the Republic." He had quoted the first stanza, fourth stanza, and refrain of this hymn on other occasions, most importantly three years earlier when speaking to fifty thousand people after the march from Selma to Montgomery.[10] He ended that oration, "Our God Is Marching On," with these lyrics from Howe's song:

Mine eyes have seen the glory of the coming of the Lord!
He is trampling out the vintage where the grapes of wrath are stored.
He has loosed the fateful lightning of his terrible swift sword.
His truth is marching on!

He has sounded forth the trumpet that shall never call retreat!
He is sifting out the hearts of men before His judgment seat.
O, be swift my soul to answer him!
Be jubilant my feet!
Our God is marching on!

Glory hallelujah!
Glory hallelujah!
Glory hallelujah!
His truth is marching on!

In "I've Been to the Mountaintop," when King cites "Mine eyes have seen the glory of the coming of the Lord!" he strong implies the same lines from "Battle Hymn of the Republic" that he had quoted in "Our God Is Marching On." He does so for four reasons.

First, by ending the two speeches similarly, he signals an important relationship between the speeches and invites listeners to recall the entire quotation that he had used earlier in "Our God Is Marching On."

Second, most in King's audience were quite familiar with Howe's lyrics. Many generations of choirs and congregations kept belting out "Battle Hymn of the Republic" well into the 1950s and 1960s, and huge numbers of people learned the lyrics in churches and schools. When many people hear a single line of a beloved song, they automatically remember its other lines. That happened in this case with King's use of Howe's anthem—and that still happens when people read or hear "I've Been to the Mountaintop."

Third, in Howe's initial sentence, the narrator announces a vision of the Second Coming—a declaration that logically entails the first and fourth stanzas and the refrain, which explain the vision. Howe's phrase "the glory of the coming of the Lord" *means* that he is "trampling out the vintage where the grapes of wrath are stored" and releasing "the fateful lightning of His terrible swift sword."

Fourth, a great, palpable excitement seized Mason Temple as soon as King entered the sanctuary. After he approached the pulpit and started speaking, a sense of wonder and amazement began to overtake the audience. As his voice intensified while his cadences grew firmer, indicating his approach to his "landing strip," a sense of triumph and elation overwhelmed the audience and King himself. When he ended by reciting the first line of "Battle Hymn of the Republic," he left the impression that, in Coretta Scott King's words, he "intended to finish the quotation" but stopped short because he was "overcome" with "exaltation."[11] His listeners could complete the quotation in their minds in part because they sensed that he was unable to do so.

When King quoted Howe, he reached back an entire century. Produced at the height of the Civil War, "Battle Hymn of the Republic" began not as a barn burner, but simply as a poem. A certified member of the Boston Brahmin, Julia Ward Howe associated with such abolitionist beacons as Charles Sumner, Theodore Parker, William Lloyd Garrison, Wendell Phillips, and Thomas Wentworth Higginson. In 1862 she visited wounded Northern soldiers who were lying in a makeshift, tent hospital in Washington, D.C. After comforting the troops, she retired to the posh Willard Hotel, where politicians from Capitol Hill jabbered while fogging the corridors with endless clouds of cigar smoke. Waking before dawn and careful not to disturb her sleeping baby, she penned "Battle Hymn of the Republic." Appearing originally in *Atlantic Monthly*, her poem was set to music and quickly became, in her words, "one of the leading lyrics" of the Civil War.[12] Union soldiers enthusiastically embraced it, and Abraham Lincoln reportedly cried when he heard it.[13]

Writing her poem that became an anthem for a culture drenched in the Bible, Howe extrapolates biblical language of judgment and eschatology. Skillfully abstracting and fusing several clusters of biblical metaphors, she refashions portions of Hebrew scripture that resurface in the Christian Bible, especially in Revelation.

By altering tropes from Hebrew narratives and prophecy, the author of Revelation reworks those narratives and that prophecy. By adapting metaphors from Revelation, Howe reworks Revelation. By quoting Howe in a speech about garbage workers, King reworks Howe. Perhaps one might conceive of these intertextual relations as a set of nesting boxes, each of which bears some resemblance to the others but is also distinctive. The tiniest box consists of passages from the Hebrew Bible. Portions of Revelation comprise a small box that reframes the tiniest box. "Battle Hymn of the Republic" is a larger box that, in turn, reframes the biblical segments, especially Revelation. And "I've Been to the Mountaintop" is the largest box that encapsulates Howe's lyrics and the boxes inside it. Even though this analogy might be tempting, it fails to account for the dialogic interplay that each later author establishes with the earlier texts. Understanding this entire dialogic relationship is crucial to understanding the climactic final line of King's final speech.

Consider the relation between "Battle Hymn of the Republic" and biblical texts. When Howe writes, "Mine eyes have seen the glory of the coming of the Lord!" her narrator conveys ecstasy through the metaphor of "seeing" (a concrete verb) the "glory" (an abstract noun) of the Lord's arrival. Always expressing religious bliss, this trope appears, in slightly different forms, on scores of occasions throughout the Bible.

After this exhilarating opening, Howe offers a provocative assertion: "He is trampling out the vintage where the grapes of wrath are stored!" She shapes this declaration by adapting and refining portions of Hebrew scripture. One such passage is the declaration in Malachi that the righteous should

> tread down the wicked.
> (Malachi 4:3)

Another is the testimony in Habakkuk that God

> trampled the nations in anger.[14]
> (Habakkuk 3:12)

When she writes "He is trampling out the vintage where the grapes of wrath are stored!" she refashions other scriptural passages as well. Many sacred Hebrew books repeatedly associate grapes with the fecundity of the soil and with the rhythms of nature and community—associations established through many images of planting, harvesting, meals, wine, weddings, celebrations, joy, and prosperity. Reversing the overwhelmingly positive associations that other biblical texts establish, Joel declares that righteous people stamp on evildoers. In a gruesome image, Joel then equates the juice from smashed grapes to the blood of crushed sinners:

> Go in [righteous people,] tread,
> for the winepress is full.
> The vats overflow,
> for their wickedness is great.
> (Joel 3:13)

In a similarly frightful passage in (Third) Isaiah, the prophet, speaking for God, states that God treads the winepress, pounding the guilty in rage and freely shedding their blood:

> I have trodden the winepress alone;
> And of the people there was none with me:
> I trod them in my anger
> And trampled them in my fury;
> And their blood is sprinkled upon my garments;
> And I have stained all my raiment.
> For the day of vengeance was in mine heart....
> I trod down the people in my anger.
> I made them drunk in my wrath,
> And I poured their lifeblood on the earth.
> ([Third] Isaiah 63:3–6)[15]

In her next line, "He hath loosed the fateful lightning of his terrible swift sword," Howe again recasts imagery from the Hebrew Bible. Psalms portrays God wielding lightning to destroy the wicked.[16] (Second) Isaiah and Daniel present the sword as an instrument of destruction.[17] Ezekiel merges the metaphors of lightning and sword into a single trope:

A glittering sword ... is made like lightning[18]
(Ezekiel 21:15, 21:28)

and

A sword, a sword is sharpened and polished,
sharpened for slaughter,
polished to flash like lightning.
(Ezekiel 21:9)[19]

Further, Jeremiah links the metaphor of God rendering judgment by treading grapes to one of God rendering judgment by wielding a sword:

The Lord shall roar from on high....
He shall mightily roar upon his habitation;
He shall give a shout, as they that tread the grapes,
Against all the inhabitants of the earth.
A noise shall come even to the ends of the earth;
For the Lord hath a controversy with the nations,
He will plead with all flesh;
He will give them that are wicked to the sword.
(Jeremiah 25:30–31)[20]

Like Ezekiel and Jeremiah, Howe uses metaphors of sword and lightning to evoke divine judgment.

Howe's declaration, "He is sounding forth the trumpet that shall never call retreat!" alludes to God's instruction in Numbers that the Israelites should play the trumpet during warfare and to a single verse in Zechariah that articulates God's judgment through images of lightning and trumpet.[21] As well, her affirmation recalls the climactic moment in Joshua in which priests dramatically blow seven trumpets to collapse the walls of Jericho, thereby allowing the Hebrews to complete the Exodus from Egypt to Canaan.[22] By packing so many allusions into a very few lines, Howe encapsulates the climax of the Exodus and vibrant elements of Hebrew narrative and prophecy.

The author of Revelation recasts the earlier figures of winepress, lightning, sword, and trumpet from sacred Jewish texts. When Howe refashions these four metaphors from the Hebrew Bible, she simultaneously retools the same tropes as they appear in the Christian Bible, especially in Revelation. When King refashions Howe, he extends Howe's process of remaking these tropes.

To understand this process, one must first examine Revelation. Written as a letter to early Christians who either suffered or expected persecution under the Roman Empire, Revelation is a phantasmagorical text that gained inestimable importance when editors selected it as the culminating book of the Christian Bible.[23] Over the centuries, readers' responses to Revelation have varied greatly. To a casual reader, Revelation may seem the undiluted raving of a certifiable psychotic. Yet, for hundreds of years, many have interpreted Revelation as a coded prediction into a distant future that is divinely determined. As many scholars explain, the author of Revelation sought to counter the prevalent, imperial ideology of the Roman Empire. Citing this purpose, Richard Bauckham claims that Revelation is "a book of profound theology, intense prophetic insight and dazzling literary accomplishment." Bauckham maintains that Revelation "has inspired the martyrs, nourished the imagination of visionaries, artists, and hymn-writers, resourced prophetic critiques of oppression in state and church, sustained hope and resistance in the most hopeless situations."[24]

King once explained, "For many people the Book of Revelation is a strange book and puzzling to decode. It is often cast aside as an enigma wrapped in mystery." But he avowed that, underneath its "peculiar jargon" and "prevailing apocalyptic symbolism, we find many challenging and profound truths."[25] Refusing to present an enigma wrapped in mystery, Howe and King adapt Revelation quite cogently.

The author of Revelation, John of Patmos, was, in his own way, an exceedingly careful student of Hebrew scripture. Instead of quoting Hebrew materials directly, this seer reshaped them into his own version of apocalypse and eschatology. He did a lot of reshaping. The just over four hundred verses of Revelation contain so many allusions to the Hebrew Bible that scholars don't know how to count them all. They cannot decide whether Revelation refers to Hebrew scripture 195 times or 500 times (and a few researchers have located even more than 500 allusions).[26] Even if Revelation features only 195 allusions—the lowest proposed number—it is obvious that, as Jan Fekkes notes, Revelation is "virtually saturated" with the "texts and traditions" of the Hebrew Bible.[27] This cornucopia of allusions establishes a gigantic intertext between Revelation and as many as thirty-one Hebrew books, including such major texts as Exodus, Isaiah, Jeremiah, Ezekiel, and Daniel. Although some of these references are clear (such as the allusion to Moses on Mount Pisgah), coping with this intertext is a formidable task that confounds and spurs readers and scholars alike. G. K. Beale observes that, during the 1980s and 1990s alone, six academics published what he calls "significant" books about the relationship between sacred Hebrew texts and Revelation.[28]

As Bauckham notes, when John of Patmos reworks and complicates sanctified Hebrew literature, he departs from his predecessors in relying heavily on his "heightened visual imagination" as opposed to the "narrative prophecy" that held an "important place" in Hebrew scripture. Bauckham observes that John of Patmos supplies "comparatively little" narrative prophecy, "replacing it with visionary material."[29] Drawing on Hebrew imagery and on his visual and aural imagination, John of Patmos repeatedly presents trumpet, lightning, and sword as instruments of God's Final Judgment. From (Third) Isaiah, Joel, and Jeremiah, John of Patmos seizes and reworks the gruesome image of the winepress as a vehicle for divine retribution:

> ... the great winepress of the wrath of God.
> And the winepress was trodden without the city
> And blood came out of the winepress,
> even unto the horse bridles.
> (Revelation 14:19–20)[30]

Like the author of Jeremiah, John of Patmos links the image of the winepress with that of the sword:

> And out of his mouth goes a sharp sword,
> That with it he should smite the nations:
> And he shall rule them with a rod of iron:
> And he treads the winepress of the fierceness and wrath
> of Almighty God.
> (Revelation 19:25)[31]

Valuing the allusive sensibility and visual imagination of John of Patmos, Howe turns repeatedly to Revelation, the only biblical book that features all four metaphors of devastation—trumpet, winepress, lightning, and sword—that she adapts for "Battle Hymn of the Republic."

As I mentioned, when she writes, "He has sounded forth the trumpet that shall never call retreat!" she evokes passages in Numbers, Zechariah, and Joshua. John of Patmos reinvents and re-fulfills the plotline of Joshua when Revelation announces that blowing trumpets, which had earlier crashed the walls of Jericho, will now herald the Final Judgment and Christ's Kingdom.[32] Similarly, John of Patmos reconfigures and re-fulfills the sacred Hebrew metaphors of winepress, sword, and lightning as instruments of God's judgment.

Howe's line, "He is sifting out the hearts of men before his judgment seat!" clearly refers to II Corinthians, which mentions

> the judgment seat of Christ,
> (II Corinthians 5:10)

and to Romans, which highlights

> the judgment seat of God.
> (Romans 14:10)

To those who expect the cosmic end-time, the image of God's "judgment seat" definitely emphasizes the Second Coming and Final Judgment and contrasts to the image of God's "mercy seat" that appears in Exodus and Leviticus.[33]

The sheer familiarity of Howe's lyrics masks their complexity, which stems not simply from the dizzying abundance of her biblical allusions, but also from her treatment of time, which parallels that of John of Patmos.

Without doubt, Revelation presents time in an extraordinary fashion. Many biblical texts proceed from the ordinary assumption that time advances straightforwardly, like an arrow rushing ahead. Many familiar biblical characters appear in a chronological sequence: Adam and Eve definitely precede Abraham, who precedes Moses, who precedes Jeremiah, who precedes Jesus, who precedes Paul. Whenever biblical writers and editors present a straightforward chronology, they affirm that time and history consist of sequential events. John of Patmos, however, replaces this view of time. As Leonard Thompson observes, "Time takes a curious turn in the Book of Revelation, for past, present, and future are not separated by fixed, absolute boundaries."[34] Rather, Thompson asserts, the metaphors in Revelation create "complex boundaries in space and time that cannot be charted in an ordinary space-time grid."[35] Time is highly elastic in this book, which presents widely separated moments as collapsing upon each other. As Thompson notes, Revelation simultaneously explains both "what is and what is to take place hereafter" while presenting "a protean world where God alone is the master of all boundary transactions."[36]

Related to the extraordinary treatment of time in Revelation is what numerous researchers and ordinary believers identify as its main theme—the "Already and Not Yet." According to many moderate and liberal Christians, the language of eschatology in the four gospels and in Revelation refers not only to Christ's return in the future, but also to the present. Christians passionately proclaim that the sacrifice of Christ transformed history. The Kingdom of God, they believe, began to enter history at the birth of Jesus, entered more fully at the resurrection, and continues to break into history. Yet, they affirm, the Kingdom is not altogether here and will not completely reveal itself until the Second Coming. The Kingdom of God, thus, is "Already and Not Yet." According to this interpretation, John of Patmos invokes the redemption history and redemption oracles of the Hebrew Bible for two purposes: first, to indicate that the advent of the Christ aids all Christians every day; second, to sketch the end of time.

Consider Howe's relationship to the Bible. Noticing few of the many biblical references in the "Battle Hymn of the Republic," Edmund Wilson, a famous literary critic, interprets Howe's anthem simply as a response to the Civil War. He claims that Howe flatly equates the Union army with "the coming of the Lord."[37] Similarly, Mary Grant contends that—like William Lloyd Garrison, John Greenleaf Whittier, and Henry James Sr.—Howe uses biblical images to emphasize the theme of national rebirth through the violent collision of the North and South. Grant argues, "In writing her poem, [Howe] translated the Civil War into eschatology."[38]

Howe certainly *was* reflecting, in part, on the Civil War. Her initial audience undoubtedly used the lyrics of "Battle Hymn of the Republic" as a lens for interpreting the monumental clash between the Union and the Confederacy. The less familiar second and third stanzas of this hymn depict a "hundred circling camps" and "burnished rows of steel"—images that apparently refer to the Northern army.[39] Accustomed to hearing Frederick Douglass and other abolitionists emphasize God's mandate to end slavery, her immediate audience could readily view a Northern triumph over Southern bondage as a biblically based sign that would eventually culminate in the Second Coming.

But "Battle Hymn of the Republic" is not only about the Civil War. Indeed, the interpretations of Wilson and Grant are simplistic and reductive, for Wilson and Grant fail to recognize the richness of Howe's artistry. Their readings cannot in any way account for the great popularity of "Battle Hymn of the Republic" for many, many decades *after* the Civil War. Unlike many other nineteenth-century hymns, it remained widely beloved at least through the 1950s and 1960s. No hymn can retain its popularity if it is only seen as a historical artifact. Congregations only treasure hymns that they believe speak to their current circumstances.

Significantly, King did not quote the second and third stanzas from "Battle Hymn of the Republic," stanzas that seem to refer to the Civil War. Instead, in 1965 he quoted the first stanza, fourth stanza, and refrain of this song. Those well-known lines retained their popularity partly because they *never* explicitly refer to Lincoln, slavery, the Union, or the Confederacy. Indeed, those lines never explicitly refer to anything American at all. For this portion of her lyrics, especially, Howe preferred highly symbolic language with grand biblical resonance, language that could easily cover human experience *after* the Civil War. Even though the large, enduring significance of Howe's symbolic language eluded Wilson and Grant, millions of ordinary churchgoers understood and embraced that resonance. "Battle Hymn of the Republic" is a formidable poem and a formidable hymn not because it translates the Civil War into eschatology, but because it both addresses and extends beyond the circumstance of the Civil War in the same way that Revelation both addresses and extends beyond the circumstance of first-century Christians.

Like Revelation, "Battle Hymn of the Republic" revives sacred metaphors of winepress, sword, and lightning both to explain a current situation *and* to highlight the centuries-old, yet ever-fresh clash between good and evil. In both Revelation and "Battle Hymn of the Republic," this clash is moving inexorably toward the millennium. As they propound the theme of "Already and Not Yet," John of Patmos and Howe do not simplistically mirror contemporary political and military events. Nor do they narrowly interpret such events. Rather, they quarry complex, charged, biblical symbolism for the purpose of reflecting on concerns that are simultaneously immediate, recurring, and ultimate.

Even though Revelation is an entire book and the lyrics of "Battle Hymn of the Republic" fit onto a single page, one could usefully apply much of Leonard Thompson's interpretation of Revelation to Howe's anthem. Like John of Patmos, Howe wrenches apart time and space. In Howe's lyrics, as in Revelation, Hebrew oracles have been fulfilled and will be fulfilled again, the life of Jesus ended and did not end, and utter desolation and blissful fulfillment both loom.

Despite Howe's reconceptualization of horrifying biblical tropes about God's powers of judgment and destruction, choirs invariably belt out "Battle Hymn of the Republic" in an upbeat tempo with robust, heartfelt tones. The anthem always sounds hopeful, even exuberant. The repeated lines of Howe's refrain

> Glory, glory, hallelujah!
> Glory, glory, hallelujah!
> Glory, glory, hallelujah!

articulate simple praise and wonder. But Howe's lyrics also recast troubling biblical images. How can she create such a resplendent, joyful lyric while summoning profoundly disconcerting biblical symbols of massive devastation and death?

She does so through two main strategies. First, she dampens the sense of destruction by beginning her poem with a cry of exaltation about the Second Coming: "Mine eyes have seen the glory of the coming of the Lord!" In Christian scripture and tradition, the Second Coming will be an altogether glorious, awe-inspiring, and welcome end of history, an event that obviously warrants exaltation.

Second, she raises biblical images of destruction to a level of abstraction. When she reworks scriptural passages about God's fury toward evildoers, her lyrics never mention the destruction of people. Instead her lyrics refer more abstractly to the destruction of evil itself. So, whereas, in Joel, (Third) Isaiah, Jeremiah, and Revelation, wicked people bleed copiously and die in the winepress, only the "grapes of wrath" are crushed in Howe's lyrics. And, while Ezekiel and Revelation note that God's lightning and sword smite evildoers, in "Battle Hymn of the Republic" they only attack evil itself. By abstracting and softening biblical symbols of destruction, Howe crafts lyrics as buoyant as her melody.

King concludes "I've Been to the Mountaintop" by orchestrating visions of catastrophe and promise that he locates in Hebrew oracles, Revelation, and "Battle Hymn of the Republic." In the Bible, the eschatology of Revelation fulfills earlier books of narrative and prophecy. In "Battle Hymn of the Republic," Howe revives those narratives, that prophecy, and that eschatology. In "I've Been to the Mountaintop," King's conclusion caps the biblical narrative and prophecy that he has articulated throughout the speech. Through his biblical logic, his narrative and prophecy now find their fulfillment in eschatology.

The theme of persecution/triumph that King has developed throughout his speech is essential to his biblical logic and eschatology. He began his time travel by noting that Pharaoh's persecution of the Hebrews preceded the Exodus and by implying that the persecution of Luther preceded the Reformation, the destruction of the Civil War preceded the Emancipation Proclamation, and the hardships of the Great Depression preceded prosperity after World War II. At every stop in his time machine, he implies, persecution, loss, and/or calamity accompany a sublime achievement.

Just before King discusses current upheavals in the new Exodus-like drama, he cites a maxim that explains the paradox of persecution/triumph: "Only when it's dark can you see the stars." King maintains that the pattern of persecution/triumph also structures current affairs in Memphis:

> Now we're going to march again and we've got to march again in order to ... force everybody to see that there are thirteen hundred of God's children here suffering. Sometimes going hungry, going through dark and dreary days, wondering how this thing is going to come out.... And we've got to say to the nation: We know how it's coming out. For when people get caught up with that which is right and they are willing to sacrifice for it, there is no stopping point short of victory.

He then contends that the Memphis strike will parallel the grand, national victory in Birmingham, where, he explains, agitators emerged supreme against such recalcitrant racists as Bull Connor because their inward, Jeremiah-like holy fire and the sacred water of their Christian Baptism countered the watery assault of Connor's fire hoses.

King's quotations from Amos, Jeremiah, and (Third) Isaiah further reinforce his argument about persecution/loss/triumph. Many in King's audience understood his biblical subtext. They realized that Amos weighs loss and triumph by supplying overabundant oracles of utter catastrophe as well as the magisterial vision, "Let justice roll down like waters and righteousness like a mighty stream," that King quotes in "I've Been to the Mountaintop." King's biblically literate listeners would have realized that the same Jeremiah who had "fire shut up in his bones" also prophesied the impending disaster of exile and captivity in Babylon and, later, during that exile and captivity, announced the possibility of a glorious return to the Israelite homeland. A number in Mason Temple may have known that the passage from (Third) Isaiah, "The Spirit of the Lord is upon me," that King invokes was probably written after the Babylonian exile, during the period of the Second Temple, when the Hebrews keenly remembered the heartbreak of the exile. Further, for King's immediate audience and for other Christians, despite the string of calamities experienced by the Israelites, Jesus fulfills the oracle from (Third) Isaiah, thereby replacing oppression and loss with triumph.

King's explication of the Parable of the Good Samaritan provides yet another variation of persecution/triumph. In King's retelling of the parable, the traveler is beaten, robbed, discarded, and ignored before the Good Samaritan arrives to dispense compassion. King contends that, in a parallel manner, supporters of the maltreated workers in Memphis can uplift these new roadside victims, creating another victory from persecution.

Near the end of the address, when King reaches the "If I had sneezed" refrain about his near-assassination, he extends the paradigm of persecution/triumph that he has exemplified throughout the speech and that he has affirmed as the single, great pattern of the Bible and of history. In this argument, every monumental, historical breakthrough provides a glimmer of the Second Coming and serves as its harbinger.

King choreographs these breakthroughs by interpreting time in two distinct ways. In three portions of the speech, he organizes historical moments in their chronological order. In the first segment, he relates the Exodus as an event prior to Plato and Aristotle in ancient Greece. Next he portrays ancient Greece preceding ancient Rome. Then he presents ancient Rome preceding the Renaissance, the Renaissance preceding Martin Luther, Luther preceding Abraham Lincoln, Lincoln preceding Franklin Roosevelt, and Roosevelt preceding current agitation for freedom in Africa and the United States.

In a second segment, King mentions events of the civil rights movement in their proper chronological sequence: first, Lunch Counter Sit-Ins; then Freedom Rides; then Albany; then Birmingham; then "I Have a Dream"; then Selma; then, finally, Memphis.

King also frames developments in Memphis chronologically: initially, the mayor treated city laborers deplorably; then the workers decided to strike; next police maced the clergy; then King led a march that turned chaotic; then the newspapers misrepresented the violence; then a judge issued an injunction against a future march; finally, King is now organizing large-scale boycotts and a new march.

As King aligns each of these three sequences—landmarks in world history, key episodes in the civil rights movement, and events in Memphis—time moves steadily forward, one occurrence follows another, each event is irreversible, and chronology and history are unshakably linear and real.

Yet "I've Been to the Mountaintop" reflects the biblical pattern of presenting time as an arrow *and* time as a cycle. King portrays time as a cycle when the Exodus narrative churns through history, returning in old, yet new forms as the Reformation, the Emancipation Proclamation, the New Deal, and recent racial unrest in Africa and the United States. The Exodus now spirals into Memphis, King asserts, where Pharaoh enslaves the trash collectors. Also, in King's argument, Hebrew prophecies return when the fire in Jeremiah's bones reappears and flames again in Birmingham and Memphis. In Luke, Jesus revives and invokes the sacred commission recorded in (Third) Isaiah. King maintains that the same commission now summons ministers in Memphis, some of whom—including James Lawson, Billy Kyles, and Ralph Jackson—have responded to it.

The portrait of time as a cycle is especially pronounced when King completes his theme of persecution/triumph by crowning his oration with eschatology:

> And He's allowed me to go up to the mountain. And I've looked over and I've seen the Promised Land! I may not get there with you, but I want you to know tonight that we, as a people, will get to the Promised Land! And so I'm happy tonight! I'm not worried about anything! I'm not fearing any man! Mine eyes have seen the glory of the coming of the Lord!

Here, when he recounts his glimpse of the Promised Land, "And he's allowed me to go up to the mountain. And I've looked over and I've seen the Promised Land!" he openly compares himself to Moses, who, at the end of Deuteronomy, gazes at the Promised Land shortly before, in Joshua, the Hebrews enter the Promised Land. When King glimpses the Promised Land, what does he see? In his words, "Mine eyes have seen the glory of the coming of the Lord!" One would expect that King would manifest his vision of the Promised Land by presenting imagery from biblical books about the Exodus (Exodus, Leviticus, Numbers, or Deuteronomy) or from the biblical text about the arrival in the Promised Land (Joshua). But he fails to do so. He does not express his vision of the Promised Land by orchestrating imagery from any portion of the Exodus narrative at all. Rather, by quoting Howe, he expresses his vision of the Promised Land while offering clusters of metaphors that appear in Hebrew prophecies that appeared centuries *after* the Exodus. He also manifests his vision of Canaan by evoking clusters of metaphors that reverberate in Revelation, which surfaced centuries *after* the Hebrew prophecies. He further expresses this vision of the Promised Land by evoking clusters of metaphors that Howe marshaled centuries *after* John of Patmos wrote Revelation.

How can this be? In King's rhetoric, Moses glimpses the Promised Land, but the content of this Mosaic vision did not appear until centuries and centuries later. How can this bundle of post-Moses metaphors embody a sight that Moses beheld centuries earlier? Here King's chronology is anything but linear.

By itself, this conundrum is not enough for King. He compounds it by fusing the Mosaic vision not only to eschatology, but also to his anticipation of his own impending death: "I may not get there with you." Projecting Moses's vision of the Promised Land, he simultaneously predicts his own assassination and prophesies the final curtain. He thus represents the last vision of Moses as one that, in some sense, recycles and resonates in Hebrew oracles, Revelation, "Battle Hymn of the Republic," his own epiphany about his death, and the Second Coming. King thereby establishes the following rough equivalencies:

Moses		Hebrew Prophets		Narrator		Howe	
Vision of Promised Land (prior to his death)	=	Visions of Doom and Salvation	=	of *Revelation* Vision of Final Judgment, New Jerusalem, and Second Coming	=	Vision of Final Judgment and Second Coming	=

King		King
Vision of Promised Land (prior to his own death)	=	Vision of Second Coming

Clearly, time here does not proceed like an arrow. Rather, like John of Patmos and like Howe, King wrenches apart time and space, then reimagines them. His memories, prophecies, and visions persistently recirculate and re-emerge in forms that are different, yet recognizable.

King's last speech thus presents time both as an arrow and as a cycle. Does this paradox make sense? How can these quite distinct representations of time be reconciled? King joins biblical writers in eschewing any myth of eternal cycles, that is, any set of cycles that spin endlessly and mindlessly forever.[40] Rather, like the authors of (Second) Isaiah, Jeremiah, Ezekiel, Amos, and Luke, King embraces and transforms religious cycles even as he acknowledges the weight and irreversibility of history. In his last speech, as in biblical texts, cycles never erase historical particulars. Like the authors of (Second) Isaiah, Jeremiah, Ezekiel, Amos, and Luke, King reconciles the metaphors of time-as-arrow and time-as-cycle by portraying time as a wheel that turns constantly, yet moves forward. Like the author of Revelation, King portrays the wheel turning and moving onward, toward the last days. In this interpretation, as the wheel moves, the sublime moments of history parallel, echo, sustain, and illuminate each other.

Interpreting time as a wheel allows King to affirm what many regard as the central eschatological theme of Revelation—the "Already and Not Yet." For King and many others, the Kingdom of God has arrived, but not yet fully. Or, as King explained on another occasion, the Kingdom of God "may be post-historical" while simultaneously existing "right now, as an inner power within you," a power that signifies "the final refusal to give up."[41] In "I've Been to the Mountaintop," he suggests that the message of Christ— which he affirms by quoting the commission from (Third) Isaiah and Luke and by interpreting the Good Samaritan—will prevail both during the strike in Memphis and at the Final Consummation.

Earlier in this speech King mentioned a prominent trope in Revelation—the New Jerusalem, a heavenly city that drops to earth at the time of the final curtain. Beginning with King David's earthly city of Jerusalem, the exceedingly rich image of the celestial Jerusalem pulls a long train of biblical signifiers. Of course, the New Jerusalem signifies the Final Redemption at the endtime. Admonishing ministers, King asserted, "It's all right to talk about the New Jerusalem. But one day God's preacher must talk about the new New York, the new Atlanta, the new Philadelphia, the new Los Angeles, and the new Memphis, Tennessee." He thereby scolded certain clergy for focusing way too much on the "Not Yet" half of the millennial theme to the exclusion of the "Already" half of the same theme. He urged them to balance the importance of the current social struggle (the "Already") against any anticipation of the last days (the "Not Yet"). This same theme of the "Already and Not Yet" radiates from the final sentence of "I've Been to the Mountaintop." Like Howe, when King declares, "Mine eyes have seen the glory of the coming of the Lord!" he affirms the "Already"—his eyes have already seen the glory, the radiance—and the "Not Yet," as he and other believers continue to await the Second Coming.

Earlier I discussed Kenneth Burke's rejection of literary form as a set of formal structures and his conception of literary form as entelechy, "the creation of an appetite" on the part of readers and the "satisfying of that appetite."[42] Certain biblical writers define biblical narrative as entelechy that continues to unfold because, in Burke's words, of the "possibilities of perfection which reside in the form as such and *toward* which all sorts of stories might gravitate."[43] For example, (Second) Isaiah, Jeremiah, and Ezekiel portray an impending return from Babylonian exile as a new Exodus. In their argument, the return from Babylon will both fulfill and surpass the splendor of the original Exodus and will thereby realize an entelechial potential within the Pentateuch. Similarly, John of Patmos taps entelechial possibilities within Israelite oracles as he adapts the oracles for a much later audience of early Christians.

In a roughly parallel fashion, Howe and King explore further entelechial potential within the Bible toward which additional imagery and stories might gravitate. Howe and King implicitly argue that the very magnificence of the Bible lies partly in its potential to release new, related stories. By quoting Howe, King not only presents a vision with biblical resonance, but also cites a precedent for the possibility of doing eschatology *after* the biblical era. The status of "Battle Hymn of the Republic" as a classic American song lends strength to King's argument that eschatology remains important and that it can continue to inspire. He implicitly maintains that, if, as late as the 1860s, Howe can discern further entelechial possibilities in biblical form, then such possibilities can also extend into the 1960s.

When King explores the Exodus narrative, prophecy, entelechy, and eschatology, he chafes at the closing of the biblical canon. Jewish authorities finalized the Hebrew Bible about the time of Jesus or shortly afterward. In a process that lasted several hundred years, early Christian leaders fixed the canon of Christian scripture. Throughout the varied branches of Judeo-Christianity, religious officials wrangled for centuries as they sifted a multitude of texts before selecting a relatively small number of books worthy of forming the Bible. When authorities pruned their final choices, they further determined that no additional writings would ever be eligible for inclusion. Their decision to freeze the biblical canon created, if not an outright contradiction, then at least a deep and perplexing paradox. Even though the main message of the Bible is that God is alive, sealing the canon appears to petrify God's revelations in the past, a past that would eventually recede many hundreds of years. Cementing the canon might suggest that, insofar as no recent revelations merit the status of scriptural representation, the living God appeared in a more compelling fashion in ancient times rather than any time lately.

But, in the interpretation of King and many others, the Bible itself addresses this problem by defying and subverting Claude Levi-Strauss's analysis of literary conclusions: "Mythical thought always progresses from the awareness of oppositions toward their resolution."[44] Both the Hebrew Bible and the Christian Bible resist resolution because, unlike later authorities who padlocked the canon, biblical authors dialogued incessantly with their predecessors as they reimagined and reworked biblical narratives and biblical theology. To them, in Mikhail Bakhtin's words, "Even *past* meanings, that is, those born in dialogue of past centuries, can never be stable (finalized, ended once and for all)" for "there will always be ... subsequent future development of the dialogue."[45] The Jewish Bible also refuses resolution because a major focus of the text—the destiny of the Jewish people—is not yet settled.

When King affirms, "Mine eyes have seen the glory of the coming of the Lord!" his climactic final sentence undergirds his earlier rhetorical moves: his projection of Memphis strikers into the Exodus narrative; his re-animation of divine commissions from Jeremiah, Amos, and (Third) Isaiah/Luke; his inscription of the sanitation workers into the Parable of the Good Samaritan; his account of his own near-assassination; his discussion of facing new death threats; and his Moses-like glimpse of the Promised Land. By ending his speech with these words, "Mine eyes have seen the glory of the coming of the Lord!" King indicates that every segment of "I've Been to the Mountaintop," including each persecution and triumph, serves as a building block that reaches toward eschatology.

King thereby defines his entire speech as a modern, Bible-like revelation.

As King does so, he, like Howe, mutes and abstracts the biblical metaphors of winepress, sword, lightning, trumpet, and judgment seat into symbols of the destruction of wickedness. Like the Hebrew prophets, King seesaws as he summons the possibilities for both doom and redemption. Near the beginning of his speech, after imagining his time travel, he refers to the prospect of nuclear annihilation: "Men for years now have been talking about war and peace. But now no longer can they just talk about it. It is no longer a choice between violence and nonviolence in this world. It's nonviolence or nonexistence. That is where we are today." He adds that privileged people must stop oppressing those with dark skin, who suffer from "their long years of poverty, their long years of hurt and neglect." If a "human rights revolution" does not occur, he warns ominously, then "the whole world is doomed." Like the Hebrew prophets, King portrays the human race as teetering between, on one side, an Exodus-like redemption and, on the other, utter damnation and loss. Faithfulness to God could create one fate, faithlessness the other.

King frames his last address as a scripture-like revelation because at Mason Temple he develops and sharpens biblical themes and eschatology. He also frames this speech as a scripture-like revelation because its conclusion partially fulfills the most famous passage of his entire oratory—the dream litany in "I Have a Dream."[46] After King eloquently articulates his dream of racial harmony, even in the tortured states of Mississippi and Alabama, he climaxes his "I have a dream" refrain by proclaiming, "I have a dream that one day every valley shall be exalted, every hill and mountain shall be made low, the rough places will be made plain, the crooked places will be made straight, the glory of the Lord shall be revealed and all flesh shall see it together!" Of course, he was quoting (Second) Isaiah, whose words explain a vision of the Israelites freed from Babylonian captivity and exile:

> Every valley shall be exalted,
> Every hill and mountain shall be made low,
> The rough places will be made plain,
> The crooked places will be made straight,
> The glory of the Lord shall be revealed
> And all flesh shall see it together!
>   ([Second] Isaiah 40:4–5)

According to this vision, the Hebrews will venture from Babylon through a wilderness and a desert that God will rearrange in order to assist their return to Canaan. (Second) Isaiah repeatedly emplots this entire experience as another Exodus. Matthew, Mark, Luke, and John all directly quote or compress these verses from (Second) Isaiah in order to herald the arrival of Christ.[47] All four of these passages underlie King's "I have a dream" litany in "I Have a Dream," just as other biblical texts buttress his final address.

Think of the last image in the "I have a dream" refrain and reflect on the verbs: "The glory of the Lord shall be revealed, and all flesh shall see it together!" Despite the sunny, uplifting tone of this quotation, King uses it to claim that racism covers the eyes of Americans. For that reason, they have not witnessed "the glory of the Lord." But, King imagines, "The glory of the Lord shall be revealed" and "all flesh" that is, all eyes, everyone, will see it.

The remainder of "I Have a Dream" does not affirm any such current revelation of this glory. Instead, in the renowned conclusion of "I Have a Dream," King organizes and extends the trope of a ringing bell to indicate what *might* or *will* happen in a future of racial equality. But throughout "I Have a Dream"—including the "I have a dream" refrain and the "Let freedom ring" ending—King anticipates visualizing "glory of the Lord" at some future time.

Compare these words at the end of the dream passage in "I Have a Dream," "The glory of the Lord shall be revealed, and all flesh shall see it together!" to these at the end of "I've Been to the Mountaintop": "Mine eyes have seen the glory of the coming of the Lord!" The words and meaning of these two sentences seem so very close. The phrase "the glory of the Lord" in "I Have a Dream" is almost identical to the phrase "the glory of the coming of the Lord" in "I've Been to the Mountaintop." Further, both sentences feature forms of the same verb: "to see." On both occasions the glory cannot be heard or touched or tasted or smelled. Rather, like the preponderance of imagery in Revelation and "Battle Hymn of the Republic," the glory can be seen.

But the sentences also differ. In the sentence from "I Have a Dream," "all flesh" serves as the subject for the verb "shall see." This sentence means that all eyes will see. In the sentence from "I've Been to the Mountaintop," "Mine eyes" serves as the subject of the verb "have seen." This sentence indicates that one person's eyes have seen. Also, although both sentences use a form of the same verb, "to see," the verb tenses differ. In the passage from "I Have a Dream," King attests to a vision of the Lord that everyone will see in the future. In the sentence in "I've Been to the Mountaintop," he affirms that his eyes have *already* seen a vision of the Lord.

The conclusion of King's final speech thus, in part, fulfills the climax of the "I have a dream" refrain in "I Have a Dream." In 1968 King witnesses that he *has finally seen* what, in "I Have a Dream," he proclaimed that all people *would see in the future.* Thus, what was distant in 1963 is now closer and, King testifies, has partly arrived. This future, King implies, could, in all its fullness, include the demise of poverty and racism in Memphis and the United States.

Suggesting that the end of poverty and racism will serve as a prelude to the millennium, King exults that he has glimpsed the radiance of the Second Coming. He evokes or presents monumental events: the crossing of the Red Sea; Moses's glimpse of the Promised Land; divine commissions in Amos, Jeremiah, (Third) Isaiah, and Luke; oracles of devastation in Joel, (Third) Isaiah, Jeremiah, and Ezekiel; the Parable of the Good Samaritan; apocalyptic prophecy in Revelation; the Reformation; renewed prophecy in "Battle Hymn of the Republic"; the Emancipation Proclamation; revolutions in Africa, Lunch Counter Sit-Ins, Freedom Rides, "I Have a Dream"; Birmingham; and Memphis. He contends that, even though persecution and loss accompany each of these episodes, each of them anticipates the Final Judgment and Final Redemption. Further, he witnesses to his vision of the Lord's glory, a vision that is now disclosed and evident. This divine splendor, he avows, can sustain an embattled yet hopeful labor union in Memphis and, eventually, uplift oppressed people everywhere.

CHAPTER 8

If I Had Merely Sneezed, I Would Have Died

King's Biblical Interpretation

As an undergraduate at Morehouse College, King enrolled in two courses in the Bible taught by George Kelsey. A respected professor, Kelsey favored a scientific and historical approach that King had not encountered before. He warmed to Kelsey's instruction and, in his second course from Kelsey, earned his only A at Morehouse. Later, during his years at Crozer Theological Seminary, King became more deeply immersed in the assumptions and practices of modern biblical criticism. One of his professors, Morton Enslin, had already served as president of a large, national scholarly organization called the Society of Biblical Literature; another of his professors, James Pritchard, later became a celebrated archeologist who led Bible-related excavations in the Middle East. King also studied the Bible with G. W. Davis, his favorite faculty member at the seminary.

Acting as rationalist historians, Kelsey, Pritchard, Enslin, Davis, and other liberal researchers treated the Bible as a set of ancient documents that were written, edited, and assembled by many people over hundreds of years. Pritchard and Enslin emphasized the relation of the Bible to other ancient, Middle Eastern texts that they required King and their other students to study. All these scholars responded to what Norman Perrin identifies as huge challenges facing the entire enterprise of biblical criticism:

> The Enlightenment and the rise of the natural and historical sciences created a grave problem for the world of New Testament scholarship, for the New Testament narratives are full of references to things that clearly have no place

in the post-Enlightenment world in which the natural sciences are so convincing: angels, demons, miracles, resurrection and ascension, the (second) coming of Jesus on the clouds of heaven, and much more.[1]

Perrin might have added that a very similar "grave problem" confronted scholars of the Hebrew Bible. Beginning at least as early as Spinoza in the seventeenth century, rationalist researchers stripped mythology and folklore from the Bible in an effort to examine scientifically the actual history of the Israelites, Jesus, and the early church. Instead of assuming that the Bible was a smooth, harmonious book that dropped from heaven, they viewed the Bible as a palimpsest and sought to unveil its multitudinous layers of text that ancient scribes had composed, edited, re-edited, and compiled over a period of centuries. They often spied gaps and fissures in the ancient text.

In the numerous essays that King wrote in seminary, he clearly followed Pritchard, Enslin, and Davis in attempting to examine the Bible historically and scientifically.[2] In one seminary essay, King declared, "The interpretation of any portion of the Bible must be both objective and disinterested."[3]

Yet, throughout his public career, King never attempted an objective and disinterested interpretation of the Bible. Instead, he performed a U-turn from the views that he frequently espoused in his seminary papers. In literally hundreds of sermons between 1955 and 1968, he rejected the perspective of Pritchard, Enslin, and Davis and, instead, veered in the direction of his grandfather, his father, Benjamin Mays, and many other preachers. Making no attempt to provide detached and impartial histories of the Bible, they focused on what they defined as the dynamic interface between the Bible and the present. They did so in response to what Robert McCracken called, in the title of a book of sermons, *Questions People Ask*.[4] Like A. D. Williams, King Sr., Mays, and other preachers, the mature King constantly shoved the Bible into the present.

In 1969, the year after King's death, Hans George Gadamer famously claimed that the circumstances of an interpreter inevitably shape that person's comprehension of the past. In Gadamer's words,

> Our usual relationship to the past is not characterized by distancing and freeing ourselves from tradition. Rather, we are always situated within traditions, and this is no objectifying process—i.e., we do not conceive of what tradition says as something other, something alien. It is always part of us, a model or exemplar.[5]

For that reason, Gadamer continues, "Understanding is to be thought of less as a subjective act than as participating in an event of tradition, a process of transmission in which past and present are constantly mediated."[6] He adds: "The abstract antithesis between tradition and historical research, between history and the knowledge of it, must be discarded."[7] Nor, he contends, do the original author and the original audience determine the final, non-negotiable significance of a text. He explains,

> The real meaning of a text, as it speaks to the interpreter, does not depend on the contingencies of the author and his original audience.... Not just occasionally but always, the meaning of a text goes beyond its author. That is why understanding is not merely a reproductive, but always a productive activity as well.[8]

Because King Sr., Mays, Harry Emerson Fosdick, George Buttrick, and other preachers strongly held that the Bible was universally applicable and eternally valid, they viewed the world very differently than did Gadamer. Yet, unlike modernist biblical critics, preachers may have, surprisingly, in certain ways, anticipated Gadamer's claim that understanding a text is not merely a reproductive activity, but always a productive one as well. They did so when they typically and overtly acknowledged that their immediate circumstances helped frame their interpretation of the Bible.

Adapting African American oratorical traditions and the idiom of such liberal white preachers as Fosdick and Buttrick, King constructed his own interpretation of the Bible that includes five chief features: transforming the entire direction of biblical interpretation, affirming Judaism as the basis of Christianity, embracing the Bible (and the civil rights movement) as a narrative of the human body, highlighting the dialogic interplay of biblical authors, and trumpeting God as the source of emancipation and justice. This chapter now addresses these five features of King's biblical hermeneutic.

First, bypassing the rationalist perspectives that he learned in seminary, King switches the whole focus of biblical interpretation. Recall Perrin's observation that the Scientific Revolution and Enlightenment posed a "grave problem" for interpreting scripture. Two scholars maintain that liberal Protestant theologians and biblical scholars responded to the rise of rationalism by developing the "key idea" that "Christianity must accommodate itself to the triumph of modernity."[9] For many liberal theologians and biblical critics, that was indeed the key idea. Yet King definitely sidestepped that grave problem and that key idea, rejecting the dominant concern of modern biblical researchers.

King greatly valued science and, in a sermon adapted from Fosdick, vigorously defended Copernicus, Galileo, and Darwin as unjustly persecuted heroes.[10] The civil rights preacher also faced modernity when he explicitly repudiated atheism.[11] But, quite unlike Pritchard and Enslin—not to mention many other rationalist scholars—the mature King did not generate his biblical hermeneutic primarily in response to science, the Enlightenment, or modernity. He did not even come close. Further, unlike generations of biblical critics operating for well over three hundred years, the mature King never seriously investigated biblical history for its own sake. Instead, he characteristically addressed another question altogether: What does the Bible offer to oppressed people? Before and during King's lifetime, rationalist scholars never seriously posed such a query. King, however, addressed it frequently throughout his books, essays, speeches, and sermons.

Second, King strongly affirms the importance of the Hebrew Bible and the significance of Judaism for Christianity. In a seminary paper, King embraced the developmentalist view that the Hebrew Bible starts with a coarse view of a furious, destructive God before stumbling toward the revelation in the Christian Bible of God as a loving father.[12] But, reversing his youthful interpretation, the mature King rejected developmentalist and supersessionist Christianity in favor of a Christianity based soundly on Judaism. He spoke before Jewish audiences without trying to convert them. Quoting Amos 5:24 more often than any other verse of the entire Bible, he adopted the sprightly translation of this passage made by his friend, Jewish theologian Abraham Heschel.[13] Susannah Heschel, the daughter of Abraham Heschel, remembers that, in conversation, King respectfully and affectionately referred to Abraham Heschel as "my rabbi."[14]

In addition, throughout his career, King often emphasized Moses, the Exodus, and the Hebrew prophets. He implicitly, but strongly, argues that Judaism—especially Moses and the prophets—serves not as a "primitive" historical backdrop, but instead as the unavoidable foundation for Christianity. In "Letter from Birmingham Jail," he highlights ties between ancient Hebrew and Christian texts by explicitly linking Amos to Paul. He spotlights such links again when, at a crucial moment in "I Have a Dream," he quotes a familiar passage in Hebrew scripture that resonates repeatedly in the Christian Bible. All four Christian gospels—Matthew, Mark, Luke, and John—encapsulate or quote the lines from (Second) Isaiah that King cites in "I Have a Dream."

Before King could begin "I've Been to the Mountaintop," many members of his audience could read the large banner above his head that brandished a quotation from Zechariah:

> "Not By Might, Nor by Power, But By My Spirit
> Saith the LORD OF HOSTS." Zechariah 4:6

Because many of his listeners could see and absorb these words even before King spoke, Zechariah, a prophetic book from the Hebrew Bible, might be said to launch his address. The line from Zechariah could easily be read as indicating divine sanction for religious nonviolence. In the speech itself, after King refers to the Exodus and quotes Amos and Jeremiah, he cites a portion of (Third) Isaiah that Luke places on the lips of Jesus. Through double-sourced quotations from Isaiah/Luke in "I Have a Dream" and in his final oration, King notes that Luke and Jesus both depend on Isaiah. And, in "I've Been to the Mountaintop," King also relies on Isaiah/Luke to announce the prophetic function of preachers in Memphis. Near the end of his last address, King's earlier narrative about Moses, Amos, Jeremiah, and Third Isaiah serves as a building block for his interpretation of the Parable of the Good Samaritan. In his final speech King underscores thematic ties between the two testaments when he combines the liberation theme in Exodus, several prophetic commissions, a lesson from a parable, and a vision of the Second Coming that the author of Revelation derives largely from Hebrew scripture.

In the universe of King's rhetoric, the official leaders of Memphis discard Judaism, and that decision proves catastrophic. According to King, Mayor Loeb (a practicing Episcopalian) and his many allies—including the police, newspaper editors, bankers, Coca Cola executives, and a federal judge—utterly fail to grasp the liberatory mission of Moses.[15] By rejecting Moses, King indicates, these power brokers (plus the moderate clergy) embrace a deeply flawed version of Christianity that serves to enhance oppression instead of removing it. Only by turning to Moses and the prophets, he strongly implies, can they begin to understand Christian scripture, the mission of Jesus, and racial injustice in Memphis.[16]

King's rejection of Christian supersessionism is extremely noteworthy because it strongly counters any tendency toward anti-Semitism. Throughout much of its long history, Christianity generated anti-Semitism, frequently with horrifying consequences. The arguments of Julius Wellhausen (and numerous other prominent modernist scholars) about the allegedly stifling legalism of the post-exilic Second Temple had the effect of denigrating Judaism and reinforcing anti-Semitism in Germany prior to the rise of Adolph Hitler. Robert Ericksen and Susannah Heschel convincingly argue that many eminent German theologians promulgated Christian supersessionist theology that helped fuel extreme anti-Semitism in Germany prior to the unspeakable genocide committed by the Nazis. Nor was the United States immune to anti-Semitism, which remained a repugnant feature of American culture throughout King's lifetime. Stoutly resisting Christian supersessionism and the anti-Semitism that it often spawns, King clearly attests that Judaism serves as the wellspring of Christianity.

But why would King reject racism and Christian supersessionism in a single speech? By combining his repudiation of white supremacy with his repudiation of supersessionism, he arguably anticipated J. Kameron Carter's argument (in 2008) that the centuries-old, close relationship among supersessionism, anti-Semitism, and white supremacy is no accident. Rather, Carter maintains, Christian supersessionism (both conceptually and historically) entailed both anti-Semitism and white supremacy. As he notes, "supersessionism articulates itself through race generally and through whiteness more specifically."[17] In Carter's argument, when white Europeans developed Christian supersessionism, they facilitated the process of transforming Jews into despised others and, simultaneously, made possible the entire, enormous project of white supremacy, a project that defined all non-whites as despised others.[18]

King's project of reconfiguring Hebrew prophecy clearly confirms his emphasis on the importance of Judaism. By assuming the mantle of prophet, he affirms that prophecy did not end at the close of the biblical era and argues for its continued importance, even in a putatively Christian or putatively post-Christian nation. He holds that the widespread acceptance of doctrinal Christianity does not automatically entail a just society. Rather, in the universe of his discourse, prophets must continually resurface for the purpose of denouncing and rectifying injustice.

Third, *King presupposes that the Bible provides an invaluable framework for interpreting past, present, and future.* King assumes that, in the words of John Barton, "we might almost say that stories recorded in the Bible turn into parables of how human life unfolds ... and predictions turn into assurances that it will continue to follow the same pattern in the future."[19] Although King sometimes appeals to science and other sources of knowledge, he frequently taps the common notion among African American Christians (and certain other Christian groups as well) that the Bible comes reasonably close to offering what Barton calls a "complete interpretive framework within which to make sense of all experience."[20] King further assumes that, as Langdon Gilkey comments, "the contradictory, confusing, and hence apparently irrational stuff of ordinary experience can be made much more intelligible by means of the biblical categories. They clarify ... vast puzzles of experience that alternative categories fail to clarify."[21] Following such an assumption, King uses scripture as a lens for re-interpreting the puzzle of Memphis and Memphis as a lens for re-interpreting scripture.

Like Fosdick and Buttrick, King explains that biblical principles are current. But, unlike them, King also proclaims that biblical stories extend into the present; and he narrates that extension. In his rhetorical universe, no one in Memphis escapes biblical narrative, especially what he defines as the core narrative of the Exodus, Hebrew prophecy, Jesus, and eschatology. For King, any detachment from biblical narrative is simply impossible. Throughout his career as a civil rights leader, King proffered a biblical interpretation that is far more narrative than it is abstract and propositional. In his rhetoric, the biblical story shapes Americans—past, present, and future—as it unfolds over time. Through an exercise of free will, one can choose one's role in the story, but God wrote the story and keeps writing it.

Even as King scholars frequently extrapolate a philosophical and abstract theology from his rhetoric, they fail to recognize that his theology and his biblical hermeneutic are predominantly narrative, rather than abstract. King certainly defines and affirms biblical and theological principles. But, unlike, say, Thomas Aquinas or Paul Tillich, the mature King consistently avoids a system of abstract, philosophical theology.[22] Instead, he consistently situates theological principles (e.g., love, justice) within his Bible-based narrative of history, a narrative that encompasses the recent, episode-laden agitation for racial equality. His biblical principles reveal themselves in concrete moments as a historical narrative unfolds, just as, in the Bible, biblical precepts reveal themselves in concrete moments as a historical narrative unfolds. Further, in King's discursive universe, the entelechial possibilities of biblical narrative do not exhaust themselves either during the biblical era or, for that matter, in Memphis during the 1960s. Rather, in King's rhetoric, the biblical narrative is ongoing and will continue to unfold until the Second Coming of Christ.

King's ongoing biblical narrative is extremely imaginative, in part, because he explains the Bible as a narrative of the body as well as the mind. The principle of Incarnation is crucial to Christian doctrine. According to that precept, the birth of Jesus signifies that God intervenes in history and, thereby, dramatically transforms human life. Christians constantly affirm the doctrine of incarnation: Jesus is God incarnate, Jesus embodies God, Jesus is God in the flesh. As King reflects on the Bible, he generates a hermeneutic that is conceptual, but also profoundly physical. His theology is a theology of embodiment, and his biblical hermeneutic is a hermeneutic of embodiment. Such a theology and such a hermeneutic thoughtfully and ably explain the civil rights movement, which consisted mainly of bodily acts of dissent. Physical protests began when thousands of African Americans in Montgomery walked (or drove) miles every day for a year while boycotting buses. And, as he eloquently explains in "I've Been to the Mountaintop," embodied agitation continued when hundreds of thousands marched, sat down at lunch counters, traveled on interstate buses, held songfests, rode in paddy wagons, sustained beatings, withstood jailings, faced water cannons, endured police dogs, and survived police macing. And, of course, NAACP organizer Medgar Evers and other agitators were murdered. Throughout the entire 1950s and 1960s, civil rights activism was *at least* as much physical as it was conceptual.

For King, his father, Fred Shuttlesworth, and thousands of other black ministers, preaching itself is a very physical act that often involves calm-to-storm delivery, hypnotic rhythms, cliff-hanging pauses in mid-sentence, one hand sweeping the air, the other hand dramatically waving the Bible, a fist hammering the pulpit, leaping listeners, exuberant call-backs, and electrifying conclusions that often provoke grateful churchgoers to stand, stomp, dance, cheer, shout, applaud, and sometimes faint.

Consider the prominence of the body in King's best-loved writings and orations. In *Stride toward Freedom*, he explains that people achieved a great racial advance by managing, for an entire year, to remove their bodies from the buses of Montgomery. In *Stride toward Freedom* and "Our God Is Able," he announces that a literal voice threatened his life over the phone in Montgomery, precipitating his kitchen revelation, which, David Garrow explains, served as the pivotal moment of his entire life.[23] Then, King continues, racists exploded the porch of his home; and, soon afterward, he arrived there to deliver his "Sermon on the Porch," which calmed a furious African American mob bent on avenging the bombing. In "Shattered Dreams" he celebrates Paul, who was "held captive in a little prison cell" and who was "beaten and bloody, his feet chained."[24] In the same sermon he lauds "early Christians" in Rome, who confronted "hungry lions in the arena and the excruciating pain of the chopping block"; he also recalls southern slaves "chained to ships like beasts" and "bone-weary in the sizzling heat" with "the marks of whip lashes freshly etched on their backs." And he remembers slave women who were "forced to satisfy the biological urges of white masters."[25] In "Suffering and Faith" he narrates the stabbing he received in Harlem and applies to himself Paul's assertion in Galatians: "I bear on my body the marks of the Lord Jesus Christ."[26]

In "Letter from Birmingham Jail," King again supplies a list of biblical and post-biblical martyrs and again quotes Paul's testimony: "I bear on my body the marks of the Lord Jesus Christ."[27] The title of "Letter from Birmingham Jail" indicates that his body languishes in jail, just as Paul's often did. In the same letter, King criticizes the Birmingham police, whose dogs were "sinking their teeth into unarmed, nonviolent Negroes."[28] The March on Washington summoned two hundred thousand people to venture dozens, hundreds, or thousands of miles to the Lincoln Memorial. Delivering "I Have a Dream" there, King consoled agitators whose bodies were, he explained, "battered by the storms of persecution and staggered by the winds of police brutality." Soon afterward he delivered a eulogy for four African American girls whose lifeless bodies were extracted from the ruins of a church bombed one Sunday morning in Birmingham. He joined hikers for part of the strenuous, blister-producing fifty-mile march from Selma to Montgomery. At the conclusion of that trek, he interpreted it as an extension of Joshua's march around Jericho. In the same speech he catalogued a list of recent martyrs who surrendered their bodies and their lives for racial equality.[29]

King begins "I've Been to the Mountaintop" by saluting his listeners for their physical gesture of driving to the church in defiance of a heavy storm. He then links the physical exploitation of slaves under Pharaoh, water hoses aimed at demonstrators in Birmingham, Jeremiah's fire in his bones, the Good Samaritan's assistance to the traveler's mugged body, and his own near-death experience when he was knifed in the chest. He also advocates the radical, far-reaching, physical acts of a city-wide work stoppage and a city-wide school walkout throughout Memphis. Each of these examples of King's discourse provides a biblical narrative of the body.

For King, Christianity is not mainly a system of formal theology, but, instead, a lived narrative that is at once thoroughly spiritual and thoroughly embodied. While he definitely conceptualizes his theology and his biblical hermeneutic, he also creatively and emphatically enacts and performs that theology and that hermeneutic in the flesh. Like the authors of the Pentateuch and the books of Hebrew prophecy—and unlike Plato and Descartes—King emphatically denies any separation among mind, body, and spirit. For that reason "Letter from Birmingham Jail" explicitly repudiates moderate churches that "commit themselves to a completely otherworldly religion which makes a strange, un-biblical distinction between the body and the soul, between the sacred and the secular."[30]

King's biblical hermeneutic and theology sharply contrast to the hermeneutics and theology of most of his predecessors and contemporaries. Emphasizing abstract conceptualizations and often prizing systematic theology, theologians before and during his lifetime did not theorize or analyze the body as King did. Nor did they pen letters while sitting in jail, as King did. With a few striking exceptions—most notably Dietrich Bonhoeffer—the preponderance of well-known European and American biblical scholars, theologians, and pastors just before and during King's lifetime did not often assume serious physical risks.

Another imaginative dimension of King's biblical interpretation is his proposal that the biblical narrative now manifests itself through a racial struggle. Rather than adopt modern scholars' assumption that race has nothing to do with the Bible, King—like Shuttlesworth, Fannie Lou Hamer, James Bevel, and certain other civil rights leaders—posits that race has *everything* to do with the Bible. In King's discursive universe, the struggle against racism is a new manifestation of the long-lasting, cosmic battle between good and evil. He presupposes that only passionate, religious devotion—not rational calculation—would spur impoverished African Americans in the Mississippi Delta to risk their lives in order to vote. He also assumes that only such devotion would prompt others to invite injury from the ferocious police of Birmingham. He strongly implies that the oppressed have the right to interpret the Bible precisely because they are living the Bible. Again, he presents the Bible as an engulfing drama, and new events keep tumbling out of ancient texts—in Montgomery, Greensboro, Albany, Birmingham, Selma, and Memphis.

Unlike his professors of biblical studies, King implicitly contends that the failure of the oppressed to become biblical historians and scholars is entirely irrelevant to their ability to interpret the Bible. He implies that the oppressed do not need to learn ancient Hebrew, ancient Greek, and other foreign languages in order to grasp the Bible. He also implies that racial outcasts and the poor do not need to examine formidable scholarly tomes or other ancient texts in order to understand the Bible. In his later discourse, especially, King presupposes that the oppressed need to interpret the Bible precisely because only God—not America—provides a reliable source of hope. In King's rhetorical universe, America often defaults on promises, but God always keeps promises. King implicitly, but strongly, claims that the oppressed must fathom the Bible in order to fathom their own lives and to lift themselves above the persistent exploitation that they doggedly endure. In King's argument, there is no other solution—none.

King further argues that those who engage in racial protest enjoy a perspective for interpreting scripture that is invaluable not only for themselves, but for the whole nation. This perspective obviously contrasts to the detachment of the college seminar room and the serenity of a minister's study, a detachment and a serenity that others sought.

King consistently refuses any such intellectual and emotional detachment, constantly jetting from one site of racial friction to another. Explicating the Bible from the basis of his own social engagement grants King an exceptional capacity to remind his audience that Moses, the Hebrew prophets, Jesus, Paul, and the earliest readers of Jewish and Christian scripture were all socially engaged, not aloof or detached. As the civil rights leader regularly suggests or implies, the writers who generated the Hebrew Bible regularly focused on the vitality and the sheer existence of the Jewish people, whose cultural integrity and physical survival were frequently threatened. And, as he directly notes in "Letter from Birmingham Jail," the Christian Bible was written by Paul and other early Christians who often faced persecution. Early Christians, King continues, were so socially involved that they were sometimes jailed or beaten and occasionally devoured by lions or decapitated. African American protestors, he attests, also undergo persecution during their struggles, as they are jailed, beaten, and sometimes killed by white racists.

Fourth, King's interpretation of the Bible is, to use Mikhail Bakhtin's term, *dialogic.* Hans-George Gadamer explains: "The discovery of the true meaning of a text or a work of art is never finished; it is in fact an infinite process. . . . [N]ew sources of understanding are continually emerging that reveal unsuspected elements of meaning."[31] While recognizing that every specimen of literature was spawned in a specific context, Bakhtin supplies an argument similar to Gadamer's. In Bakhtin's words, great literary productions "break through the boundaries of their own time" and "live for centuries" in a way that is "more intense and fuller than are their lives within their own time."[32] He continues, "[Shakespeare] included in his works immense treasures of potential meaning that could not be fully revealed or recognized in his epoch" but remained for later interpreters to unveil.[33] Adding that the significance of sterling literature is determined dialogically, Bakhtin notes the "unfinalizability" of Doestoevsky's fiction.[34] Elaborating his definition of "dialogic," Bakhtin explains that, with respect to the interpretation of exemplary literature, "there is neither a first nor a last word and there are no limits to the dialogic context (it extends into the boundless past and the boundless future)."[35] As the dialogue ensues, the author's creation need not morph into an unrecognizable shape. Bakhtin declares, "There are immense, boundless masses of forgotten contextual meanings, but at certain moments of the dialogue's subsequent development along the way they are recalled and invigorated in a renewed form (in a new context)."[36]

Biblical writers themselves interpret the Bible dialogically. As Andre LaCocque and Paul Ricoeur explain,

> Textual dynamism is found in almost every one of the genres represented in biblical literature. The very anonymity of the biblical texts can be interpreted from this point of view, the "original authors" being aware from the beginning of the irremediable incompleteness of their work.

LaCocque and Ricoeur add that biblical writing "asks to be re-modeled, to be re-actualized by the community."[37] And, as Gerhard von Rad, Walter Zimmerli, Brevard Childs, Donald Gowan, James Sanders, Walter Brueggemann, and other scholars comment, entire generations of biblical writers and editors (including the authors of Isaiah) did exactly that. Sanders, Gowan, and others view Hebrew scripture as literature whose themes and texts were dramatically reconstituted and hugely reshaped after the Babylonian exile of 527 BCE. And, as various interpreters explain, the authors of the Christian Bible quote and reconfigure Hebrew lines and themes so often that one can easily interpret not only Revelation, but the entire Christian Bible as a hermeneutic of the Hebrew Bible.

By explicating the Bible as an ongoing process, rather than a fossilized text, King engages dialogically with biblical texts while he extends them.

Consider two examples—one from "I Have a Dream" and the other from "I've Been to the Mountaintop." First, the author of (Second) Isaiah interprets the Pentateuch dialogically by arguing that the Babylonian exile provides a fresh context for understanding Egyptian slavery and the Exodus. In "I Have a Dream," King quotes (Second) Isaiah and maintains that the exile and slavery of African Americans provides another fresh context for understanding Egyptian slavery, the Exodus, and Babylonian exile.

Second, the author of Luke interprets (Third) Isaiah dialogically by claiming that an ancient Hebrew prophecy is refulfilled centuries later when Jesus appears. In "I've Been to the Mountaintop," King quotes this passage and contends that the Memphis strike supplies yet another fresh context for understanding the prophetic commission from (Third) Isaiah/Luke.

For the authors and editors of Isaiah and Luke—and for King—the meaning of the Bible is continually refashioned and continually re-enacted. In King's rhetoric, the Bible lives precisely on the boundary between past and present, in the interface between ancient history and today. According to King's interpretation, the Bible, by its very nature, thrives in great time and will continue to disclose new meanings in every new arena.

Rejecting the popular tendency to petrify biblical narrative and prophecy, King discovers the Bible in Memphis and Memphis in the Bible. He uses the Bible to narrate Memphis and Memphis to narrate the Bible. In doing so, he spotlights and rekindles what I would call the dialogic biblical interpretation practiced in (Second) Isaiah and Luke. He simultaneously anticipates important portions of the now-famous literary interpretation proclaimed by Gadamer and Bakhtin. That is, King *simultaneously* resuscitates biblical writers' own, centuries-old hermeneutic of scripture *and* presages the views of Gadamer and Bakhtin, who burst on the American scene after King's death. King thereby leaps beyond his professors' approaches to the Bible and beyond the interpretive practice of Fosdick, Buttrick, and other popular preachers as well. Even today, biblical scholars and preachers alike have barely begun to plumb Bakhtin's literary hermeneutics as a means to probe the Bible.

When King generates his interpretation of the Bible, he scrapes against the decision to close the biblical canon. As he implies in "I Have a Dream" and in his last speech, the biblical text itself resists completion because the authors of the Bible dialogued incessantly with their predecessors. King also implies that the Bible resists resolution because the fate of "God's children" is undecided. By quoting Julia Ward Howe, he spotlights Revelation and Howe's abstract portrait of the Second Coming and Last Judgment. As he proclaims in his final sentence, only "the glory of the coming of the Lord" can resolve history. That is, he implicitly claims that the Bible can conclude only when the Second Coming and Last Judgment *actually occur*. In King's argument, until the final curtain drops, all human experience—including the moment that you are reading these lines—is contained within the arc of the biblical narrative. Until all life ends, he implies, the long-running biblical drama will keep unfolding, in Memphis and everywhere else. For him, the task of preachers is to define the current manifestation of that drama and to identify its newest actors. In his final address, he also urges preachers themselves to assume a role in the biblical drama that they are explaining—the role of the prophet.

Fifth, King unequivocally interprets the God of the Bible as a God of justice and freedom. As King invokes the Bible to inspire demonstrators and to frame the civil rights movement, he invariably argues that God emancipates. In "Letter from Birmingham Jail" he declares, "Just as the Apostle Paul left his village of Tarsus and carried the gospel of Jesus Christ to the far corners of the Greco-Roman world, so I am compelled to carry the gospel of freedom beyond my own home town."[38] With these words, he announces his own attempt to emulate Paul on the new, modern stage of Birmingham while equating Paul's Christian gospel to his own "gospel of freedom."

In the final twelve sentences of "I Have a Dream," King projects a possible future as he reiterates the word "freedom" eleven times and the word "free" three times. His final sentence is a phrase from a spiritual: "Thank God Almighty we're free at last!" Those words positively and unambiguously affirm that God liberates. Presaging such later figures as Desmond Tutu, King unmistakably attests that God constantly works to end oppression and to secure justice and freedom. Based largely on the Bible, that interpretation of God—not a theory of political science—empowers King repeatedly to call for the end of all racism, all war, all poverty. Political theorists usually promote compromises and realpolitik. Elected leaders characteristically choose pragmatic half-measures. But, as King regularly reminds his audiences, the Bible does not countenance half-measures and instead declares: swords can be beaten into plowshares, justice can roll down like waters, and segregation can vanish. Because he champions a God who frees oppressed people, his biblical hermeneutic must be called emancipatory.

+++

As I mentioned in the introduction, many people *only* view this speech as King's prediction of his own assassination the next evening.[39] Actually, King *often* publicly and privately predicted the possibility, or likelihood, that he would be murdered. He first did so publicly in 1956, during the Montgomery Bus Boycott. In his 1958 book about that boycott, he explains that, at one point, his telephone jangled with an increasing number of death threats. "Soon," he notes, "I felt myself faltering and growing in fear.... For the first time I realized that something could happen to me." He reports that, at one mass meeting of the boycott, he ominously warned, "'If one day you find me sprawled out dead, I do not want you to retaliate with a single act of violence.'"[40] Within his hundreds of subsequent orations, he occasionally scattered additional projections of his own assassination. At Ebenezer Church, two months before his assassination, he delivered "Drum Major Instinct," a sermon based largely on a homily by J. Wallace Hamilton. Instead of mentioning death threats, King appeared to assume that his home congregation was quite aware of the constant danger that surrounded him. Even though he was a healthy thirty-nine-year-old, he jumped off Hamilton's text to tell his eulogist what to say at his funeral.[41] Further, at his speech in Memphis on March 18, 1968, sixteen days before his final oration, he repeated a riff that he had used on earlier occasions: "Sometimes I feel discouraged, having to live under the threat of death everyday.... Sometimes I feel discouraged. But then the Holy Spirit revives my soul again!"[42]

After the murders of NAACP leader Medgar Evers and President John Kennedy, King fully realized that some trigger-happy bigot might easily aim the next round of bullets at him. His concern was rational, for the threat was palpable. Yet nothing required him to discuss in public the possibility of his own assassination. He *chose* to do so, and he made that choice fairly often. Jailed by segregationists, harried by the FBI, and threatened with death, he resisted intimidation and refused to be silenced. Instead of shirking at the horrifying prospect of assassination, he managed to turn his opponents' violent threats to his own rhetorical advantage. By hounding and victimizing him, his opponents created the rhetorical space that he needed to construct himself not only as a prophet, but also as a hounded and victimized prophet. In "Letter from Birmingham Jail" and before television cameras in Birmingham, he also generated a synecdoche, a figure of speech in which the part stands for the whole.[43] In this appeal, his unjust jailing in Birmingham served as a single incident that crystallized the victimization that millions of blacks experienced away from the news media. He relied on another synecdoche as well: the actual and threatened violence against him epitomized white oppressors' frequent violence against African Americans.

Before the civil rights coalition began to fragment during the middle 1960s, King's discourse contributed mightily to a remarkable solidarity and shared sense of purpose among many civil rights activists. Adam Fairclough maintains that King's rhetoric about his menacing abusers helped him to unify large numbers of African Americans.[44] King could not do so simply by relating the plentiful incidents of threatened or actual violence that were visited upon African Americans in general and civil rights workers in particular. Instead, he faced the challenge of amalgamating and shaping threats and tragic incidents into an effective argument; he did so largely by explaining African American suffering as an extension of the persecution experienced by biblical prophets and apostles. He rhetorically reversed the obvious interpretation of African American pain and loss as emblems of defeat, treating pain and loss instead as precursors to victory. Recall his fervent desire to avoid the riots that so recently devastated Watts and Detroit: "We don't need any Molotov cocktails!" In the universe of King's rhetoric, even the shock and calamity of Watts and Detroit can prove temporary roadblocks on the march to justice. He argues that African American unity is possible because the logic of the Bible dictates that the woebegone centuries of auction blocks, overseers' whips, rape, lynching, disfranchisement, Jim Crow, poverty, and hunger remain surmountable.

King's rhetoric is rooted in the interpretation of the Bible generated by those slaves and subsequent African American who celebrated Moses while stoutly resisting white supremacist versions of Christianity. Although Fosdick and Buttrick seldom discussed race, King's treatment of the Bible also reflects, adjusts, and transforms their Social Gospel. In his hands, all these rhetorical resources proved powerful. Of course, after the advent of Black Power and after rioters and police left much of Watts and Detroit in ruins, King's task of invigorating his listeners and prodding the federal government proved far more difficult. Yet he undertook this severe challenge. Weaving the sanitation workers of Memphis into a biblical tapestry meant relocating their city in ancient Egypt, casting it as the site of prophecy, identifying holiness within activists' bodies, placing the garbage workers along the "Bloody Pass" to Jericho, and invoking the principle of the "Already and Not Yet."

Just as King reimagined Memphis, so did the sanitation workers. After King's assassination the next day, they remained united until Mayor Loeb finally capitulated, recognized their union, and raised their salaries. Continuing and winning their strike meant continuing King's process of reinventing their city and reinventing America.

Appendix A

Text of "I've Been to the Mountaintop"

Thank you very kindly, my friends. As I listened to Ralph Abernathy in his eloquent and generous introduction and then thought about myself, I wondered who he was talking about. It's always good to have your closest friend and associate say something good about you. And Ralph is the best friend that I have in the world.

I'm delighted to see each of you here tonight in spite of a storm warning. You reveal that you are determined to go on anyhow. Something is happening in Memphis, something is happening in our world.

As you know, if I were standing at the beginning of time, with the possibility of general and panoramic view of the whole human history up to now, and the Almighty said to me, "Martin Luther King, which age would you like to live in?"—I would take my mental flight by Egypt through, or rather across the Red Sea, through the wilderness on toward the promised land. And in spite of its magnificence, I wouldn't stop there. I would move on by Greece, and take my mind to Mount Olympus. And I would see Plato, Aristotle, Socrates, Euripides, and Aristophanes assembled around the Parthenon as they discussed the great and eternal issues of reality.

But I wouldn't stop there. I would go on, even to the great heyday of the Roman Empire. And I would see developments around there, through various emperors and leaders. But I wouldn't stop there. I would even come up to the day of the Renaissance, and get a quick picture of all that the Renaissance did for the cultural and esthetic life of man. But I wouldn't stop there. I would even go by the way that the man for whom I'm named had his habitat. And I would watch Martin Luther as he tacked his ninety-five theses on the door at the church in Wittenberg.

But I wouldn't stop there. I would come on up even to 1863 and watch a vacillating president by the name of Abraham Lincoln finally come to the conclusion that he had to sign the Emancipation Proclamation. But I wouldn't stop there. I would even come up to the early thirties and see a man grappling with the problems of the bankruptcy of his nation. And come with an eloquent cry that we have nothing to fear but fear itself.

But I wouldn't stop there. Strangely enough, I would turn to the Almighty and say, "If you allow me to live just a few years in the second half of the twentieth century, I will be happy." Now that's a strange statement to make, because the world is all messed up. The nation is sick. Trouble is in the land. Confusion all around. That's a strange statement. But I know, somehow, that only when it is dark enough can you see the stars. And I see God working in this period of the twentieth century in a way that men, in some strange way, are responding—something is happening in our world. The masses of people are rising up. And wherever they are assembled today—whether they are in Johannesburg, South Africa; Nairobi, Kenya; Accra, Ghana; New York City; Atlanta, Georgia; Jackson, Mississippi; or Memphis, Tennessee—the cry is always the same: "We want to be free."

And another reason that I'm happy to live in this period is that we have been forced to a point where we're going to have to grapple with the problems that men have been trying to grapple with through history, but the demand didn't force them to do it. Survival demands that we grapple with them. Men, for years now, have been talking about war and peace. But now, no longer can they just talk about it. It is no longer a choice between violence and nonviolence in this world; it's nonviolence or nonexistence.

That is where we are today. And also in the human rights revolution, if something isn't done, and in a hurry, to bring the colored peoples of the world out of their long years of poverty, their long years of hurt and neglect, the whole world is doomed. Now, I'm just happy that God has allowed me to live in this period, to see what is unfolding. And I'm happy that He's allowed me to be in Memphis.

I can remember; I can remember when Negroes were just going around as Ralph has said, so often, scratching where they didn't itch and laughing when they were not tickled. But that day is all over. We mean business now, and we are determined to gain our rightful place in God's world.

And that's all this whole thing is about. We aren't engaged in any negative protest and in any negative arguments with anybody. We are saying that we are determined to be men. We are determined to be people. We are saying that we are God's children. And that we don't have to live like we are forced to live.

Now, what does all of this mean in this great period of history? It means that we've got to stay together. We've got to stay together and maintain unity. You know, whenever Pharaoh wanted to prolong the period of slavery in Egypt, he had a favorite, favorite formula for doing it. What was that? He kept the salves fighting among themselves. But whenever the slaves get together, something happens in Pharaoh's court, and he cannot hold the slaves in slavery. When the slaves get together, that's the beginning of getting out of slavery. Now let us maintain unity.

Secondly, let us keep the issues where they are. The issue is injustice. The issue is the refusal of Memphis to be fair and honest in its dealings with its public servants, who happen to be sanitation workers. Now, we've got to keep attention on that. That's always the problem with a little violence. You know what happened the other day, and the press dealt only with the window-breaking. I read the articles. They very seldom got around to mentioning the fact that 1,300 sanitation workers were on strike and that Memphis is not being fair to them and that Mayor Loeb is in dire need of a doctor. They didn't get around to that.

Now we're going to march again, and we've got to march again, in order to put the issue where it is supposed to be. And force everybody to see that there are thirteen hundred of God's children here suffering, sometimes going hungry, going through dark and dreary nights wondering how this thing is going to come out. That's the issue. And we've got to say to the nation: we know it's coming out. For when people get caught up with that which is right and they are willing to sacrifice for it, there is no stopping point short of victory.

We aren't going to let any mace stop us. We are masters in our nonviolent movement in disarming police forces; they don't know what to do; I've seen them so often. I remember in Birmingham, Alabama, when we were in that majestic struggle there we would move out of the Sixteenth Street Baptist Church day after day; by the hundreds we would move out. And Bull Connor would tell them to send the dogs forth and they did come; but we just went before the dogs singing, "Ain't gonna let nobody turn me round." Bull Connor next would say, "Turn the fire hoses on." And as I said to you the other night, Bull Connor didn't know history. He knew a kind of physics that somehow didn't relate to the transphysics that we knew about. And that was the fact that there was a certain kind of fire that no water could put out. And we went before the fire hoses; we had known water. If we were Baptist or some other denomination, we had been immersed. If we were Methodist, and some others, we had been sprinkled, but we knew water.

That couldn't stop us. And we just went on before the dogs and we would look at them; and we'd go on before the water hoses and we would look at it, and we'd just go on singing, "Over my head I see freedom in the air." And then we would be thrown in the paddy wagons, and sometimes we were stacked in there like sardines in a can. And they would throw us in, and old Bull would say, "Take them off," and they did; and we would just go in the paddy wagon singing, "We Shall Overcome." And every now and then we'd get in the jail, and we'd see the jailers looking through the windows, being moved by our prayers, and being moved by our words and our songs. And there was a power there, which Bull Connor couldn't adjust to; and so we ended up transforming Bull into a steer, and we won our struggle in Birmingham.

Now we've got to go on to Memphis just like that. I call upon you to be with us Monday. Now about injunctions: We have an injunction and we're going into court tomorrow morning to fight this illegal, unconstitutional injunction. All we say to America is, "Be true to what you said on paper." If I lived in China or even Russia, or any totalitarian country, maybe I could understand the denial of certain basic First Amendment privileges because they hadn't committed themselves to that over there. But somewhere I read of the freedom of assembly. Somewhere I read of the freedom of speech. Somewhere I read of the freedom of the press. Somewhere I read that the greatness of America is the right to protest for right. And so just as I say, we aren't going to let any injunction turn us around. We are going on.

We need all of you. And you know what's beautiful to me is to see all of these ministers of the Gospel. It's a marvelous picture. Who is it that is supposed to articulate the longings and aspirations of the people more than the preacher? Somehow the preacher must have a kind of fire shut up in his bones and, whenever injustice is around, he must tell it. Somehow the preacher must be an Amos and say, "Let justice roll down like waters and righteousness like a mighty stream." Somehow, the preacher must say with Jesus, "The spirit of the Lord is upon me, because he hath anointed me to deal with the problems of the poor."

And I want to commend the preachers, under the leadership of these noble men: James Lawson, one who has been in this struggle for many years; he's been to jail for struggling; but he's still going on, fighting for the rights of his people. Rev. Ralph Jackson, Billy Kyles; I could just go right on down the list, but time will not permit. But I want to thank them all. And I want you to thank them because, so often, preachers aren't concerned about anything but themselves. And I'm always happy to see a relevant ministry.

It's all right to talk about "long white robes over yonder," in all of its symbolism. But ultimately people want some suits and dresses and shoes to wear down here. It's all right to talk about "streets flowing with milk and honey," but God has commanded us to be concerned about the slums down here and his children who can't eat three square meals a day. It's all right to talk about the new Jerusalem, but one day, God's preachers must talk about the new New York, the new Atlanta, the new Philadelphia, the new Los Angeles, the new Memphis, Tennessee. This is what we have to do.

Now the other thing we'll have to do is this: Always anchor our external direct action with the power of economic withdrawal. Now, we are poor people, individually; we are poor when you compare us with white society in America. We are poor. Never stop and forget that collectively, that means all of us together, collectively we are richer than all the nations in the world, with the exception of nine. Did you ever think about that? After you leave the United States, Soviet Russia, Great Britain,

West Germany, France, and I could name the others, the Negro collectively is richer than most nations of the world. We have an annual income of more than thirty billion dollars a year, which is more than all of the exports of the United States, and more than the national budget of Canada. Did you know that? That's power right there, if we know how to pool it.

We don't have to argue with anybody. We don't have to curse and go around acting bad with our words. We don't need any bricks and bottles; we don't need any Molotov cocktails; we just need to go around to these stores, and to these massive industries in our country, and say, "God sent us by here to say to you that you're not treating his children right. And we've come by here to ask you to make the first item on your agenda fair treatment, where God's children are concerned. Now, if you are not prepared to do that, we do have an agenda that we must follow. And our agenda calls for withdrawing economic support from you."

And so, as a result of this, we are asking you tonight to go out and tell your neighbors not to buy Coca-Cola in Memphis. Go by and tell them not to buy Sealtest milk. Tell them not to buy—what is the other bread?—Wonder Bread. And what is the other bread company, Jesse? Tell them not to buy Hart's bread. As Jesse Jackson has said, up to now, only the garbage men have been feeling pain; now we must kind of redistribute the pain. We are choosing these companies because they haven't been fair in their hiring policies; and we are choosing them because they can begin the process of saying they are going to support the needs and the rights of these men who are on strike. And then they can move on downtown and tell Mayor Loeb to do what is right.

But not only that, we've got to strengthen black institutions. I call upon you to take your money out of the banks downtown and deposit your money in Tri-State Bank—we want a "bank-in" movement in Memphis. So go by the savings and loan association. I'm not asking you something we don't do ourselves at SCLC. Judge Hooks and others will tell you that we have an account here in the savings and loan association from the Southern Christian Leadership Conference. We're just telling you to follow what we're doing. Put your money there. You have six or seven black insurance companies in Memphis. Take out your insurance there. We want to have an "insurance-in."

Now these are some practical things we can do. We begin the process of building a greater economic base. And at the same time, we are putting pressure where it really hurts. I ask you to follow through here.

Now, let me say as I move to my conclusion that we've got to give ourselves to this struggle until the end. Nothing would be more tragic than to stop at this point, in Memphis. We've got to see it through. And when we have our march, you need to be there. Be concerned about your brother. You may not be on strike. But either we go up together, or we go down together.

Let us develop a kind of dangerous unselfishness. One day a man came to Jesus, and he wanted to raise some questions about some vital matters in life. At points, he wanted to trick Jesus and show him that he knew a little more than Jesus knew, and through this, throw him off base. Now that question could have easily ended up in a philosophical and theological debate. But Jesus immediately pulled that question from mid-air and placed it on a dangerous curve between Jerusalem and Jericho. And he talked about a certain man who fell among thieves. You remember that a Levite and a priest passed by on the other side. They didn't stop to help him. And finally a man of another race came by. He got down from his beast, decided not to be compassionate by proxy. But he got down with him, administered first aid, and helped the man in need. Jesus ended up saying this was the good man, this was the great man because he had the capacity to project the "I" into the "thou" and to be concerned about his brother. Now you know, we use our imagination a great deal to try to determine why the priest and the Levite didn't stop. At times we say they were busy going to church meetings—an ecclesiastical gathering—and they had to get on down to Jerusalem so they wouldn't be late for their meeting. At other times we would speculate that there was a religious law that "One who was engaged in religious ceremonials was not to touch a human body twenty-four hours before the ceremony." And every now and then we begin to wonder whether maybe they were not going down to Jerusalem, or down to Jericho, rather to organize a "Jericho Road Improvement Association." That's a possibility. Maybe they felt that it was better to deal with the problem from the causal root, rather than to get bogged down with an individual effort.

But I'm going to tell you what my imagination tells me. It's possible that these men were afraid. You see, the Jericho road is a dangerous road. I remember when Mrs. King and I were first in Jerusalem. We rented a car and drove from Jerusalem down to Jericho. And as soon as we got on that road, I said to my wife, "I can see why Jesus used this as a setting for his parable." It's a winding, meandering road. It's really conducive for ambushing. You start out in Jerusalem, which is about 1,200 miles, or rather 1,200 feet above sea level. And by the time you get down to Jericho, fifteen or twenty minutes later, you're about 2,200 feet below sea level. That's a dangerous road. In the days of Jesus it came to be known as the "Bloody Pass." And you know, it's possible that the priest and the Levite looked over that man on the ground and wondered if the robbers were still around. Or it's possible that they felt that the man on the ground was merely faking. And he was acting like he had been robbed and hurt in order to seize them over there, lure them there for quick and easy seizure. And so the first question that the Levite asked was, "If I stop to help this man, what will happen to me?" But then the Good Samaritan came by. And he reversed the question: "If I do not stop to help this man, what will happen to him?"

That's the question before you tonight. Not, "If I stop to help the sanitation workers, what will happen to all of the hours that I usually spend in my office every day and every week as a pastor?" The question is not, "If I stop to help this man in need, what will happen to me?" "If I do not stop to help the sanitation workers, what will happen to them?" That's the question.

Let us rise up tonight with a greater readiness. Let us stand with a greater determination. And let us move on in these powerful days, these days of challenge to make America what it ought to be. We have an opportunity to make America a better nation. And I want to thank God, once more, for allowing me to be here with you.

You know, several years ago, I was in New York City autographing the first book that I had written. And while sitting there autographing books, a demented black woman came up. The only question I heard from her was, "Are you Martin Luther King?"

And I was looking down, writing, and I said yes. And the next minute I felt something beating on my chest. Before I knew it I had been stabbed by this demented woman. I was rushed to Harlem Hospital. It was a dark Saturday afternoon. And that blade had gone through, and the X-rays revealed that the tip of the blade was on the edge of my aorta, the main artery. And once that's punctured, you drown in your own blood—that's the end of you.

It came out in the *New York Times* the next morning that, if I had sneezed, I would have died. Well, about four days later, they allowed me, after the operation, after my chest had been opened and the blade had been taken out, to move around in the wheelchair in the hospital. They allowed me to read some of the mail that came in, and from all over the states, and the world, kind letters came in. I read a few, but one of them I will never forget. I had received one from the President and the Vice President. I've forgotten what those telegrams said. I'd received a visit and a letter from the Governor of New York, but I've forgotten what the letter said. But there was another letter that came from a little girl, a young girl who was a student at the White Plains High School. And I looked at that letter, and I'll never forget it. It said simply, "Dear Dr. King: I am a ninth-grade student at the White Plains High School." She said, "While it should not matter, I would like to mention that I am a white girl. I read in the paper of your misfortune, and of your suffering. And I read that if you had sneezed, you would have died. And I'm simply writing you to say that I'm so happy that you didn't sneeze."

And I want to say tonight—I want to say that I am happy that I didn't sneeze. Because if I had sneezed, I wouldn't have been around here in 1960, when students all over the South started sitting-in at lunch counters. And I knew that as they were sitting in, they were really standing up for the best in the American dream. And taking the whole nation back to those great wells of democracy which were dug deep by the Founding Fathers in the Declaration of Independence and the Constitution. If I had sneezed, I wouldn't have been around here in 1961, when we decided to take a ride for freedom and ended segregation in interstate travel. If I had sneezed, I wouldn't have been around in 1962, when Negroes in Albany, Georgia, decided to straighten their backs up. And whenever men and women straighten their backs up, they are going somewhere, because a man can't ride your back unless it is bent. If I had sneezed, I wouldn't have been here in 1963, when the black people of Birmingham, Alabama, aroused the conscience of this nation and brought into being the Civil Rights Bill. If I had sneezed, I wouldn't have had a chance later that year, in August, to try to tell America about a dream that I had had. If I had sneezed, I wouldn't have been down in Selma, Alabama, been in Memphis to see the community rally around those brothers and sisters who are suffering. I'm so happy that I didn't sneeze.

And they were telling me, now it doesn't matter now. It really doesn't matter what happens now. I left Atlanta this morning, and as we got started on the plane, there were six of us, the pilot said over the public address system, "We are sorry for the delay, but we have Dr. Martin Luther King on the plane. And to be sure that all of the bags were checked, and to be sure that nothing would be wrong with the plane, we had to check out everything carefully. And we've had the plane protected and guarded all night."

And then I got to Memphis. And some began to say the threats or talk about the threats that were out. What would happen to me from some of our sick white brothers?

Well, I don't know what will happen now. We've got some difficult days ahead. But it doesn't matter with me now. Because I've been to the mountaintop. And I don't mind. Like anybody, I would like to live a long life. Longevity has its place. But I'm not concerned about that now. I just want to do God's will. And He's allowed me to go up to the mountain. And I've looked over. And I've seen the promised land. I may not get there with you. But I want you to know tonight, that we, as a people, will get to the promised land. And I'm happy, tonight. I'm not worried about anything. I'm not fearing any man. Mine eyes have seen the glory of the coming of the Lord!

Appendix B

The Parable of the Good Samaritan, as Told in Luke 10:25–37

And behold, a certain lawyer stood up and made trial of him, saying, Teacher, what shall I do to inherit eternal life? And [Jesus] said unto him, What is written in the law? how readest thou? And he answering said, Thou shalt love the Lord thy God with all thy heart, and with all thy soul, and with all thy strength, and with all thy mind; and thy neighbor as thyself. And he said unto him, Thou hast answered right: this do and thou shalt live. But, he, desiring to justify himself, said unto Jesus, And who is my neighbor? Jesus made answer and said, A certain man was going down from Jerusalem to Jericho; and he fell among robbers, who both stripped him and beat him, and departed, leaving him half dead. And by chance a certain priest was going down that way: and when he saw him, he passed by on the other side. And in like manner a Levite also, when he came to the place, and saw him, passed by on the other side. But a certain Samaritan, as he journeyed, came where he was: and when he saw him, he was moved with compassion, and came to him, and bound up his wounds, pouring on them oil and wine; and he set him on his own beast, and brought him to an inn, and took care of him; and on the morrow he took out two shillings, and gave them to the host, and said, Take care of him; and whatsoever thou spendest more, I, when I come back again, will repay thee. Which of these three, thinkest thou, proved neighbor unto him that fell among the robbers? And he said, He that showed mercy on him. And Jesus said unto him, Go, and do thou likewise.

(The above translation is one that George Buttrick excerpted from the American Standard Edition of the Revised Bible [New York: Nelson, 1901].)

Appendix C

The Murray/Buttrick Intertext

In explicating the Parable of the Good Samaritan, George Buttrick in *The Parables of Jesus* (1928) borrowed directly from George Murray's *Jesus and His Parables* (1914). (Conceivably, Buttrick borrowed this passage from some writer other than Murray. In *The Parables of Jesus*, however, Buttrick cites Murray. By far, the most likely possibility is that Buttrick directly mirrored Murray's text.) Consider these two writers' overlapping descriptions of the road from Jerusalem to Jericho:

> Murray: "Jerusalem is more than 2000 feet above sea-level and Jericho nearly a thousand below it, while the distance between the two towns was little more than a dozen miles.... [I]t lies through a limestone region, abounding in caves and shelters, where robbers ... found convenient resort for their nefarious trade. The road ... had a name of evil omen, the Pass of Blood" (47).

> Buttrick: "Jerusalem was some two thousand feet above sea level and Jericho over one thousand feet below it. The twenty miles between the cities wound through mountainous country, whose limestone caves offered ambush for brigand bands, and whose sudden turns exposed the traveler to unforeseen attack. The road became known as the 'Bloody Pass'" (150).

Appendix D

The Luccock/Buttrick Intertext

In *The Parables of Jesus* (1928), Buttrick borrowed directly from Halford Luccock's *Studies in the Parables of Jesus* (1917). Compare their similar descriptions of the road from Jerusalem to Jericho and of the relationship between the Jewish priest and the Jewish victim:

> Luccock: "It was a very common experience for travelers to be robbed and beaten on the Jericho road, so common, in fact, that in Jesus' time it was know as 'the red or bloody way'" (57).

> Buttrick: "[The road from Jerusalem to Jericho] exposed the traveler to unforeseen attack. The road became known as the 'Bloody Pass'" (150).

> Luccock: "The cruelty of the priest was all the more blameworthy because he was bound to this traveler by ties of special obligation, race, and religion" (57).

> Buttrick: "The priest was a fellow Jew and withal a pillar of the Temple. By birth and by sacred calling he was a 'neighbor' to the robbed and wounded man, but he left him to his fate" (151).

The gospel account fails to directly suggest the motive of the priest and Levite, teasing many readers, including Luccock and Buttrick, to speculate about possible motives:

> Luccock: "People 'pass by' because they are 'too busy.' ... [The priest and Levite] could easily think of others whose business it was rather than theirs. They might be willing to report the case to a Travelers' Aid Society. ... We may be sure that the priest and Levite did not regard themselves as heartless monsters" (58–59).

"One excuse was danger. They could easily reason that the robbers might still be near. It was safer to hurry on" (60).

Buttrick: "Perhaps [the priest and Levite] were 'too busy.'... Moreover, it was better to cure injustice at the source.... In print the conduct of the priest and Levite seems monstrous.... [It was] so dangerous a road. Besides, how were [the priest and Levite] to know that the man was not himself a brigand, some victim of a robbers' wretched feud?" (151–152).

Here Luccock and Buttrick both indicate that the priest and Levite might be "too busy," both suggest that the priest and Levite might think that some formal organization should treat the source of the problem, both suggest that the priest and Levite might or might not be "monsters/monstrous," and both suggest that the two passersby might avoid the victim from fear of being beaten themselves.

The parallels continue:

Luccock: "The service of the Good Samaritan was personal.... Organized charity is absolutely necessary, but it need not become hard and unsympathetic. It needs much personal contact to save it" (61–62).

Buttrick: "The model neighbor rendered *a personal service*.... Philanthropy must be organized.... But the wellspring of neighborliness is personality" (153–154).

Further, Luccock and Buttrick both claim that the parable undercuts a popular tendency to divide people into cultural and racial categories:

Luccock: "[Certain] people ... profess to believe in the brotherhood of man but ... call some of those who make up that brotherhood 'dagos' and 'sheenies' and 'niggers'" (62).

Buttrick: "Rarely do we see people; rarely do we wish to see.... We say, 'He is an American,' a 'Japanese,' a 'negro'" (153).

As the two writers summarize the broad implications of the parable, Luccock quotes Robert Trench (and credits Trench by placing his last name in parentheses). Buttrick's wording is strikingly similar:

Luccock: "Jesus ... declared that love does not ask for limits but looks for openings.... 'Love ..., like the sun, does not inquire upon what it shall shine, or whom it shall warm, but shines or warms by the very law of its own being' (Trench)" (56).

Buttrick: "True neighborliness is not curious to know where its boundaries run; it cares as little for boundaries as sun and rain care about contour lines upon our maps. It seeks not for limits, but for opportunities" (152).

Not only are several of their passages similar, so are the overall interpretations that Luccock and Buttrick supply.

Appendix E

The Buttrick/King Intertext

For his analysis of the Parable of the Good Samaritan, King borrowed directly from George Buttrick's *The Parables of Jesus* (1928). This appendix demonstrates the overlap between Buttrick's text and King's "On Being a Good Neighbor" and "I've Been to the Mountaintop."

Buttrick: "The story begins in a theological controversy and ends in a description of 'first aid' at a roadside....

"The question was asked by an expert in the Jewish law: 'Teacher, what shall I do to inherit eternal life?' . . . Perhaps in self-confidence he was taking up the cudgels of debate. It was disconcerting to have Jesus reply, 'What is written in the law? How readest thou?' as if to say, 'The law is *your* profession. You ought to know.' But he rallied from the retort and recited smoothly: 'Thou shalt love the Lord thy God . . . and thy neighbor as thyself.' Then came the conclusive word: 'Continually do that, and you *shall* live'" (149).

"The scribe was placed in a poor light. He appeared to have asked a needless question, whose sufficient answer was the best-known pronouncement of the law in which he was an expert. A sorry ending to a promising debate! He must absolve himself in the eyes of the bystanders. He must show Jesus that he was not without discernment. Jesus' reply, as he would demonstrate, was far from conclusive. So, 'desiring to justify himself,' he said, 'And who is my neighbor?'" (149–150).

"[Jesus] lifted the question out of the atmosphere of controversy . . . and set it down—where? He set it down on a dangerous road in Palestine!" . . .

"'A certain man . . . went down from Jerusalem to Jericho.' Jerusalem was some two thousand feet above sea level and Jericho over one thousand feet below it. The twenty miles between the cities wound through mountainous country, whose limestone caves offered ambush for brigand bands, and whose sudden turns exposed the traveler to unforeseen attack. The road became known as the 'Bloody Pass'" (150).

"[The Samaritan] was a half-breed, of a race which the Jews counted religiously in disrepute and with which they had 'no dealings.' But 'when he saw him, he was moved with compassion'...

"Perhaps [the priest and Levite] shrank, as we naturally do, from 'getting mixed up' in such a case. Moreover, it was better to cure injustice at the source" (151).

"Besides, how were they to know that the man was not himself a brigand, some victim of a robber's wretched feud?" (152).

"'Who is my neighbor?' 'I do not know,' Jesus retorts; 'but life will reveal him to you. He is not of one class or nation. He is anybody—in need!... He is "a certain man" —any man needy at your roadside.' Thus Jesus replies not in a definition but by an instance" (152–153).

"We say, 'He is an American,' a 'Japanese,' a 'negro'; it is astonishing how the 'national' sheath can save our sympathies" (153).

King, "On Being a Good Neighbor" (1963): "The ethical concern of this man is expressed in a magnificent little story, which begins with a theological discussion on the meaning of eternal life and concludes in a concrete expression of compassion on a dangerous road. Jesus is asked a question by a man who had been trained in the details of Jewish law: 'Master, what shall I do to inherit eternal life?' The retort is prompt: 'What is written in the law? How readest thou?' After a moment the lawyer recites articulately: 'Thou shalt love the Lord thy God... and thy neighbor as thyself.' Then comes the decisive word from Jesus: '... this do, and thou shalt live.'...

"The lawyer was chagrined. 'Why,' the people might ask, 'would an expert in law raise a question that even the novice can answer?' Desiring to justify himself and to show that Jesus' reply was far from conclusive, the lawyer asks, 'And who is my neighbour?' The lawyer was now taking up the cudgels of debate.... But Jesus... pulls the question from mid-air and places it on a dangerous curve between Jerusalem and Jericho....

"Finally, a certain Samaritan, a half-breed from a people with whom the Jews had no dealings, appeared....

"We see men as Jews or Gentiles, Catholics or Protestants, Chinese or American, Negroes or whites....

"Who is my neighbor? 'I do not know his name,' says Jesus in essence. 'He is anyone toward whom you are neighborly. He is anyone who lies in need at life's roadside. He is neither Jew nor Gentile; he is neither Russian nor American; he is neither Negro nor white....' So Jesus defines a neighbor, not in a theological definition, but in a life situation" (20–21).

"Maybe the priest and the Levite believed that it is better to cure injustice at the causal source than to get bogged down with a single individual effect....

"The Jericho Road was a dangerous road. When Mrs. King and I visited the Holy Land, we rented a car and drove from Jerusalem to Jericho. As we traveled slowly down that meandering, mountainous road, I said to my wife, 'I can now understand why Jesus chose this road as the setting for his parable.' Jerusalem is some two thousand feet above and Jericho one thousand feet below sea level. The descent is made in less than twenty miles. Many sudden curves provide likely places for ambushing and expose the traveler to unforeseen attacks. Long ago the road was known as the Bloody Pass....

"So it is possible that the Priest and the Levite were afraid that if they stopped, they too would be beaten. Perhaps the robbers were still nearby. Or maybe the wounded man on the road was a faker, who wished to draw passing travelers to his side for quick and easy seizure" (24–25).

King, "I've Been to the Mountaintop" (1968): "But Jesus immediately pulled [the man's] question from midair and placed it on a dangerous curve between Jerusalem and Jericho.

"Maybe [the priest and Levite] felt that it was better to deal with the problem from the causal root, rather than to get bogged down with an individual effort.

"You see, the Jericho Road is a dangerous road. I remember when Mrs. King and I were first in Jerusalem. We rented a car and drove from Jerusalem down to Jericho. And as soon as we got on that road I said to my wife, 'I can see why Jesus used this as the setting for his parable.' It's a winding, meandering road. It's really conducive for ambushing. You start out in Jerusalem, which is about twelve hundred miles, or, rather, twelve hundred feet above sea level. And by the time you get down to Jericho fifteen or twenty minutes later, you're about twenty-two hundred feet below sea level. That's a dangerous road. In the days of Jesus, it came to be known as the Bloody Pass.

"And you know, it's possible that the priest and the Levite looked over that man on the ground and wondered if the robbers were still around. Or it's possible that they felt that the man on the ground was merely faking, and he was acting like he had been robbed and hurt in order to seize them over there, lure them there for quick and easy seizure."

Appendix F

The Murray/Buttrick/King Intertext

This appendix only lists the overlapping segments among texts by George Murray, George Buttrick, *and* King.

> Murray: "Jerusalem is more than 2000 feet above sea-level and Jericho nearly a thousand below it, while the distance between the two towns was little more than a dozen miles.... [I]t lies through a limestone region, abounding in caves and shelters, where robbers ... found convenient resort for their nefarious trade. The road ... had a name of evil omen, the Pass of Blood" (47).

> Buttrick: "Jerusalem was some two thousand feet above sea level and Jericho over one thousand feet below it. The twenty miles between the cities wound through mountainous country, whose limestone caves offered ambush for brigand bands, and whose sudden turns exposed the traveler to unforeseen attack. The road became known as the 'Bloody Pass'" (150).

> King, "On Being a Good Neighbor": "The Jericho Road was a dangerous road. When Mrs. King and I visited the Holy Land, we rented a car and drove from Jerusalem to Jericho. As we traveled slowly down that meandering, mountainous road, I said to my wife, 'I can now understand why Jesus chose this road as the setting for his parable.' Jerusalem is some two thousand feet above and Jericho one thousand feet below sea level. The descent is made in less than twenty miles. Many sudden curves provide likely places for ambushing and expose the traveler to unforeseen attacks. Long ago the road was known as the Bloody Pass" (24).

> King, "I've Been to the Mountaintop": "You see, the Jericho Road is a dangerous road. I remember when Mrs. King and I were first in Jerusalem. We rented a car and drove from Jerusalem down to Jericho. And as soon as we got on that road I said to my wife, 'I can see why Jesus used this as the setting for his parable.' It's a winding, meandering road. It's really conducive for

ambushing. You start out in Jerusalem, which is about twelve hundred miles, or, rather, twelve hundred feet above sea level. And by the time you get down to Jericho fifteen or twenty minutes later, you're about twenty-two hundred feet below sea level. That's a dangerous road. In the days of Jesus, it came to be known as the Bloody Pass."

Appendix G

The Luccock/Buttrick/King Intertext

This appendix indicates *only* the overlap among texts by Halford Luccock, George Buttrick, *and* King.

> Luccock: "It was a very common experience for travelers to be robbed and beaten on the Jericho road, so common, in fact, that in Jesus' time it was know as 'the red, or bloody way'" (57).
> "One excuse [of the priest and Levite] was danger [on that road]" (60).
>
> Buttrick: "[The road from Jerusalem to Jericho] exposed the traveler to unforeseen attack. The road became known as the 'Bloody Pass'" (150).
> "[It is] so dangerous a road" (152).
>
> King, "On Being a Good Neighbor": "The Jericho Road was a dangerous road. Long ago the road was known as the Bloody Pass" (24).
>
> King, "I've Been to the Mountaintop": "You see, the Jericho Road is a dangerous road.... In the days of Jesus, it came to be known as the Bloody Pass."
>
> Luccock: "[The priest and Levite] could easily think of others whose business it was rather than theirs. They might be willing to report the case to a Travelers' Aid Society" (59).
>
> Buttrick: "Moreover, it was better to cure injustice at the source" (151).
>
> King, "On Being a Good Neighbor": "Maybe the priest and the Levite believed that it is better to cure injustice at the causal source than to get bogged down with a single individual effort" (24).

King, "I've Been to the Mountaintop": "Maybe [the priest and Levite] felt that it was better to deal with the problem from the causal root, rather than to get bogged down with an individual effort."

Luccock: "One excuse was danger. [The priest and Levite] could easily reason that the robbers might still be near. It was safer to hurry on" (60).

Buttrick: "[It was] so dangerous a road. Besides, how were [the priest and Levite] to know that the man was not himself a brigand, some victim of a robbers' wretched feud? Wise men steer clear of vendettas" (152).

King, "On Being a Good Neighbor": "So it is possible that the Priest and the Levite were afraid that if they stopped, they too would be beaten. Perhaps the robbers were still nearby. Or maybe the wounded man on the road was a faker, who wished to draw passing travelers to his side for quick and easy seizure" (24–25).

King, "I've Been to the Mountaintop": "And you know, it's possible that the priest and the Levite looked over that man on the ground and wondered if the robbers were still around. Or it's possible that they felt that the man on the ground was merely faking, and he was acting like he had been robbed and hurt in order to seize them over there, lure them there for quick and easy seizure."

Luccock: "[Certain] people . . . profess to believe in the brotherhood of man but . . . call some of those who make up that brotherhood 'dagos' and 'sheenies' and 'niggers'" (62).

Buttrick: "Rarely do we see people; rarely do we wish to see. . . . We say, 'He is an American,' a 'Japanese,' a 'negro'" (153).

King, "On Being a Good Neighbor": "We see men as Jews or Gentiles, Catholics or Protestants, Chinese or American, Negroes or whites" (21).

Appendix H

Liberal Protestant Commonplaces in "I've Been to the Mountaintop"

Here I align observations that, starting at least as early as 1841, various Protestant writers articulated and repeated when discussing the Parable of the Good Samaritan. Given the popularity of these points in print, one deduces that they almost certainly circulated orally as well, with different preachers expounding them from different pulpits. When writers and preachers borrowed these notions from each other, they often massaged the wording, but not always. In his analysis of the Parable of the Good Samaritan, Halford Luccock sometimes indicates his sources (including Robert Trench), but sometimes fails to do so. In his discussion of the same parable, George Buttrick sometimes footnotes his sources (including Marcus Dods and George Hubbard). In his explication of another parable, Buttrick mentions Luccock. But in his exegesis of the Parable of the Good Samaritan, Buttrick does not mention Luccock, even though he mirrored points that he read directly in Luccock's text.

In "On Being a Good Neighbor" and "I've Been to the Mountaintop," King directly borrowed a large portion of his analysis of the Parable of the Good Samaritan from Buttrick's *The Parables of Jesus*, and *not* from any other source. Three reasons very, very strongly support this conclusion. First, King borrowed heavily from Buttrick's *The Parables of Jesus* on many occasions (especially when preaching on the Parable of Dives and Lazarus and on the Parable of the Rich Fool). King simply liked Buttrick. Second, in King's treatment of the Parable of the Good Samaritan in "On Being a Good Neighbor" and "I've Been to the Mountaintop," *all* his intertextual material overlaps Buttrick's. In other words, once one observes the parallels between King's treatment of the parable and Buttrick's treatment, there is no additional overlap to consider. Third, in "On Being a Good Neighbor" and "I've Been to the Mountaintop," King borrows *some* material from Buttrick that does *not* appear in any of these other texts.

Even though King probably never read this succession of partially overlapping texts about the parables, this succession of texts matters for two reasons. The train of texts illustrates the frequency with which Protestant scholars and ministers borrowed from each other and, when added to other evidence about homiletic borrowing, demonstrates that King's tendency to borrow was fairly typical, not anomalous.

Further, beginning at least as early as 1841, numerous, now-forgotten writers actually composed motifs and lines that King repeated in "On Being a Good Neighbor" and "I've Been to the Mountaintop." When King echoed lines from Buttrick, he echoed some that Buttrick originated and others that previous Protestant authors had handed down to each other and to Buttrick. All these authors deserve recognition for helping compose a great American speech.

Below I list Luccock's and Buttrick's own books, plus mainly books that Luccock and/or Buttrick directly indicate that they read. And I add a book by King's mentor Benjamin Mays that appeared long after Luccock and Buttrick wrote their books. Although King did not directly borrow from Mays's brief exegesis of the Parable of the Good Samaritan, Mays's treatment may have helped shape King's general understanding of the parable. (For Mays's entire discussion of the parable, see Appendix I.)

Below, I directly quote these texts when the wording is strikingly similar. When the observations are parallel, but the wording is not strikingly similar, I simply list the writers and dates.

<u>Because bandits victimized many travelers on the road from Jerusalem to Jericho, people recognized the road as so dangerous that they called it the "Bloody Way" or the "Bloody Pass."</u>

> Robert Trench, *Notes on the Parables of Our Lord* (1841): "The road leading from [Jerusalem to Jericho] was at one place called the Red or the Bloody Way, from the blood which had been there shed [by bandits]" (315).
>
> A. B. Bruce, *The Parabolic Teachings of Christ* (1882): "The rugged, rocky pass from Jerusalem to Jericho [has a] bad renown as the 'Way of Blood' [or] 'the Bloody Way'" (346).
>
> Marcus Dods, *The Parables of Our Lord* (1886): "So notorious had that road become for robbery and violence that it was called 'the red or bloody way'" (25).
>
> George Murray, *Jesus and the Parables* (1916): "[The road from Jerusalem to Jericho] had a name of evil omen, the Pass of Blood" (47).
>
> Halford Luccock, *Studies in the Parables of Jesus* (1917): "It was a very common experience for travelers to be robbed and beaten on the Jericho road, so common, in fact, that in Jesus' time it was know as 'the red, or bloody way'" (57).

George Buttrick, *The Parables of Jesus* (1928): "[The road from Jerusalem to Jericho] exposed the traveler to unforeseen attack. The road became known as the 'Bloody Pass'" (150).

Martin Luther King Jr., "On Being a Good Neighbor" (1963): "The Jericho Road was a dangerous road. Long ago the road was known as the Bloody Pass" (24).

Martin Luther King Jr., "I've Been to the Mountaintop" (1968): "You see, the Jericho Road is a dangerous road. . . . In the days of Jesus, it came to be known as the Bloody Pass."

<u>The priest and Levite were Jewish officials who would have been especially expected to help the roadside victim, who was also a Jew.</u>

Trench (1841)
Dods (1886)
Charles Reynolds Brown, *Two Parables* (1898)
George Hubbard, *The Teachings of Jesus in Parables* (1907)
Murray (1916)
Luccock (1917)
Buttrick (1928)
King (1963 and 1968)

<u>Though the gospel writer does not suggest motives for the priest and Levite, they must have had reasons for neglecting the roadside victim, and readers can should ponder what those reasons might be.</u>

Trench (1841)
Bruce (1882): "Nothing [is] so easy as to invent excuses for [the priest and Levite]. Every commentator suggests a list of excuses, each one inventing his own list—so plentiful are they" (349).
Dods (1886)
Luccock (1917)
Buttrick (1928)
King (1963 and 1968)

<u>The priest and Levite may have feared that robbers would also attack them.</u>

Trench (1841)

Bruce (1882)
Dods (1886)
Luccock (1917)
Buttrick (1928)
King (1963 and 1968)

<u>The priest and Levite might rationalize that, instead of helping the roadside victim, they would work on an institutional solution to highway crimes.</u>

Luccock (1917)
Buttrick (1928)
Benjamin Mays, *Seeking to Be Christian in Race Relations* (1957): Mays humorously mentions that the Samaritan failed to seek an institutional solution to roadside banditry.
King (1963 and 1968)

<u>The Samaritan belonged to a religious group that stood dramatically apart from the Jews. Those who heard Jesus would not expect a Samaritan to help a Jew who was beaten and robbed.</u>

Trench (1841): "[Samaritans were] excommunicated [and] synonymous with heretic" (317–318).
Bruce (1882): "[The Samaritan was a] stranger of a different race" (343). "[The Samaritan was a] heretic [and an] alien" (346).
Dods (1886): "[The Samaritan] was not bound to the man by any tie of country, he was not even a mere foreigner, but was of the Samaritans, who had no dealings with the Jews" (33).
Brown (1898): "[The Samaritan was a] heretic" (3).
Hubbard (1907): "[The Samaritan was of a different] nationality" (426).
Murray (1916): The Samaritan was a "wretched heretic" and was "despised" as an "unknown alien" (46, 49, 50).
Luccock (1917): "[The Samaritan was] alien or heretical" (57).
Buttrick (1928): "[The Samaritan was] of a race ... with which [the Jews] had 'no dealings'" (151).
Mays (1957): "[The Samaritan was] despised" (21).
King (1963): "[The Samaritan was] from a people with whom the Jews had no dealings." (27)

The Samaritan offered personal service.

Brown (1898): "The Samaritan's service was also intensely personal" (19).
Luccock (1917): "The service of the Good Samaritan was personal" (61).
Buttrick (1928): "The [Samaritan] rendered *a personal service*" (153).

Compassion obeys no limits.

Trench (1841): "Love [is] like the sun, which does not inquire upon what it shall shine, or whom it shall warm, but shines and warms by the very law of its own being, so that nothing is hidden from its light and heat" (328).
Dods (1886)
Hubbard (1907)
Murray (1916): "[Christian charity] is like the sun above us, shining impartial" (352).
Luccock (1917): "Jesus ... declared that love does not ask for limits but looks for openings. ... Love finds a neighbor in every one that is in need and can be helped. 'Love ... , like the sun, does not inquire upon what it shall shine, or whom it shall warm, but shines or warms by the very law of its own being' (Trench)" (56).
Buttrick (1928): "True neighborliness is not curious to know where its boundaries run; it cares as little for boundaries as sun and rain care about contour lines upon our maps. It seeks not for limits, but for opportunities" (152).
Mays (1957)
King (1963)

When compassion observes no limits, that means that compassion acknowledges no racial or cultural boundaries.

Bruce (1882)
Dods (1886)
Luccock (1917): "[Certain] people ... profess to believe in the brotherhood of man but ... call some of those who make up that brotherhood 'dagos' and 'sheenies' and 'niggers'" (62).
Buttrick (1928): "Rarely do we see people; rarely do we wish to see. ... We say, 'He is an American,' a 'Japanese,' a 'negro'" (153).
Mays (1957)

King (1963): "We see men as Jews or Gentiles, Catholics or Protestants, Chinese or American, Negroes or whites" (21).

Appendix I

Parallels for Segments of "I've Been to the Mountaintop"

Martin Luther King Sr., in his "Moderator's Annual Address, Atlanta Missionary Baptist Association" (1940), writes:

> Quite often we say the church has no place in politics, forgetting the words of the Lord, the spirit of the Lord is upon me because he hath anointed me to preach the Gospel to the poor, he hath sent me to heal the brokenhearted, to preach deliverance to the captives, and the recovering of sight to the blind, to set at liberty them that are bruised....
> In this we find we are to do something about the broken-hearted, poor, unemployed, the captive, the blind, and the bruised.
> How can people be happy without jobs, food, shelter, and clothes?...
> God hasten the time when every minister will become a registered voter and a part of every movement for the betterment of our people....
> As ministers a great responsibility rests upon us as leaders. We cannot expect our people to register and become citizens until we as leaders set the standard. (34)

William Holmes Borders, in "'Thy Word Is as a Fire Shut Up in My Bones'—Are the Words of Jerimiah [sic]" (1943), writes, "'Thy word is as a fire shut up in my bones'" (41).

Benjamin Mays, in *Seeking to Be Christian in Race Relations* (1957), writes:

> Although the good Samaritan did not do the job of a modern social worker and initiate a program to clear the Jericho Road of thieves ...
> Then came a Samaritan, a member of a group despised by the Jews, who stopped to help. He dressed the injuries of the wounded man, took him on his own beast to an inn, and left money for his expenses. Jesus declared that this man who showed mercy was a neighbor to the one who fell among thieves, rather than the members of his own group.
> In modern speech, this means that neighborliness is not defined in terms

of nationality or race. It cannot be defined in terms of geography. A true neighbor is one who responds helpfully and sympathetically to human needs. ...[W]hoever ministers to them is a real neighbor.... [E]very one who walks the earth is a neighbor to every one who is in need....

...to preach good news to the poor...to proclaim release to the captives, sight to the blind, set at liberty those who are oppressed. (21–22)

Benjamin Mays, in "The Vocation of a Christian—In, but Not of, the World" (1964), declares: "Your word is like a fire shut up in my bones" (232).

NOTES

Introduction

1. The excellent historian Adam Fairclough, for one, writes that "many consider" "I've Been to the Mountaintop" to be King's "best" speech (*To Redeem*, 380). Rhetorical critic Michael Osborne simply notes that the speech "was surely an awesome performance" (148).
2. Beifuss, 276.
3. Ibid., 277.
4. See Branch, *At Canaan's Edge*, 755.
5. See Beifuss, 277.
6. Abernathy, 430.
7. Marian Logan, a board member of King's Southern Christian Leadership Conference, also strenuously objected to the Poor People's Campaign.
8. See McKnight, 33; Green, 276.
9. Robinson, "James Robinson," 303.
10. Ibid., 304.
11. Qtd. in Honey, *Going*, 61.
12. Qtd. in Bello, 3A.
13. Robinson, "James Robinson" 305.
14. Qtd. in Honey, *Going*, 55.
15. See Honey, *Going*, 34.
16. See Beifuss, 30.
17. Young, *Easy*, 449.
18. Qtd. in Beifuss, 20–21.
19. Rogers, 296.
20. See Honey, *Going*, 149.
21. Ibid., 219–220.
22. Qtd. in Honey, *Going*, 283.
23. Ibid., 284, 285.
24. Qtd. in Green, 216. Green is quoting an interview that originally appeared in *Tri-State Defender*, the African American newspaper in Memphis. For more on this rally, see Green, 216–217; and Honey, *Going*, 30–31.

25. See Honey, *Going*, 30–31. The participant was Russell Sugarmon, a candidate for city commissioner and a local organizer.

26. Young, *Easy*, 450.

27. Like the reports of Mark Twain's death, the size of Mason Temple and the size of the audience for King's oration, "The Dignity of Labor," on March 18 have been greatly exaggerated. Frank claims that the sanctuary of Mason Temple "easily held 10,000" (49). Clemmons also claims that it seated 10,000 (180). Several prominent scholars declare that 15,000 people assembled to hear King on that occasion. (See Branch, *At Canaan's Edge*, 755; Burns, 424–425; and Ling, 284–285.) Honey, the best historian of the strike in Memphis, numbers the attendees at between 9,000 and 15,000 (*Going*, 292). Andrew Young, who heard "The Dignity of Labor," claims that the crowd amounted to "more than ten thousand" (*Easy*, 450). Billy Kyles, who also listened to this speech, estimates an audience of "at least 6,000"—a much lower number (*At the River I Stand* [DVD]). Instead of pews, the sanctuary of Mason Temple features bolted seats. In 2006 and 2011 I visited Mason Temple and personally counted every seat in its sanctuary. Adding together the twelve loose chairs in the chancel and all the bolted seats, I counted *exactly* 3,734 seats in the sanctuary. The sanctuary has changed relatively little since its dedication in 1945, and *no* evidence suggests that there ever were more seats in that sanctuary. My own examination of the space within Mason Temple impels my conclusion that no more than 4,000 (or, at the *absolute most*, 4,300) people could ever conceivably jam into its reasonably large, but definitely not massive, sanctuary. Ever. There is simply no way that that sanctuary could hold a larger number. A few more might have listened to King's oration from the vestibule, but not many because the vestibule is definitely small. In her discussion of "The Dignity of Labor," Beifuss reports an "overflowing crowd . . . spilling outside Mason Temple" (193). Curiously, Beifuss and others do not claim that an outside loudspeaker was used to broadcast "The Dignity of Labor" outside the church. But I assume that the usually reliable Beifuss is accurate and that some listeners did congregate outside Mason Temple. On one side of the temple is its parking lot. Beifuss does not observe that these extra attendees filled that parking lot. They almost certainly did not fill it because they would have parked their cars there. (There were no other nearby parking lots. Mason Temple faced and still faces a narrow street that held and still holds very few cars—a tiny fraction of the vehicles that listeners drove to Mason Temple on March 18. The parking lot would have been filled with cars because it was the only available place to park a significant number of cars.) Even if the parking lot of Mason Temple were somehow entirely devoid of cars and even if the crowd did somehow occupy the entire parking lot, the lot is fairly small and could not have held anywhere close to 10,000 people. There is simply no

way. When empty, the lot might conceivably have held, at most, 3,000 or 4,000 folks. But the lot would not have been empty. Further, the lawn between the front of the Mason Temple and the street is extremely tiny and would hold 100 or less. On the opposite side of the church from the parking lot is a side lawn, with trees, that might accommodated several hundred people, or possibly a thousand or so, who could have heard King's address, if one assumes that an outside loudspeaker was used. If one assumes that the crowd swarmed the sanctuary, the vestibule, the parking lot, the miniscule front lawn, and the larger side lawn, then the absolute maximum conceivable number of listeners would be about 8,000. But in that case, except for people seated in the sanctuary, most individual bodies would press sardine-like against the bodies of several others. That seems very unlikely. For King's speech on March 18, I estimate that the crowd actually amounted to between 5,000 and 6,000 people. This estimate is close to that of Billy Kyles.

Why does the number of listeners for this address matter? Some writers clearly imply—or directly claim—that the audience for King's last speech was seven times smaller or five times smaller than it was on March 18. That simply is not the case. Given the severity of the rainstorm, the turnout for "I've Been to the Mountaintop" was even more impressive than researchers have noted. How did scholars originate their supposed number of 15,000? Perhaps that number stemmed from a conversation between James Lawson, Jesse Epps, and King. Apparently, when Lawson and Epps picked up King at the Memphis airport on March 18 to drive him to Mason Temple, they attempted to bolster his morale by teasing him about a surprisingly large audience of 15,000. (See Frank, 16; and Branch, *At Canaan's Edge*, 755.) I assume that Lawson and Epps may well have actually teased King about the size of the crowd and may well have intentionally or unintentionally exaggerated the size of the audience by boasting about 15,000 folks. Still, 5,000 or 6,000 listeners comprised a considerably larger crowd than the ones that King usually attracted in the South.

28. When King stepped into the pulpit to deliver a sermon, he normally began by supplying the title of his homily. But he normally didn't do that with speeches. His speeches are often titled as his (or someone else's) afterthought, and that person normally selects an important phrase from the speech as its title. Apparently, no one has ever created a title for his oration of March 18. I hereby jump into this vacuum by grabbing an important phrase from the speech and christening the speech "The Dignity of Labor."

29. Qtd. in Beifuss, 194.

30. Ibid., 195. See also Fairclough, *To Redeem*, 371.

31. Qtd. in Fairclough, *To Redeem*, 371.

32. See Honey, *Going*, 348.

33. Abernathy states that only five hundred people where present when King arrived at Mason Temple (430, 432). Other estimates of the number of attendees are uniformly much higher. A DVD documentary of the Memphis strike, *At the River I Stand*, includes shots made by cameras panning the crowd. In these camera images, roughly 80 or 90 percent of the seats on the floor of the sanctuary seem occupied during the speech, indicating a number far higher than five hundred.

34. Young, *Easy*, 461; and Young, "Introduction," 204.

35. I reproduce the wording, italics, and capitalization of this banner as it appears in photos. While one scholar deserves credit for noticing the banner, he misarranges some of the words on the banner and incorrectly capitalizes all of its words, only some of which were actually capitalized. See Branch, *At Canaan's Edge*, 718.

36. For the rain jacket, see Honey, *Going*, 415–416; for King walking down the main aisle of the sanctuary, see Abernathy, 432.

37. The minister was James E. Smith. See J. Smith, 466.

38. There were and are no pews in Mason Temple.

39. On a visit to Mason Temple, I counted these seats and took these measurements myself. Since 1968, workers have installed air conditioners and a lower ceiling in the sanctuary of Mason Temple. Apart from those changes (plus moving a tomb to a less prominent spot in the vestibule), the vestibule and sanctuary have changed very little since 1968.

40. For the size of the audience, see Honey, *Going*, 415.

41. Young, "Introduction," 204; Young, *Easy*, 462.

42. Qtd. in Beifuss 277. The minister was Rev. Malcolm Blackburn.

43. Young remembers Abernathy's talk as lasting "at least an hour" (*Easy*, 461). Honey states that it took twenty-five minutes (*Going*, 415–416). Abernathy does not estimate the length of his introduction, but he implies that it was long (433).

44. Abernathy, 433.

45. Thomas Jackson strongly argues that King advocated economic justice and embraced a version of socialism throughout his entire adult life. According to Jackson, King moderated his views in some of his speeches, including "I Have a Dream," in deference to the more moderate colleagues in his civil rights coalition.

46. See Burns, 313–316.

47. See Garrow, "Measuring," R3.

48. For analyses of this tradition, see Howard-Pitney; and K. Miller, "'Plymouth Rock.'"

49. See Vander Lei and Miller.

50. See John 3:3 and 3:7.

51. For "I Have a Dream" as an interpretation of the Bible, see K. Miller, "Second Isaiah."

52. King's interpretation of the Exodus narrative has drawn a certain amount of scholarly analysis. (See, for example, Selby.) But scholars generally fail to delve into the many rich dimensions of King's Exodus references and also fail to relate King's interpretation of the Exodus to his exegesis of the Bible as a whole.

53. Rieder addresses this topic more than anyone else does.

54. In my earlier book about King, I very briefly mention this source, but do so *only* in an endnote in a book that contains hundreds of endnotes. In that brief endnote, I do not *demonstrate* that King uses this source. No one else has ever mentioned this source in print. In my endnote, I do not even mention any of the other, earlier sources of commonplaces that impact King's explication of this parable. I discovered these earlier sources in the summer of 2010, when researching this book.

55. Bakhtin, *Speech Genres*, 169.

56. Claassens, 131.

57. For more on the Judeo-Christian qualities of the civil rights movement, see Chappell and two books by Marsh.

Chapter 1

1. King Sr., *Daddy King*, 85.

2. Ibid., 89; Carson, Luker, and Russell, "Introduction," 13–18. For the best scholarly overview of the lives of King's great-grandparents, grandparents, and parents, see Carson, Luker, and Russell, "Introduction."

3. See King Sr., *Daddy King*, 23, 45, 61.

4. See Carson, Luker, and Russell, "Introduction," 33. See also King Sr., *Daddy King*, 98–101. Writing decades later, King Sr. misdates this march.

5. Qtd. in Carson, Luker, and Russell, "Introduction," 34. See (Third) Isaiah 61:1–2; Luke 4:16–19.

6. See Genovese, 248–255; and Berlin, 206–209.

7. Qtd. in Raboteau, 32–33.

8. Raboteau, 32, 33–34.

9. Cone, 122. See also L. Baldwin, 168–169.

10. See anthology by Foner and Branham, which features Exodus-minded speeches by each of these orators.

11. Carter, 149.

12. Acts 2.

13. See Dennis, 635.

14. Shuttlesworth, "Address," 768.

15. Qtd. in Manis, 109. Shuttlesworth referred to Daniel in the lion's den, an episode recounted in Daniel 6:1–28. The "'three boys'" whom Shuttlesworth mentioned were Shadrach, Meshach, and Abednego, whose episode in the fiery furnace of King Nebuchadnezzar appears in Daniel 3:1–30. For Shuttlesworth's brief account of his house bombing, see "Fred Shuttlesworth."

16. Shuttlesworth, "Call," 466. For an excellent analysis of Shuttlesworth's rhetoric, see a forthcoming book by David Holmes.

17. See Fager, 82–83. See also Burns, 272–273. Bevel referred to Acts 12:2–3 and Esther 4:16.

18. Qtd. in Lomax, 126. Smith adapted the phrase "never said a mumbling word" from a spiritual.

19. E. King, 784.

20. Manis, 131.

21. Spike, 673.

22. See King, "Why"; and King, "Three Dimensions," April 9, 1967.

23. King, "Address," 200.

24. King, "Birth," 20.

25. Ibid., 20, 28.

26. Ibid., 29.

27. Ibid., 34.

28. King, "Death of Evil," 74.

29. Ibid., 75.

30. Qtd. in Morris, 98.

31. One striker was Leslie Moore. See Baird. The other was James Robinson. See Robinson, 309.

32. Manis, 109.

33. See Numbers 13–14.

34. Burns, 270–271.

35. For Abernathy's use of eschatological imagery from Revelation 7:9, see Rieder, 230.

36. Qtd. in Rieder, 205. King is adapting Revelation 7:9.

37. Barr, 139.

38. Childs, *Introduction*, 671.

39. See King, "Address."

40. See Miller and Lewis; Vander Lei and Miller. For King and Carey, see K. Miller, "Voice Merging" and *Voice*. In "I Have a Dream" King also derives his pat-

terns of metaphors from African American gospel songs. See K. Miller, "Beacon Light."

41. See also Zechariah 3:10, I Kings 4:25, II Kings 1831, (First) Isaiah 36:16.

42. Gowan, 55.

43. Ibid., 101.

44. Ibid., 55.

45. King, "I Have a Dream," 81.

46. For views of the Hebrew Bible that are consistent with Gowan's interpretation, see Childs, *Introduction*; and J. Sanders.

47. Will Campbell, a maverick white preacher, advocated this oratorical direction in 1960 when he urged civil rights leaders to base their appeals exclusively on Christianity and to drop references to American "cultural landmarks." See Campbell, 387.

48. King, "Beyond Vietnam," 163.

49. King, "Drum Major Instinct," 264.

50. Sometimes "Our God Is Marching On" is titled "How Long?" or simply "Address at the Conclusion of the Selma to Montgomery March."

51. For excellent accounts of Selma, see Fager; and Garrow, *Protest*.

52. King, "Our God Is Marching On," 119–120.

53. Ibid., 125.

54. Ibid., 125–126.

55. Ibid., 126–127.

56. Ibid., 127.

57. Ibid., 127.

58. Ibid., 128–129.

59. Ibid., 128.

60. Ibid., 131–132.

61. Ibid., 129–130. See Amos 5:24.

62. King, "Our God Is Marching On," 127. See Micah 6:8.

Chapter 2

1. For more on Mays, see his two autobiographies, *Born to Rebel* and *Lord*. Troy Jackson also provides a valuable perspective on Mays's relationship with King Jr.

2. King also knew other African Americans in Atlanta, such as William Holmes Borders, who had pursued graduate education in the North.

3. King, *Stride*, 145.

4. For more on Fosdick, see the excellent biography by Robert Miller.

5. See Carson, Luker and Russell, "King's Personal Library." For information about Fosdick, Buttrick, Luccock, Mays, and Thurman, see K. Miller, *Voice*.

6. See Carey. For the discovery that King borrowed from Carey, see K. Miller, "Voice Merging." Carey and King were personally acquainted.

7. See K. Miller, *Voice* 73.

8. Dodd, 5.

9. Buttrick, *Parables*, 233.

10. Author's interview with David Buttrick, August 1983.

11. King's letter to Coretta King is reprinted in Branch, *Parting*, 363.

12. For King's debt to Hamilton and Buttrick, see K. Miller, *Voice*.

13. Compare Buttrick, "Life," to King, "Why" and "Man."

14. Compare Buttrick, "Springs," to King, "Impassable Gulf."

15. Compare Buttrick, "Springs" and (especially) "Life," to King, "Dignity."

16. See Appendix H. Of course, it is possible that more than six authors characterized the road this way and that neither I nor anyone else has located their texts. It is often difficult to trace who borrowed which interpretive commonplace from whom because many commonplaces almost certainly floated from pulpit to pulpit as well as from page to page. Also, sometimes a preacher or writer may have heard or read boilerplate more than once before deciding to reuse it. In that case, there is no single source, but rather two or more sources for a minister's decision to reuse a commonplace.

17. Buttrick, in *Parables*, footnotes Trench, Dods, Hubbard, Murray, and Luccock in different places in his book. In one footnote, Buttrick calls Luccock's book "valuable" (58). In his discussion of the Parable of the Good Samaritan, Buttrick borrows material without acknowledgement from both Murray and Luccock.

18. For his oration "Sleeping through a Revolution," King borrowed from Luccock's "Sleeping through a Revolution," which appeared in Luccock's *Marching off the Map*. But no evidence suggests that King directly read Luccock's *Studies in the Parables of Jesus*.

19. Luke 10:25–37.

20. See King, "On Being a Good Neighbor," and Fosdick, "The Cross."

21. Bruce, 349.

22. Buttrick says "Japanese"; King says "Chinese."

Chapter 3

1. See Watters, 195–196.

2. As White observes, researchers in general pay little attention to COGIC. See White, 2.

3. Honey, *Going*, 295.

4. The architect of New Concord Baptist Church in New York City was one of many who made this mistake. King preached at that church, which was led by Rev. Gardner Taylor, his friend and political ally.

5. Honey, *Going*, 149.

6. Ibid., 219–220.

7. Ibid., 397.

8. For the involvement of members of COGIC in the strike, see Clemmons, 127.

9. Honey, *Going*, 297.

10. A historical marker at Mason Temple states that C. H. Mason was born in 1862. But Mary Mason's book from 1924, which was completed with the cooperation of C. H. Mason, gives his birth date as 1866 (19). Clemmons, Courts, and Daniels agree with Mary Mason.

11. See Courts, 15–16.

12. Qtd. in Mason, 26.

13. See Olsen; and Owens.

14. See Acts 2:1–4.

15. Qtd. in Mason, 26–27.

16. For the phenomenal growth of Pentecostalism around the world, see Cox.

17. Pleas, 11.

18. Qtd. in Maxwell, 25–26. Another scholar observes that Mason continued "the charismatic style of old slave preachers." See White, 17.

19. For a report of one million members, see Maxwell, 26.

20. Butler, 12. See also Butler, 2.

21. Butler, 118.

22. This leader was Arenia Mallory. See Butler, 109–116.

23. See Butler, 153.

24. Ibid., 130.

25. See Pleas, 18–22.

26. Qtd. in Butler, 131.

27. Qtd. in Butler, 130. Making a similar observation, another scholar calls Mason Temple "the largest black-built structure at the time." Maxwell, 25.

28. For the mistaken view that the sanctuary of Mason Temple was "cavernous," see Young, *Easy*, 450; Branch, *At Canaan's Edge*, 718; Green, 251; and Sides, 92. Carlsbad Caverns is cavernous. Mammoth Cave is cavernous. Mason Temple has never been cavernous. It has never been even close to cavernous. Even though the sanctuary now features a lower ceiling than it did in 1968—virtually the only physical change to the sanctuary between 1968 and 2006—the ceiling was never

high enough to create a "cavernous" effect because the roof is relatively low. Frank inaccurately describes the sanctuary as a "huge vaulted hall" (48); Posner erroneously calls the sanctuary a "grand, vaulted hall" (20). There was and is no vault anywhere in Mason Temple. Nor is there anything resembling a vault. Frank also wrongly refers to the sanctuary of Mason Temple as a "huge auditorium" (49). It is not and never was an auditorium. It is a sanctuary in a church. Sides incorrectly terms the same sanctuary "massive"; he also incorrectly locates it in downtown Memphis (92). It has never been massive and is now and has always been several miles from downtown Memphis. The usually reliable Young misremembers not only the size of the sanctuary at Mason Temple, but also its name. He calls it "Masonic Temple" (*Easy*, 450) even though the temple has never had anything to do with anything Masonic. Perhaps the relatively small size of other black churches in the South prompts writers to greatly exaggerate the size of Mason Temple.

29. For Robeson's concert, see Honey, *Going*, 19. A sign on the outside wall on the front of Mason Temple states that White and Evers spoke there. I assume that this information is accurate. Mason Temple would have been a rather obvious site for Evers to speak because of his well-known work as an NAACP organizer in Mississippi, particularly in Jackson and in the Mississippi Delta, which are fairly close to Memphis.

30. Mason's associate, Charles Pleas, identifies the architect as Elder W. H. Taylor (18–22). But the cornerstone of the Mason Temple identifies the architect only as H. Taylor. A permanent historical marker on an attached building identifies the elders of the church, including "Elder H. Taylor." Pleas, the cornerstone, and the historical marker almost certainly point toward the same person, but it is unclear whether his name was W. H. Taylor or H. Taylor.

31. The banner with the quotation from Zechariah hung above the pulpit where King spoke. The two other banners flanked that central banner.

32. The tomb is now at the far end of the vestibule, away from the front door. But, in 2006, church officials told me that the tomb had been moved fairly recently and that it had been close to the front doors when King gave his final speech. In 2011 Clyde Milton, who leads tours of Mason Temple, also indicated a spot right beside the front doors where, he stated, the tomb was located in April 1968. Those statements are consistent with Abernathy's experience of "shock" when he saw the tomb in the vestibule. He was shocked because the tomb was readily visible within the vestibule.

33. See Abernathy, 431.

34. Abernathy claims that King walked "down the aisle" of the sanctuary, which

indicates that he strode from the vestibule, past Mason's tomb, and through the middle aisle, in full view of the crowd (432).

35. Tinney, 240–241.
36. Ibid.
37. Ibid.
38. C. Sanders, 66.
39. These other church historians include Townsend-Gilkes, Daniels, and Courts.
40. Daniels, 184.
41. Ibid., 185–187.

Chapter 4

1. Sellers, 208.
2. Kerner Commission, 20.
3. Ibid., 3.
4. Lowell, 607.
5. Ibid.; Hersey, 90–91.
6. For the number of dead, see Hersey, 352. For his count of the deceased, Hersey cites a detailed investigation conducted by the *Detroit Free Press*. Branch accepts Hersey's number (*At Canaan's Edge*, 633). Kotz claims that thirty-seven people died (381).
7. Kerner Commission, 20, 22, 25, 27, 33, 40, 43, 51, 59.
8. Qtd. in Hersey, 90–91.
9. See Kotz, 381.
10. Breslin, 603.
11. I realize that many scholars think that the Exodus is not a historical event, but rather a fiction. King was taught this view in seminary. For the purpose of this speech, however, he constructs the Exodus both as a historical event and as an ongoing drama.
12. See Dudziak, 153.
13. LaCocque and Ricoeur, 8.
14. See Genesis 1:9–10.
15. See Exodus 14:21–30.
16. Fretheim, 12–14, 153, 159–169. See also Childs, *Book of Exodus*, 237–238.
17. Anderson, 185.
18. See Psalms 114:1–5 and (Second) Isaiah 51:9–10. In the late eighteenth century, scholars began to argue that Isaiah 1–39 was written during the eighth century

BCE, before the period of Hebrew captivity in Babylon, and that later portions of Isaiah were written roughly two hundred years later, during the period of captivity that began in 587 BCE. Critics therefore began to distinguish between First Isaiah, the author of chapters 1–39, and Second Isaiah, the author of the subsequent chapters. In the 1920s scholars began to decide that Isaiah 55–66 was probably written after the time of Second Isaiah and began to refer to the author(s) of these chapters as Third Isaiah. Although virtually all scholars now accept the divisions between (First) Isaiah, (Second) Isaiah, and (probably) (Third) Isaiah, distinguishing among these sections of Isaiah took centuries in part because biblical editors worked hard to connect the three segments of Isaiah thematically and (in some ways) lexically, combining the three texts into a single document that partly succeeded in fusing the texts produced by First Isaiah, Second Isaiah, and (probably) Third Isaiah. Because Isaiah both is and is not a unified text, I use the phrase "(First) Isaiah" to refer to Isaiah 1–39, the phrase "(Second) Isaiah" to refer to Isaiah 40–55, and the phrase "(Third) Isaiah" to refer to Isaiah 55–66.

19. It is not clear whether Second Isaiah read the text of what we now call Genesis 1:9–10 or heard it through an oral tradition. In either event, by the time that Second Isaiah encountered the creation narrative that surfaced in Genesis, that narrative was already a canonized portion of Hebrew religion.

20. Anderson, 185.

21. Fishbane, 356.

22. For a broader analysis of the relationship between Genesis and Exodus, see Zimmerli.

23. Gottwald, 195–196.

24. Brueggemann, *Prophetic*, 21–38, and "Trajectories," 313, 316.

25. See Exodus 12.

26. See Numbers 9:1–14; Deuteronomy 16:1–8; and Ezekiel 45:21–25.

27. J. Sanders, 4.

28. Ricoeur, 172.

29. See Matthew 26:1–29; Mark 14:1–25; Luke 22:15–20; John 13:1–30.

30. See Acts 7:17–50; Hebrews 11:23–31.

31. See I Corinthians 10:1–4; II Corinthians 3:7–18.

32. Hebrews 11:26.

33. Burke, *Rhetoric*, 19–23.

34. Margalit, 60.

35. Burke, *Attitudes*, 225–226.

36. See Joshua 4:22–23. The parallel is to Exodus 14:21.

37. See Psalms 114:1–8.

38. See (First) Isaiah 10:24–27, 11:11–16, 35:5–10; Micah 7:14–15; Hosea 2:16–17.
39. See Ezekiel 20.
40. See Zephaniah 3:20 and Ezra 1:5–6. Compare Exodus 12:35.
41. See Jeremiah 16:14–15, 23:7–8.
42. Anderson, 181.
43. Eichrodt, 234.
44. See Amos 9:7. See also I Samuel 4:7–8 and 6:6.
45. See (First) Isaiah 19.
46. Brueggemann, *Theology*, 177–178.
47. Fishbane, 543.
48. Brueggemann, *Theology*, 178.
49. Burke, *Rhetoric*, 23.
50. Fishbane, 360.
51. Burke, *Counter-Statement*, 31.
52. Ibid., 124.
53. Burke, *Kenneth Burke*, 161; Burke, *Language*, 390–391.
54. Burke, *Language*, 390–391.
55. For Malcolm X's important critique of King and other African American integrationists, see K. Miller, "Plymouth Rock."
56. Malcolm X, "God's Judgment," 126–132.

Chapter 5

1. Qtd. in Rieder, 149.
2. Gowan, 101.
3. Brueggemann, *Theology*, 636.
4. Ibid., 624.
5. Ibid., 623.
6. See, for example, Brueggemann, *Theology*, 629–630.
7. See Jeremiah 1:6 and (First) Isaiah 6:1–8.
8. See Judges 6:11–18.
9. See Jeremiah 5:30–31, 14:14–16, 23:31–40.
10. A. Heschel, x, 4, 5, 9.
11. See II Samuel 11 and 12.
12. For a similar passage, see (First) Isaiah 1:13–15
13. See Ezekiel 33:32–33; (Second) Isaiah 50:5–6; Jeremiah 26:7–8, 26:21–23, 43:1–7; Amos 7:12; and II Chronicles 24:20–32. The Bible offers two prophets named Zechariah and records that the first of these was murdered. See also Matthew 23:34–35.

14. Jeremiah 26:20–23.
15. See I Kings 19:10 and Nehemiah 9:26.
16. Hosea 9:7.
17. See Hosea 12:13.
18. See Numbers 12:6–8 and Deuteronomy 34:10.
19. See Numbers 9:1–14; Deuteronomy 16:1–8; Joshua 3:7, 4:22–23; I Samuel 4:1–8, 6:6; Ezra 1:4–6; Nehemiah 9:9–23; Psalms 18:15, 77:15–20, 74:13–14, 81:8–10, 96:6, 99:6, 106:9, 107:31–35, 114:3–4; (First) Isaiah 10:24–26, 11:15–16, 19:19–25, 30:7; (Second) Isaiah 40, 41, 42, 43, 48, 49, 51:9–10, 52; (Third) Isaiah 63, 64; Jeremiah 2:6–7, 7:22–25, 11:4–7, 16:14–15, 23:7–8, 31:32, 32:20–22, 34:13–14, 46:7–8; Ezekiel 20:5–10, 29:3–5, 32:2–8, 33, 36:22–32, 39:25–29, 45:21–25, Daniel 9:15; Hosea 2:14–17, 9:1–3, 11:1, 12:9, 13; 13:4–5; Amos 2:9–12, 3:1–2, 9:7; Micah 6:2–8, 7:14–15.
20. Gowan, 37.
21. J. Sanders, 78–79.
22. Von Rad, 217.
23. Sweeney, 86. Sweeney argues that Jeremiah parallels Jeremiah to Moses by portraying Jeremiah as one "who served as a prophet for a forty-year period; promulgated Mosaic Torah as the basis for the relationship between [God] and the people; suffered continuous abuse, isolation and rebellion in carrying out his prophetic role; and ultimately died outside the land of Israel" (86).
24. Brueggemann, *Theology*, 634; Brueggemann, "Trajectories," 313; Brueggemann, *Theology*, 635.
25. Fishbane, 543.
26. Amos 3:8.
27. Amos 5:24.
28. Aiming to speak for God, a seer avers: "From the day that your fathers came out of the land of Egypt to this day, I have persistently sent all my servants the prophets to them, day after day" (Jeremiah 7:25). See also Amos 2:11; Jeremiah 11:7; Zechariah 1:4, 7:7, 12, 8:9. Johannes Lindblom notes that the prophets who appear in the prophetic books "were only a small minority of the prophets who were active in Israel during the monarchy and the first centuries after the deportation"; he adds that "for several centuries very many prophets were active in Israel and played an important part in the national life" (202).
29. For an example of such a complaint, see Garrow, *Bearing*, 578.
30. See Green, 280.
31. Rev. Joseph Durick, one of the targets of King's criticism in "Letter from Birmingham Jail," became a liberal, activist clergy along the lines that King had urged. Having moved from Birmingham to Memphis, Durick supported the garbagework-

ers' strike. For an analysis of "Letter," Durick, and other moderate clergy in Birmingham, see Bass.

32. See Revelation 3:12, 21:02, 10.
33. One exception was *Time* magazine. See Lentz, 269–271.
34. Green, 254.
35. See Beifuss, 201–202.
36. Tri-State Bank succeeded largely because of vigorous support from African American organizations, both regional and national. T.R.M. Howard, a pioneering African American entrepreneur and political leader in the Mississippi Delta, served as vice president of Tri-State Bank in Memphis in 1948. Tri-State Bank also had a successful branch in Nashville that received funds from national African American organizations. See Beito and Beito, 63, 99–101.
37. One might be tempted to interpret King's economic emphasis here to the influence of Malcolm X. However, King had urged African Americans to patronize their own businesses, instead of those of the white power structure, during the Montgomery Bus Boycott. See Poston, 136–137.
38. See Pomerantz, 336–338; Roberts and Klibanoff, 381–382.
39. According to Lewis Baldwin, Ralph Abernathy recalled that King was capable of "whooping" (299).
40. Honey, *Going*, 421.
41. Qtd. in Beifuss, 278.
42. Qtd. in Beifuss, 279.
43. King discussed his need for an oratorical "landing strip" in a conversation with Wyatt Walker. See Lischer, 139.
44. See Abernathy, 433.
45. Qtd. in Beifuss, 280.
46. Rev. James Jordan makes this observation. See Beifuss, 280.
47. Qtd. in Frady, 226.
48. Qtd. in Beifuss, 279.
49. See Abernathy, 433.
50. The minister was James E. Smith. See J. Smith, 466.
51. Qtd. in Beifuss, 281.
52. This observer was a young girl named Barbara Brown. Qtd. in Honey, *Going*, 423.
53. For the crying, see Abernathy, 433. Middlebrook and Jordan also observed King's tears. See Honey, *Going*, 424.
54. See Ezekiel 1:1–14 and 10:1–2.
55. See Numbers 9:15–16.

56. See Exodus 13:21–22.
57. See Exodus 3.
58. Barton, 215.
59. Childs, *Introduction*, 50.

Chapter 6
1. Fishbane, 412.
2. Ricoeur, 161.
3. Acts 6:8–7:60.
4. Exodus 3:1–6.
5. Exodus 13:21.
6. Qtd. in Mason, 26, 30.
7. Powers, 788; see also C. Sanders, 64.
8. Luke is also the only gospel to record King's three other favorite parables—the Parable of the Prodigal Son, the Parable of Dives and Lazarus, and the Parable of the Rich Fool.
9. Luke 10:25–37. For the entire parable, see Appendix B.
10. See Fosdick, *Modern Use* and *Guide*.
11. See, for example, Smith and Zepp; Ansbro; Burrow; and Wills. This view also influences numerous biographies of King.
12. King provides another account of this experience in "Ultimate Doom."

Chapter 7
1. For an excellent account of this entire incident, see Pearson.
2. See Genesis 22:14; Exodus 3:1; Deuteronomy 11:29; Joshua 8:30; II Kings 4:25; (First) Isaiah 2:2, 8:18; Ezekiel 28:14.
3. See Psalms 68:16, 84:5; (First) Isaiah 4:05, 8:18, 18:07; Joel 3:17; and Micah 4:07.
4. See I Kings 16:29–18:46.
5. See Deuteronomy 34:1–8.
6. See Matthew 5:1–7:28.
7. See Mark 11:1 and Luke 19:29.
8. See Luke 24:50 and Acts 1:9–12.
9. See Mark 9:2–8.
10. See also King, "Birth."
11. C. King, 316.
12. Howe, 276.
13. See Hall, 69–70.

14. The King James Version translates the passage as "Thou [God] didst thresh the heathen in anger."
15. Compare Lamentations 1:15.
16. Psalms 144:5–6.
17. (Second) Isaiah 51:9; Daniel 11:33.
18. Ezekiel 21:15, 21:28.
19. For still further variations of this imagery, see Ezekiel 21:1–23.
20. See also Jeremiah 25:15–16.
21. See Numbers 10:9 and Zechariah 9:13–14. Also, II Chronicles 5:12–13 reports that Hebrew priests sounded trumpets.
22. See Joshua 6:1–20.
23. Many recent scholars think that Christians were subjected to scattered harassment and repression, but not intense persecution, during the time that John of Patmos was writing. In that case, he simply perceived that such persecution was occurring or feared that it was imminent.
24. Bauckham "Revelation," 1287.
25. King, "Three Dimensions," *Strength*, 82.
26. For these proposed numbers of allusions, see Fekkes, 61–62; and Beale, 77.
27. Fekkes, 61. Agreeing with Fekkes, David Aune observes that references to Hebrew scripture "permeate the composition of *Revelation*" (122).
28. Beale, 14. In 2001, Pilchan Lee produced yet another book on this topic. Before the 1980s, other scholars trained their attention on the same topic.
29. Bauckham, *Climax*, 176, 178.
30. See also Revelation 14:14–18. Fekkes observes that John of Patmos "has brought together" the two similar passages from Joel and (Third) Isaiah (195).
31. See also Revelation 19:21.
32. See Revelation 8 and 9.
33. See Exodus 25:17–22, 37:6; Leviticus 16:2.
34. Thompson, 84.
35. Ibid., 52.
36. Ibid., 84, 201.
37. Wilson, 94.
38. Grant, 139.
39. See Woodworth, 107–108.
40. Ecclesiastes is an exception to this generalization.
41. Qtd. in Fairclough, *Martin Luther King, Jr.*, 138.
42. Burke, *Counter-Statement*, 31.
43. Burke, *Language*, 390–391.

44. Levi-Strauss, 819.

45. Bakhtin, *Speech Genres*, 170.

46. For analysis of "I Have a Dream," see Hansen; Bobbitt; and Sundquist. For a very philosophical exploration of King's rhetoric, including "I Have a Dream," see Sunnemark.

47. See (Second) Isaiah 40:3–5; Matthew 3:1–12; Mark 1:1–8; Luke 3:1–20; John 1:6–15, 19–28. For a fuller discussion of this topic, see K. Miller, "Second Isaiah."

Chapter 8

1. Perrin, 21.

2. See King, "Ethics," "How," "Influence," Light," "Significant," "Study," and "What Experiences."

3. King, "How," 253. As Clayborne Carson and the other editors of the Martin Luther King Jr. Papers Project explain, King borrowed this passage from Millar Burrows.

4. King borrowed sermons from this book. See K. Miller, *Voice*.

5. Gadamer, 282.

6. Ibid., 292.

7. Ibid., 282.

8. Ibid., 296.

9. Harrisville and Sundberg, 272.

10. See Fosdick, "Crucified by Stupidity"; and King, "Love in Action." For an analysis of King's borrowing of this sermon and other sermons from Fosdick, see K. Miller, *Voice*.

11. See, for example, King, "Why" and "Three Dimensions," April 9, 1967.

12. See King, "How."

13. See Susannah Heschel, 173.

14. Qtd. in Rieder, 284.

15. For Loeb's Episcopalianism, see Honey, *Going*, 36.

16. Perhaps many of King's listeners agreed. When Jerry Wurf, a national union official, flew to Memphis to precede King in addressing the rally on March 18, 1968, the crowd in Mason Temple heartily welcomed his support. Honey explains listeners' response to Wurf: "The workers did not mind either his Jewishness or his New York accent" (*Going*, 291).

17. Carter, 149.

18. I thank J. Kameron Carter for a conversation about this point.

19. Barton, 262.

20. Ibid., 262.

21. Gilkey, 77.
22. King's most serious attempt at formal theology is his highly derivative, heavily plagiarized, abstruse dissertation that few people have read.
23. Garrow, *Bearing*, 56–58.
24. King, "Shattered Dreams," 95–96, 102.
25. Ibid., 102–104.
26. Galatians 6:17.
27. King, "Letter" (*Why We Can't Wait*), 88.
28. Ibid., 93.
29. King, "Our God Is Marching On."
30. King, "Letter" (*Why We Can't Wait*), 90.
31. Gadamer, 298.
32. Bakhtin, *Speech Genres*, 4.
33. Ibid., 5.
34. Bakhtin, *Problems*, 63.
35. Bakhtin, *Speech Genres*, 170.
36. Ibid., 170.
37. LaCocque and Ricoeur, xiii.
38. King, "Letter" (*Why We Can't Wait*), 77.
39. Even scholars mainly notice King's conclusion and often fail to discuss the rest of the speech. One notable exception is Honey.
40. King, *Stride*, 133.
41. For another occasion in which King publicly instructed his eulogist, see Garrow, *Bearing*, 555.
42. Qtd. in Burns, 425.
43. Not exactly a symbol, synecdoche is a specific figure of speech and argument. See Burke, *Grammar*.
44. Fairclough, *Martin Luther King, Jr.*, 28.

BIBLIOGRAPHY

Abernathy, Ralph. *And the Walls Came Tumbling Down.* New York: Harper, 1989.

Anderson, Bernhard. "Exodus Typology in Second Isaiah." In *Israel's Prophetic Heritage: Essays in Honor of James Muilenburg*, edited by Bernhard Anderson and Walter Harrelson, 177–195. New York: Harper, 1962.

Angelou, Maya. *I Know Why the Caged Bird Sings.* New York: Random House, 1970.

Ansbro, John. *Martin Luther King, Jr.: The Making of a Mind.* Maryknoll, NY: Orbis, 1982.

Aune, David. *Apocalypticism, Prophecy, and Magic in Early Christianity.* Tubingen, Germany: Mohr Siebeck, 2001.

Baird, Woody. "Marches in Memphis Mark Anniversary of King's Death." *Las Vegas Review-Journal* 5 (April 2008): 1A and 4A.

Bakhtin, Mikhail. *Problems of Dostoevsky's Poetics.* Edited by Caryl Emerson. Translated by Caryl Emerson. Minneapolis: University of Minnesota Press, 1984.

———. *Speech Genres and Other Late Essays.* Edited by Caryl Emerson and Michael Holquist. Translated by Vern McGeen. Austin: University of Texas Press, 1986.

Baldwin, James. *The Fire Next Time.* New York: Dial, 1963.

Baldwin, Lewis. *There Is a Balm in Gilead: The Cultural Roots of Martin Luther King, Jr.* Minneapolis: Augsburg Fortress, 1991.

Barr, James. *Old and New in Interpretation: A Study of the Two Testaments.* New York: Harper, 1966.

Barton, John. *Oracles of God.* London: Darton, 1986.

Bass, S. Jonathan. *Blessed Are the Peacemakers: Martin Luther King, Jr., Eight White Religious Leaders, and the "Letter from Birmingham Jail."* Baton Rouge: Louisiana State University Press, 2001.

Bauckham, Richard. *The Climax of Prophecy: Studies in the Book of Revelation.* New York: Clark, 1998.

———. "Revelation." In *Oxford Bible Commentary*, edited by John Barton and John Muddiman, 1287–1306. New York: Oxford University Press, 2001.

Beale, G. K. *The Book of Revelation.* Grand Rapids, MI: Eerdmans, 1998.

Beifuss, Joan. *At the River I Stand: Memphis, the 1968 Strike, and Martin Luther King.* Memphis: B & W Books, 1985.

Beito, David, and Linda Royster Beito. *Black Maverick: T.R.M. Howard's Fight for Civil Rights and Economic Power.* Urbana: University of Illinois Press, 2009.

Bello, Marisol. "Picking Up Where MLK Left Off in Memphis." *USA Today,* April 3, 2008, 3A.

Berlin, Ira. *Generations of Captivity: A History of African-American Slaves.* Cambridge, MA: Harvard University Press, 2003.

Bobbitt, David. *The Rhetoric of Redemption: Kenneth Burke's Redemption Drama and Martin Luther King, Jr.'s "I Have a Dream" Speech.* New York: Rowman and Littlefield, 2004.

Borders, William Holmes. "'Thy Word Is as a Fire Shut Up in My Bones'—Are the Words of Jerimiah [sic]." In *Seven Minutes at the "Mike" in the Deep South,* 41–44. 1943. Reprint, Atlanta: Logan, 1980.

Branch, Taylor. *At Canaan's Edge: America in the King Years, 1965–1968.* New York: Simon and Schuster, 2007.

——. *Parting the Waters: America in the King Years, 1954–1963.* New York: Simon and Schuster, 1988.

Breslin, Jimmy. "Breslin on Riot: Death, Laughter, but No Sanity." *Detroit News,* July 25, 1967. Reprinted in *Reporting Civil Rights: Part II,* 602–606.

Brooks, Phillips. "Egyptians Dead upon the Seashore." In *Selected Sermons,* edited by William Scarlett, 105–111. New York: Dutton, 1950.

Brown, Charles Reynolds. *Two Parables.* 1898. Reprint, np: General Books, 2010.

Bruce, A. B. *The Parabolic Teaching of Christ.* London: Hodder and Stoughton, 1882.

Brueggemann, Walter. *The Prophetic Imagination.* Minneapolis: Augsburg Fortress, 2001.

——. *Theology of the Old Testament: Testimony, Dispute, Advocacy.* Minneapolis: Augsburg Fortress, 1997.

——. "Trajectories of Old Testament Literature and the Sociology of Ancient Israel." In *The Bible and Liberation,* edited by Norman Gottwald, 307–333. Maryknoll, NY: Orbis, 1983.

Buber, Martin. *I and Thou.* Translated by Ronald Gregor Smith. New York: Scribner's, 1958.

Burke, Kenneth. *Attitudes toward History.* 1937. Reprint, Berkeley: University of California Press, 1984.

——. *Counter-Statement.* 1931. Reprint, Berkeley: University of California Press, 1968.

——. *A Grammar of Motives.* 1945. Reprint, Berkeley: University of California Press, 1969.

———. *Kenneth Burke on Shakespeare*. Edited by Scott Newstock. West Lafayette, IN: Parlor Press, 2007.

———. *Language as Symbolic Action*. Berkeley: University of California Press, 1966.

———. *Rhetoric of Motives*. 1950. Reprint, Berkeley: University of California Press, 1969.

Burns, Stewart. *To the Mountaintop: Martin Luther King Jr.'s Sacred Mission to Save America, 1955–1968*. New York: Harper San Francisco, 2004.

Burrow, Rufus. *God and Human Dignity: The Personalism, Theology, and Ethics of Martin Luther King, Jr.* Notre Dame, IN: University of Notre Dame Press, 2006.

Butler, Anthea. *Women in the Church of God in Christ: Making a Sanctified World*. Chapel Hill: University of North Carolina Press, 2007.

Buttrick, George, ed. *Interpreter's Bible*. Vols. 1–12. New York: Abingdon-Cokesbury, 1952.

———. "Life—and 'Much Goods': The Parable of the Rich Fool." In his *The Parables of Jesus*, 126–135.

———. *The Parables of Jesus*. New York: Harper, 1928.

———. "The Springs of Sympathy: The Parable of the Rich Man and the Beggar [Dives and Lazarus]." In his *The Parables of Jesus*, 136–146.

———. "True Neighborliness: The Parable of the Good Samaritan." In his *The Parables of Jesus*, 148–156.

Campbell, Will. "Witnessing When Cultural Landmarks Are Down." In Houck and Dixon, *Rhetoric, Religion, and the Civil Rights Movement*, 386–397.

Carey, Archibald. "Address to the Republican National Convention." In *Rhetoric of Racial Revolt*, edited by Roy Hill, 149–154. Denver: Golden Bell, 1964.

Carson, Clayborne, Ralph E. Luker, and Penny Russell. Introduction in King, *The Papers of Martin Luther King, Jr.*, vol. 1, 1–57.

———. "King's Personal Library: Selected Works." In King, *The Papers of Martin Luther King, Jr.*, vol. 6, 629–655.

Carter, J. Kameron. *Race: A Theological Account*. New York: Oxford University Press, 2008.

Chappell, David. *A Stone of Hope: Prophetic Religion and the Death of Jim Crow*. Chapel Hill: University of North Carolina Press, 2004.

Childs, Brevard. *The Book of Exodus*. Philadelphia: Westminster, 1974.

———. *Introduction to the Old Testament as Scripture*. Philadelphia: Fortress, 1979.

Claassens, Julia. "Biblical Theology as Dialogue: Continuing the Conversation on Mikhail Bakhtin and Biblical Theology." *Journal of Biblical Literature* 122 (2003): 127–144.

Clemmons, Ithiel. *Bishop C. H. Mason and the Roots of the Church of God in Christ.* Bakersfield, CA: Pneuma Life, 1996.
Cone, James. *Martin and Malcolm and America.* Maryknoll, NY: Orbis, 1992.
Corder, Jim. "Varieties of Ethical Argument, with Some Account of the Significance of *Ethos* in the Teaching of Composition." In *Selected Essays of Jim W. Corder*, edited by James S. Baumlin and Keith D. Miller, 60–101. Urbana, IL: National Council of Teachers of English, 2004.
Courts, James. *The History and Lifework of Elder C. H. Mason, Chief Apostles, and His Co-Laborers.* N.p., 1920.
Cox, Harvey. *Fire from Heaven: The Rise of Pentecostal Spirituality and Reshaping of Religion in the Twenty-First Century.* New York: DaCapo, 2001.
Daniels, David. "The Cultural Renewal of Slave Religion: Charles Price Jones and the Emergence of the Holiness Movement in Mississippi." PhD diss., Union Theological Seminary, 1992.
Dennis, Dave. "A Modern Day Moses." In Houck and Dixon, *Rhetoric, Religion, and the Civil Rights Movement*, 634–637.
Dodd, C. H. *The Parables of the Kingdom.* London: Nisbet, 1935.
Dods, Marcus. *The Parables of Our Lord.* London: Hodder and Stoughton, 1905.
Dudziak, Mary. *Cold War Civil Rights: Race and the Image of American Democracy.* Princeton, NJ: Princeton University Press, 2002.
Eichrodt, Walther. "Is Typological Exegesis an Appropriate Method?" Translated by James Barr. In Westerman, *Essays on Old Testament Hermeneutics*, 224–245.
Ericksen, Robert, and Susannah Heschel. *Betrayal: German Churches and the Holocaust.* Minneapolis: Augsburg Fortress, 1999.
Fager, Charles. *Selma 1965.* New York: Scribner's, 1974.
Fairclough, Adam. *Martin Luther King, Jr.* 2nd ed. Athens: University of Georgia Press, 1995.
———. *To Redeem the Soul of America: The Southern Christian Leadership Conference and Martin Luther King, Jr.* Athens: University of Georgia Press, 1987.
Fekkes, Jan. *Isaiah and Prophetic Traditions in the Book of Revelation.* Sheffield, UK: Sheffield Academic Press, 1994.
Fishbane, Michael. *Biblical Interpretation in Ancient Israel.* New York: Oxford University Press, 1985.
Foner, Philip, and Robert Branham, eds. *Lift Every Voice: African American Oratory, 1787–1900.* Tuscaloosa: University of Alabama Press, 1998.
Fosdick, Harry Emerson. "The Cross and the Ordinary Man." In his *Successful Christian Living*, 200–219. New York: Harper, 1937.

———. "Crucified by Stupidity. In his *Hope of the World*, 222–230. New York: Harper, 1933.

———. *A Guide to Understanding the Bible.* London: Harper, 1938.

———. *The Modern Use of the Bible.* London: Student Christian Movement, 1926.

Frady, Marshall. *Jesse: The Life and Pilgrimage of Jesse Jackson.* New York: Random House, 1996.

Frank, Gerold. *An American Death.* Garden City, NJ: Doubleday, 1972.

Franklin, C. L. "Moses at the Red Sea." In *Give Me This Mountain*, edited by Jeff Todd Titon, 107–113. Urbana: University of Illinois Press, 1989.

Fretheim, Terence. *Exodus: A Bible Commentary for Teaching and Preaching.* Louisville: John Knox Press, 1991.

Gadamer, Hans George. *Truth and Method.* 1969. Reprint, New York: Continuum, 2005.

Garrow, David. *Bearing the Cross: Martin Luther King, Jr., and the Southern Christian Leadership Conference.* New York: Morrow, 1986.

———. "Measuring His Words." *Los Angeles Times*, April 6, 2008, R3. www.davidgarrow.com.

———. *Protest at Selma.* New Haven: Yale University Press, 1978.

Genovese, Eugene. *Roll, Jordan, Roll: The World the Slaves Made.* New York: Vintage, 1976.

Gilkey, Langdon. *On Niebuhr: A Theological Study.* Chicago: University of Chicago Press, 2001.

Gottwald, Norman. *Hebrew Bible: A Socio-Literary Introduction.* Philadelphia: Fortress, 1985.

Gowan, Donald. *Theology of the Prophetic Books.* Louisville: Westminster John Knox, 1998.

Grant, Mary. *Private Woman, Public Person: An Account of the Life of Julia Ward Howe from 1819 to 1868.* Brooklyn, NY: Carlson, 1994.

Green, Laurie. *Battling the Plantation Mentality: Memphis and the Black Freedom Struggle.* Chapel Hill: University of North Carolina Press, 2007.

Hall, Florence Howe. *The Story of the Battle Hymn of the Republic.* 1916. Reprint, Freeport, NY: Books for Libraries, 1971.

Hamilton, J. Wallace. "Drum-Major Instincts." In his *Ride the Wild Horses!*, 26–38. Westwood, NJ: Revell, 1952.

———. *Horns and Halos in Human Nature.* Westwood, NJ: Revell, 1954.

Hansen, Drew. *The Dream: Martin Luther King, Jr. and the Speech that Inspired a Nation.* New York: Ecco, 2003.

Harrisville, Roy, and Walter Sundberg. *The Bible in Modern Culture: Baruch Spinoza to Brevard Childs*. Grand Rapids, MI: Eerdmans, 2002.

Hersey, John. *The Algiers Motel Incident*. New York: Knopf, 1968.

Heschel, Abraham. *The Prophets: An Introduction*. New York: Harper, 1962.

Heschel, Susannah. "Theological Affinities in the Writings of Abraham Joshua Heschel and Martin Luther King, Jr." In *Black Zion: African American Religious Encounters with Judaism*, edited by Yvonne Chireau and Nathaniel Deutsch, 168–186. New York: Oxford University Press, 2000.

Honey, Michael, ed. *Black Workers Remember: An Oral History of Segregation, Unionism, and the Freedom Struggle*. Berkeley: University of California Press, 1999.

——— . *Going Down Jericho Road: The Memphis Strike, Martin Luther King's Last Campaign*. New York: Norton, 2007.

Houck, Davis, and David Dixon, eds. *Rhetoric, Religion, and the Civil Rights Movement*. Waco, TX: Baylor University Press, 2006.

Howard-Pitney, David. *The Afro-American Jeremiad*. Philadelphia: Temple University Press, 1990.

Howe, Julia Ward. *Reminiscences, 1819–1899*. Boston: Houghton, 1900.

Hubbard, George. *The Teaching of Jesus in Parables*. Boston: Pilgrim, 1907.

Jackson, Thomas. *From Civil Rights to Human Rights: Martin Luther King, Jr., and the Struggle for Economic Justice*. Philadelphia: University of Pennsylvania Press, 2007.

Jackson, Troy. *Becoming King: Martin Luther King Jr. and the Making of a National Leader*. Lexington: University of Kentucky, 2008.

Jeremias, Joachim. *The Parables of Jesus*. New York: Scribner's, 1954.

Kerner Commission. *Report on the National Advisory Commission on Civil Disorders*. New York: Bantam, 1968.

King, Coretta. *My Life with Martin Luther King, Jr.* New York: Holt, 1969.

King, Ed. "Address at the Funeral Service for James Chaney." In Houck and Dixon, *Rhetoric, Religion, and the Civil Rights Movement*, 778–784.

King, Martin Luther, Jr. "Address to MIA Mass Meeting at Holt Street Baptist Church." In *The Papers of Martin Luther King, Jr.*, vol. 3, 199–201.

——— . *The Autobiography of Martin Luther King, Jr.* Edited by Clayborne Carson. New York: Warner, 1998.

——— . "Beyond Vietnam." In his *A Call to Conscience*, 133–164.

——— . "The Birth of a New Nation." In his *A Call to Conscience*, 13–42.

——— . *A Call to Conscience: The Landmark Speeches of Martin Luther King, Jr.* Edited by Clayborne Carson and Kris Shepard. New York: Warner, 2001.

———"A Comparison of the Conceptions of God in the Thinking of Paul Tillich and Henry Nelson Wieman." PhD diss., Boston University, 1955. Reprinted in *The Papers of Martin Luther King, Jr.*, vol. 2, 339–544.

———"Death of Evil on the Seashore." In his *Strength to Love*, 71–81.

———"The Dignity of Labor." Reprinted (in part) in *The Autobiography of Martin Luther King, Jr.*, 353–355.

———"Drum Major Instinct." In his *Testament of Hope*, 259–267. Reprinted in his *A Knock at Midnight*, 169–186.

———"The Ethics of Late Judaism as Evidenced in the Testament of the Twelve Patriarchs." In *The Papers of Martin Luther King, Jr.*, vol. 1, 195–209.

———"How Should a Christian View Communism?" In his *Strength to Love*, 96–105.

———"How to Use the Bible in Modern Theological Construction." In *The Papers of Martin Luther King, Jr.*, vol. 1, 251–256.

———"I Have a Dream." In his *A Call to Conscience*, 75–88.

———"The Impassable Gulf (The Parable of Dives and Lazarus)." In *The Papers of Martin Luther King, Jr.*, vol. 6, 235–239.

———"The Influence of Mystery Religions on Christianity." In *The Papers of Martin Luther King, Jr.*, vol. 1, 294–313.

———*A Knock at Midnight*. Edited by Clayborne Carson and Peter Holloran. New York: Time-Warner, 1998.

———"Letter from Birmingham Jail." *Christian Century* 80 (1963): 767–773.

———"Letter from Birmingham Jail." In his *Why We Can't Wait*, 76–95. New York: Harper, 1963.

———"Light on the Old Testament from the Ancient Near East." In *The Papers of Martin Luther King, Jr.*, vol. 1, 162–180.

———"Love in Action." In his *Strength to Love*, 25–33.

———"The Man Who Was a Fool." In his *Strength to Love*, 62–70.

———"The Negro and the Constitution." In *The Papers of Martin Luther King, Jr.*, vol. 1, 108–111.

———"On Being a Good Neighbor." In his *Strength to Love*, 20–29.

———"Our God Is Marching On." In his *A Call to Conscience*, 111–132.

———*The Papers of Martin Luther King, Jr.: Called to Serve*. Vol. 1. Edited by Clayborne Carson, Ralph E. Luker, and Penny Russell. Berkeley: University of California Press, 1992.

———*The Papers of Martin Luther King, Jr.: Rediscovering Precious Values*. Vol. 2. Edited by Clayborne Carson, Ralph E. Luker, Penny Russell, and Peter Holloran. Berkeley: University of California Press, 1994.

———. *The Papers of Martin Luther King, Jr.: Birth of a New Age*. Vol. 3. Edited by Clayborne Carson, Stewart Burns, Susan Carson, Peter Holloran, and Dana Powell. Berkeley: University of California Press, 1997.

———. *The Papers of Martin Luther King, Jr.: Advocate of the Social Gospel*. Vol. 6. Edited by Clayborne Carson, Susan Carson, Susan Englander, Troy Jackson, and Gerald Smith. Berkeley: University of California Press, 2007.

———. "Shattered Dreams." In his *Strength to Love*, 95–105.

———. "The Significant Contributions of Jeremiah to Religious Thought." In *The Papers of Martin Luther King, Jr.*, vol. 1, 181–195.

———. "Sleeping through a Revolution." Washington, DC, March 31, 1968. King Archives. Atlanta, GA.

———. *Strength to Love*. 1963. Reprint, New York: Pocket Books, 1968.

———. *Stride toward Freedom*. New York: Harper, 1958.

———. "A Study of Mithraism." In *The Papers of Martin Luther King, Jr.*, vol. 1, 211–225.

———. "Suffering and Faith." In his *Testament of Hope*, 41–42.

———. *Testament of Hope*. Edited by James Melvin Washington. New York: Harper, 1986.

———. "Three Dimensions of a Complete Life." In his *Strength to Love*, 82–94.

———. "Three Dimensions of a Complete Life." April 9, 1967, Chicago. King Archives. Atlanta, GA.

———. "The Ultimate Doom of Evil." *King Came Preaching: The Pulpit Power of Dr. Martin Luther King, Jr.* Edited by Mervyn Warren, 182–190. Downers Grove, IL: InterVarsity.

———. "What Experiences of Christians Living in the Early Christian Century Led to the Christian Doctrines of the Divine Sonship of Jesus, the Virgin Birth, and the Bodily Resurrection." In *The Papers of Martin Luther King, Jr.*, vol. 1, 225–230.

———. "Where Do We Go from Here?" In his *A Call to Conscience*, 165–199.

———. "Why Jesus Called a Man a Fool." In his *A Knock at Midnight*, 145–164.

King, Martin Luther, Sr. *Daddy King: An Autobiography*. With Clayton Riley. New York: Morrow, 1980.

———. "Moderator's Annual Address, Atlanta Missionary Baptist Association." 1940. Reprinted in *The Papers of Martin Luther King, Jr.*, vol. 1, 34.

Kotz, Nick. *Judgment Days: Lyndon Baines Johnson, Martin Luther King, Jr., and the Laws that Changed America*. New York: Houghton Mifflin, 2005.

LaCocque, Andre, and Paul Ricoeur. *Thinking Biblically: Exegetical and Hermeneutical Studies*. Translated by David Pellauer. Chicago: University of Chicago Press, 1998.

Lee, Pilchan. *The New Jerusalem in the Book of Revelation*. Tubingen, Germany: Mohr Siebeck, 2001.

Lentz, Richard. *Symbols, the News Magazines, and Martin Luther King*. Baton Rouge: Louisiana State University Press, 1990.

Levi-Strauss, Claude. "The Structural Study of Myth." In *Contemporary Literary Criticism*, edited by Robert Con Davis, 307–322. New York: Longman, 1986.

Lindblom, Johannes. *Prophecy in Ancient Israel*. Philadelphia: Fortress, 1962.

Ling, Peter. *Martin Luther King, Jr.* London: Routledge, 2002.

Lischer, Richard. *The Preacher King: Martin Luther King, Jr., and the Word that Moved America*. New York: Oxford University Press, 1997.

Lomax, Louis. *The Negro Revolt*. New York: Harper, 1962.

Lowell, Jon. "Guerilla War Rips 12th." *Detroit News*, July 26, 1967. Reprinted in *Reporting Civil Rights: Part II*, 607–610.

Luccock, Halford. *In the Minister's Workshop*. New York: Abingdon, 1944.

———. "Sleeping through a Revolution." In his *Marching off the Map*, 129–137. New York: Harper, 1952.

———. *Studies in the Parables of Jesus*. New York: Methodist Book Concern, 1917.

Manis, Andrew. *A Fire You Can't Put Out: The Civil Rights Life of Birmingham's Reverend Fred Shuttlesworth*. Tuscaloosa: University of Alabama Press, 1999.

Margalit, Avishai. *The Ethics of Memory*. Cambridge: Harvard University Press, 2002.

Marsh, Charles. *The Beloved Community: How Faith Shapes Social Justice, from the Civil Rights Movement to Today*. New York: Basic, 2005.

———. *God's Long Summer*. Princeton, NJ: Princeton University Press, 1999.

Mason, Mary. *The History and Life Work of Elder C. H. Mason: Chief Apostle and His Co-Laborers*. 1924. N.p., 1987.

Mays, Benjamin. *Born to Rebel*. New York: Scribner's, 1971.

———. *Lord, the People Have Driven Me On*. New York: Vantage, 1981.

———. *Seeking to Be Christian in Race Relations*. New York: Friendship Press, 1957.

———. "The Vocation of a Christian—In, but Not of, the World." In *Dr. Benjamin E. Mays Speaks: Representative Speeches of a Great American Orator*, edited by Freddie Colston, 229–233. Lanham, MD: University Press of America.

Maxwell, Joe. "Building the Church (of God in Christ)." *Christianity Today* 40 (April 8, 1996): 22–28.

McCracken, Robert. *Questions People Ask*. New York: Harper, 1951.

McKnight, Gerald. *The Last Crusade: Martin Luther King, Jr., the FBI, and the Poor People's Campaign*. Boulder, CO: Westview, 1998.

Miller, Keith D. "Beacon Light and Penumbra: African American Gospel Lyrics and

Martin Luther King, Jr.'s 'I Have a Dream.'" In *The Role of Ideas in the Civil Rights South*, edited by Ted Ownby, 55–67. Jackson: University Press of Mississippi.

———. "'Plymouth Rock Landed on Us': Malcolm X's Whiteness Theory as a Basis for Alternative Literacy." *College Composition and Communication* 56, no. 2 (2004): 199–222.

———. "Second Isaiah Lands in Washington, D.C.: Martin Luther King, Jr.'s 'I Have a Dream' as Biblical Narrative and Biblical Hermeneutic." *Rhetoric Review* 26 (2007): 405–424.

———. *Voice of Deliverance: The Language of Martin Luther King, Jr., and Its Sources.* 2nd ed. Athens: University of Georgia Press, 1998.

———. "Voice Merging and Self-Making: The Epistemology of 'I Have a Dream.'" *Rhetoric Society Quarterly* 19 (1989): 23–32.

Miller, Keith D., and Emily Lewis. "Touchstones, Authorities, and Marian Anderson: The Making of 'I Have a Dream.'" In *The Making of Martin Luther King, Jr., and the Civil Rights Movement*, edited by Brian Ward and Tony Badger, 147–161. London: MacMillan, 1996.

Miller, Robert. *Harry Emerson Fosdick: Preacher, Pastor, Prophet.* New York: Oxford, 1985.

Morris, Aldon. *Origins of the Civil Rights Movement.* New York: Free Press, 1984.

Murray, George. *Jesus and the Parables.* Edinburgh: Clark, 1914.

Myrdal, Gunnar. *An American Dilemma.* New York: Harper, 1944.

Olsen, Ted. "American Pentecost: The Story behind the Azusa Street Revival, the Most Phenomenal Event of Twentieth-Century Christianity." *Christian History* 17 (May 1998): 10–17.

Osborne, Michael. "The Last Mountaintop of Martin Luther King, Jr." In *Martin Luther King, Jr., and the Sermonic Power of Public Discourse*, edited by Carolyn Calloway-Thomas and John Lucaites, 147–161. Tuscaloosa: University of Alabama Press, 1993.

Owens, Robert. "The Azusa Street Revival: The Pentecostal Movement Begins in America." In *Century of the Holy Spirit: 100 Years of Pentecostal and Charismatic Renewal, 1901–2001*, edited by Vinson Synan. Nashville: Nelson, 2001.

Pearson, Hugh. *When Harlem Nearly Killed King.* New York: Seven Stories Press, 2002.

Perrin, Norman. *The New Testament: An Introduction.* New York: Harcourt, 1974.

Pleas, Charles. *A Period in History of the Church of God in Christ: 50 Years Achievement, 1906–1956.* Memphis: Public Relations for Church of God in Christ, n.d.

Polsgrove, Carol. *Divided Minds: Intellectuals and the Civil Rights Movement.* New York: Norton, 2001.

Pomerantz, Gary. *Where Peachtree Meets Sweet Auburn*. New York: Penguin, 1997.
Posner, Gerald. *Killing the Dream: James Earl Ray and the Assassination of Martin Luther King, Jr.* New York: Harcourt Brace, 1998.
Poston, Ted. *A First Draft of History*. Edited by Kathleen Hauke. Athens: University of Georgia Press, 2000.
Powers, Peter Kerry. "The Treacherous Body: Isolation, Confession, and Community in James Baldwin." *American Literature* 77 (December 2005): 787–814.
Raboteau, Albert. *A Fire in the Bones: Reflections on African-American Religious History*. Boston: Beacon, 1995.
Reporting Civil Rights: Part II. New York: Library of America, 2003.
Ricoeur, Paul. *Figuring the Sacred: Religion, Narrative, and Imagination*. Translated by David Pellauer. Minneapolis: Augsburg Fortress, 1995.
Rieder, Jonathan. *The Word of the Lord Is upon Me: The Righteous Performance of Martin Luther King, Jr.* Cambridge, MA: Harvard University Press, 2008.
Roberts, Gene, and Hank Klibanoff. *The Race Beat: The Press, the Civil Rights Struggle, and the Awakening of a Nation*. New York: Knopf, 2006.
Robinson, James. "James Robinson Describes the Worst Job He Ever Had." In Honey, *Black Workers Remember*, 302–309.
Rogers, Taylor. "Taylor Rogers Relives the Memphis Sanitation Strike." In Honey, *Black Workers Remember*, 293–302.
Sanders, Cheryl. *Saints in Exile: The Holiness-Pentecostal Experience in African American Religion and Culture*. New York: Oxford University Press, 1999.
Sanders, James. *Torah and Canon*. Philadelphia: Fortress, 1972.
Selby, Gary. *Martin Luther King and the Rhetoric of Freedom: The Exodus Narrative in America's Struggle for Civil Rights*. Waco, TX: Baylor University Press, 2008.
Sellers, Cleveland. *The River of No Return: The Autobiography of a Black Militant and the Life and Death of SNCC*. With Robert Terrell. New York: Morrow, 1973.
Shuttlesworth, Fred. "Address at Medgar Evers Memorial Service." In Houck and Dixon, *Rhetoric, Religion, and the Civil Rights Movement*, 766–768.
——. "Call for Reason." In Houck and Dixon, *Rhetoric, Religion, and the Civil Rights Movement*, 464–468.
——. "Fred Shuttlesworth." In *My Soul Is Rested: Movement Days in the Deep South Remembered*, edited by Howell Raines, 136–143. New York: Putnam's, 1977.
Sides, Hampton. *Hellhound on His Trail: The Stalking of Martin Luther King, Jr., and the International Hunt for His Assassin*. New York: Doubleday, 2010.
Smith, James. "James E. Smith." In *Voices of Freedom: An Oral History of the Civil Rights Movement from the 1950s through the 1980s*, edited by Henry Hampton and Steve Fayer, 466. New York: Bantam, 1990.

Smith, Kenneth, and Ira Zepp. *Search for the Beloved Community*. Valley Forge: Judson, 1974.

Spike, Robert. "Division of Home Missions." In Houck and Dixon, *Rhetoric, Religion, and the Civil Rights Movement*, 667–676.

Sundquist, Eric. *King's Dream*. New Haven, CT: Yale University Press, 2009.

Sunnemark, Frederick. *Ring Out Freedom! The Voice of Martin Luther King, Jr., and the Making of the Civil Rights Movement*. Bloomington, IN: Indiana University Press, 2003.

Sweeney, Marvin. "Latter Prophets." In *Hebrew Bible Today*, edited by Steven McKenzie and Patrick Graham, 69–94. Louisville: Westminster John Knox Press, 1998.

Thompson, Leonard. *The Book of Revelation*. New York: Oxford University Press, 1990.

Tinney, James. "A Theoretical and Historical Comparison of Black Political and Religious Movements." PhD diss., Howard University, 1978.

Townsend-Gilkes, Cheryl. "Together and in Harness: Women's Traditions in the Sanctified Church." *Signs* 10 (Summer 1985): 679–680.

Trench, Robert. *Notes on the Parables of Our Lord*. 1841. Reprint, New York: Appleton, 1861.

Vander Lei, Elizabeth, and Keith D. Miller. "Martin Luther King, Jr.'s 'I Have a Dream' in Context: Ceremonial Protest and African American Jeremiad." *College English* 62, no. 1 (1999): 83–99.

Von Rad, Gerhard. "Typological Interpretation of the Old Testament." In Westermann, *Essays on Old Testament Hermeneutics*, 17–39.

Watters, Pat. *Down to Now: Reflections on the Southern Civil Rights Movement*. New York: Random House, 1971.

Westermann, Claus, ed. *Essays on Old Testament Hermeneutics*. New York: John Knox, 1979.

White, Calvin. "In the Beginning, There Stood Two: Arkansas Roots of the Black Holiness Movement." *Arkansas Historical Quarterly* 68 (March 1, 2009): 1–22.

Wills, Richard Wayne. *Martin Luther King, Jr., and the Image of God*. New York: Oxford University Press, 2009.

Wilson, Edmund. *Patriotic Gore: Studies in the Literature of the American Civil War*. New York: Oxford University Press, 1962.

Woodworth, Steven. *While God Is Marching On: The Religious World of Civil War Soldiers*. Lawrence: University of Kansas Press, 2001.

X, Malcolm. *The End of White World Supremacy: Four Speeches*. Edited by Benjamin Goodman. New York: Merlin House, 1971.

———. "God's Judgment of White America (the Chickens Are Coming Home to Roost)." In his *The End of White World Supremacy,* 121–148.

Young, Andrew. *An Easy Burden: The Civil Rights Movement and the Transformation of America.* New York: Harpercollins, 1996.

———. "Introduction to 'I've Been to the Mountaintop.'" In King, *A Call to Conscience,* 201–205.

Zimmerli, Walter. "Promise and Fulfillment." Translated by James Wharton. In Westermann, *Essays on Old Testament Hermeneutics,* 89–122.

INDEX

Abernathy, Ralph, 3, 4, 9, 11–13, 23, 36, 50, 62, 63, 69, 74, 102, 104, 108, 206n33, 208n35, 212n32, 212–13n34, 217n39
Abolitionists, 28, 31, 49, 76, 145
African American biblical interpretation, 28–37
African American churches, 28
African American jeremiad, 25, 28, 38–39
African American Pentecostalism. *See* Pentecostalism
African American slave religion, 30
American Federation of State, County, and Municipal Workers (ASFSCME), 4, 5, 6
Angelou, Maya, 45
Anti-Semitism, 163
Atlanta, Georgia, 15, 27, 28, 77, 98, 101, 104, 152
Atlantic Monthly, 138
At the River I Stand, 206n33
Aune, David, 219n27
Azusa Street Revival. *See* Pentecostalism

Baker, Ella, 17, 33
Bakhtin, Mikhail, 24, 25, 154, 168–70
Baldwin, James, 33
Baldwin, Lewis, 217n39
Barr, James, 36, 37, 121
Barton, John, 111, 163–64

Bates, Daisy, 8, 17
"Battle Hymn of the Republic." *See* Howe, Julia Ward
Bauckham, Richard, 142–43
Beale, G. K., 143
Beifuss, Joan, 3, 204n27
Bethune, Mary McLeod, 6
Bevel, James, 4, 32, 33, 167
"Beyond Vietnam." *See* King, Martin Luther, Jr.: orations
Bible, 15–26
Biblical authors: (First) Isaiah, 169–70, 213–14n18; (Second) Isaiah, 44, 169–70, 213–14n18, 214n19; (Third) Isaiah, 169–70, 213–14n18; John of Patmos, 144–46, 219n23, 219n30; Paul, 84, 166, 168
Biblical books: Acts, 31, 65, 83, 84, 115, 116, 134; Amos, 16, 20, 23, 40, 41, 43, 44, 49, 61, 83, 90, 91, 93, 94, 96, 100, 101, 105, 106, 112, 113, 162; I Corinthians, 16, 83, 84; II Corinthians, 83, 84, 144; Daniel, 83, 208n15; Deuteronomy, 20, 83, 96, 106, 133–34; Ecclesiastes, 219n40; Exodus, 16, 26, 49, 86, 101, 110, 133, 142, 144, 151; Ezekiel, 20, 83, 86, 93, 94, 96, 109, 135, 141, 162; Ezra, 83; Galatians, 16, 166; Genesis, 78–79, 81, 133, 214n19; Habakkuk, 139; Hebrews, 83, 84; Hosea, 95, 96;

Isaiah, 16, 20, 23, 29, 30, 39, 40, 42, 43, 44, 83, 86, 94, 95, 96, 113–17, 135, 140, 162, 213–14n18; Jeremiah, 20, 23, 38, 42, 43, 83, 86, 90–96, 100, 101, 106, 109, 110, 135, 141, 162, 216n28; Job, 94; Joel, 20, 42, 43, 140; John, 16, 83, 84, 162; Joshua, 16, 48, 83, 133–34; I Kings, 95, 133; Lamentations, 43; Luke, 20, 23, 29–30, 40, 42, 43, 83, 84, 113–17, 162, 170, 218n8; Malachi, 139; Mark, 83, 84, 162; Matthew, 83, 84, 162; Micah, 16, 40, 42, 43, 44, 49, 83, 96; Nehemiah, 83, 95; Numbers, 96, 110; I Peter, 42; Proverbs, 89; Psalms, 40, 83, 96; Revelation, 20, 33, 34, 36, 83, 101, 139–43; Romans, 83, 144; I Samuel, 83; II Samuel, 92; Zechariah, 12, 162, 212n31

Biblical characters: Aaron, 80, 95; Amos, 95; Bathsheba, 92; Daniel, 32; David, 20, 82, 83, 92; Esther, 32; Ezekiel, 94, 95; Gideon, 92; Isaiah, 92, 94, 95; James, 32; Jesus, 9, 16, 20, 21, 29, 30, 33, 35, 37, 51, 55–61, 79, 83, 84, 88, 112–23, 128, 129, 134, 135, 144, 145, 147, 149, 150, 152, 153, 156, 162, 164, 165, 166, 168, 170, 171, 178, 180, 183, 184, 185, 187–93, 195–99; Jonah, 83, 92; Joshua, 47; Moses, 19, 20, 21, 30, 32, 35–36, 48, 68, 74, 76, 79–86, 88, 93, 95–96, 110–11, 115, 120–22, 130–36, 143–44, 150–51, 154, 157, 161, 168, 173; Nathan, 92; Nebuchadnezzar, 83, 208n15; Paul, 11, 83, 166, 168, 171; Pharaoh, 16, 20, 21, 35, 84–85, 93, 95, 96, 98, 118–20, 148; Samson, 83; Shadrach, Meshach, and Abednego ("the three boys"), 31, 83, 208n15; Solomon, 82; Zechariah, 95

Biblical concepts and events: "Already and Not Yet," 145–46, 152–53; Easter, 7, 35; Eschatology, 20, 44, 50, 132, 134, 142, 145–47, 148, 150, 151, 153–55; Exodus, 16, 20, 21, 23, 24, 28, 30–37, 44, 45, 47, 48, 50, 71–88, 95, 96, 97, 105–6, 109–10, 112, 115, 116, 120–22, 125, 129–31, 133–35, 141, 148–51, 153–56, 161, 162, 164, 170, 207n52, 213n11; Fall, 78–79; Fire as holiness, 109–10; New Jerusalem, 100–101, 136, 151, 152; Passover, 74, 80, 82–84, 134; Promised Land/Canaan, 16, 30, 35, 36, 47–49, 75, 76, 80, 81, 83, 87, 88, 96, 110, 126, 129–36, 151, 154, 157, 175, 182; Sermon on the Mount, 134; Second Coming of Christ, 20, 21, 37, 129, 130, 135–36, 138, 144, 145, 147, 149, 151, 153, 157, 159, 165, 171; Sinai Covenant, 74, 82–83, 96, 106, 122, 133, 134; Ten Commandments, 74, 80, 82, 83, 96, 133, 134; Time as arrow/Time as wheel, 144–52

Biblical genres: early prophetic history, 16; gospel, 16; Pauline epistle, 16; Pentateuchal narrative, 16, 20, 77–78, 80, 94, 134; prophecy, 16, 20, 23–24, 37, 39–44, 89–111, 129–57

Biblical locations: Assyria, 86, 94; Babylon, 32, 43, 83, 86, 94, 149, 153, 155, 213–14n18; Bloody Way/Bloody Pass, 57, 184, 185, 188, 190–92; Egypt, 16, 30, 35–37, 75, 77, 79, 82, 84–86, 88, 95, 119, 130, 135, 141, 173, 176; Jericho, 38, 47–49, 57–59, 60, 117, 118, 141, 144, 166, 173, 180, 183–85, 189–93, 196–97; Mount Pisgah, 20, 30, 35, 76, 80, 133–34, 136, 143; Mountains, 133–34, 136; Red Sea, 20, 30, 35, 36, 49, 71, 75, 77, 78, 80, 86, 126, 134, 157, 175

Biblical parables, 51–61; Parable of Dives and Lazarus, 9, 57, 195, 218n8; Parable of Good Samaritan, 20, 22, 23, 51–61, 116–23, 149, 162, 166, 183, 184, 195, 210n17; Parable of Prodigal Son, 56, 218n8; Parable of Rich Fool, 56, 195, 218n8

Birmingham campaign, 7, 8, 32, 109–11, 167

"Birth of a New Nation." *See* King, Martin Luther, Jr.: orations

Bobbitt, David, 220n46

Bonhoeffer, Dietrich, 167

"Book of the Seven Seals." *See* Brewster, William Herbert

Borders, William Holmes, 28, 209n2

Branch, Taylor, 213n6

Brewster, William Herbert, and "Book of the Seven Seals," 34

Brooks, Phillips, 31, 35

Broome, Nathaniel, 5

Brown, Bailey, 98–99, 104

Brown, Barbara, 217n52

Brown, Charles Reynolds, and *Two Parables* (1898), 197–99

Brown court decision, 35

Bruce, A. B., and *The Parabolic Teachings of Christ* (1882), 196–99

Brueggemann, Walter, 25, 91, 96–97, 169

Buber, Martin, and *I and Thou*, 120–21

Bunche, Ralph, 14

Burke, Kenneth, 25, 85, 87, 111, 153

Burns, Stewart, 36

Burrows, Clinton, 5

Burrows, Millar, 220n3

Butler, Anthea, 23

Buttrick, George, 51, 57–61, 118, 160, 164, 217n17; and *Parables of Jesus*, 51, 56, 184, 185–87, 188, 191–92, 193–94, 195–200

Campbell, Will, 209n47

Carey, Archibald, 54, 210n6

Carmichael, Stokely, 72

Carson, Clayborne, 207n2, 207n4, 220n3

Carter, J. Kameron, 31, 163, 220n18

Chaney, James, 33

Chappell, David, 207n57

Childs, Brevard, 36, 37, 111, 121, 169, 209n46

Christianity and Judaism, 19, 22, 24, 71–111, 161, 163

Church of God in Christ (COGIC), 21, 62, 64–69, 210n2, 211n8

Ciampa, P. F., 6, 7

Civil Rights Act of 1964, 14

Civil War, 20, 31, 36, 39, 145–46

Claassens, Julia, 24

Clark, Septima, 35

Coca-Cola, 103–4, 105, 126, 162

Commercial Appeal, 101, 102
Cone, James, 30
Connor, Bull, 109, 148
Constitution, 98–100
Crenshaw, Cornelia, 6

Davis, G. W., 158–59
"Death of Evil on the Seashore." *See* King, Martin Luther, Jr.: orations
Declaration of Independence, 15, 38, 39
Dennis, Dave, 31
Detroit, Michigan, 8, 73, 173
Detroit Free Press, 213n6
"Dignity of Labor." *See* King, Martin Luther, Jr.: orations
Dodd, C. H., 55
Dods, Marcus, 210n17; and *The Parables of Our Lord* (1886), 196–99
Douglass, Frederick, 25, 31, 38, 39, 145; and "What to the Slave Is the Fourth of July?," 25
"Drum Major Instinct." *See* King, Martin Luther, Jr.: orations
Durick, Joseph, 216–17n31
Dylan, Bob: and "A Hard Rain's Gonna Fall," 34; and "When the Ship Comes In," 34

Ebenezer Baptist Church, 27, 173
Elliot, Robert, 38
Emancipation Proclamation, 15, 39, 131, 132
Enslin, Morton, 158–59, 161
Epps, Jesse, 107, 205n27
Ericksen, Robert, 163
Ethics of Memory, The. *See* Margalit, Avishai

"Eve of Destruction." *See* McGuire, Barry
Evers, Medgar, 31, 33, 47, 48, 165, 172, 212n29

Fairclough, Adam, 173, 203n1
Fekkes, Jan, 142, 219n30
Fishbane, Michael, 97, 114
Fosdick, Harry Emerson, 37, 52–53, 121, 160, 164; and "Crucified by Stupidity," 220n6
Frank, Gerold, 212n28
Franklin, C. L., 22

Gadamer, Hans George, 159–60, 168–70, 220n5, 221n31
Galbraith, John Kenneth, 15
Garbage workers of Memphis, 4–11, 24, 102, 110, 173–74
Garnet, Henry Highland, 31, 38
Garrow, David, 165, 221n41
George, Henry, 15
Gilkey, Langdon, 164
"Go Down, Moses," 30, 31–32
"God's Judgment on White America." *See* X, Malcolm
Goodman, Andrew, 47
Gottwald, Norman, 80–81
Gowan, Donald, 42, 43, 44, 90, 169
Graham, Billy, 37, 121
Grant, Mary, 145–46
Great Depression, 23, 27–29, 45, 64–66, 75, 130, 148
Green, Laurie, 102, 203n24
Grimke, Francis, 38

Hamer, Fannie Lou, 17, 31, 167
Hamilton, J. Wallace, 54, 56, 172; and

Horns and Halos in Human Nature, 56
Hansen, Drew, 44, 220n46
"Hard Rain's Gonna Fall, A." *See* Dylan, Bob
Harlem, 73, 124–32, 166
Harper, Frances Ellen Watkins, 31, 38
Henry, Aaron, 17
Hersey, John, 213n6
Heschel, Abraham, 92, 161
Heschel, Susannah, 110, 161, 163
Holmes, David, 208n16
Honey, Michael, 204n27, 206n43, 220n16, 221n39
"How Should a Christian View Communism?" *See* King, Martin Luther, Jr.: orations
Howard, T. R. M., 17, 217n36
Howard-Pitney, David, 30
Howe, Julia Ward, 129–57, 170; background, 130, 138; and "Battle Hymn of the Republic," 20, 48–49, 129, 138–57; and Hebrew Prophets, 139–41; and Revelation, 139–42
Hubbard, George, 210n17; and *The Teachings of Jesus in Parables* (1907), 197–99

I and Thou. See Buber, Martin
"If I Had My Way." *See* Peter, Paul, and Mary
"I Have a Dream." *See* King, Martin Luther, Jr.: orations
Invaders, 10

Jackson, Jesse, 11, 12, 50, 103, 104, 107, 108, 179

Jackson, Jimmie Lee, 31
Jackson, Mahalia, 8
Jackson, Ralph, 7, 99–100, 107
Jackson, Thomas, 206n45
Jeremias, Joachim, 55, 56
Jesus. *See* Biblical characters: Jesus
Jesus and the Parables. See Murray, George
Johnson, James Weldon: and "Lift Every Voice and Sing," 45–46
Johnson, Lyndon, 14, 45
Jones, T. O., 5, 6, 7
Jordan, James, 217n46, 217n53
Judaism and Christianity. *See* Christianity and Judaism

Kelsey, George, 158, 159
Kennedy, John, 33, 172
King, Alberta, 27–28
King, Ed, 33
King, James, 27
King, Martin Luther, Jr.
  childhood, 27–28
  delivery, 106–7
  essays: "Letter from Birmingham Jail," 50, 100, 161, 166–71, 216n31; "Suffering and Faith," 166
  as icon, 16
  orations: "Beyond Vietnam," 41, 43; "Birth of a New Nation," 35, 36, 49; "Death of Evil on the Seashore," 35, 36, 49; "Dignity of Labor" (March 18, 1968), 9, 41, 57, 204–5n27; "Drum Major Instinct," 44, 172; "How Should a Christian View Communism?," 41; "I Have a Dream," 14, 15, 22, 28, 39, 41, 42, 43, 44, 49,

50, 106–8, 161, 166, 170, 206n45, 208–9n40; "I've Been to the Mountaintop," 175–82; "Love in Action," 220n10; "On Being a Good Neighbor," 51, 188–90, 193–94, 197; "Our God Is Able," 165; "Our God Is Marching On," 22, 28, 41, 44–50; "The Negro and the Constitution," 39; "Sermon on the Porch," 165–66; "Shattered Dreams," 166; "Three Dimensions of a Complete Life," 220n11; "Ultimate Doom of Evil," 218n12; "Where Do We Go from Here?," 15–16; "Why Jesus Called a Man a Fool," 220n11
as prophet, 89–111
radicalism of 1967 and 1968, 13, 14, 15, 16
Stride toward Freedom, 165–66
themes: "Already and Not Yet," 152–53; avoids rationalist interpretation of Bible, 160–61; Bible and emancipation, 171–72; Bible and racial struggle, 167–71; Bible as dialogic, 168–71; Bible as narrative, 163–71; body, 123–26, 165–67; boycott/shutdown in Memphis, 103–4, 105; doomsday warning, 105–6; Judaism as basis for Christianity, 161–63; own assassination, 20, 129–35, 149, 172–73; persecution/triumph, 49–50, 129, 130, 132, 148–50; science, 161; time as arrow/time as cycle, 148–52; war and peace/nonviolence, 105–6

King, Martin Luther, Sr., 27–29, 159, 160
Kotz, Nick, 213n6
Kyles, Billy, 9, 99–100, 106–7, 204–5n27

LaCocque, Andre, 169
Lafayette, Bernard, 14
"Landing strip," 107, 129–32, 138, 217n43
Langston, John Mercer, 38
Lawson, James, 4, 8, 9, 10, 12, 50, 99–100, 104, 108, 205n27
Lee, Bernard, 10, 12
Lee, Pilchan, 219n28
Levison, Stanley, 11
Levi-Strauss, Claude, 154
Lewis, John, 14
Lincoln, Abraham, 15, 30
Lindblom, Johannes, 216n28
Lischer, Richard, 15
Loeb, Henry, 5, 6, 8, 9, 73–74, 85, 98, 101, 102, 103, 104, 106, 119, 162, 173–74
Logan, Marian, 203n7
Luccock, Halford, 53, 57, 58, 185–87, 193–94, 195–96, 210n17; and *Marching off the Map*, 210n18; and *Studies in the Parables of Jesus* (1917), 196–99, 210n18
Luker, Ralph, 207n2, 207n4

Manis, Andrew, 33
March in Memphis (March 28), 10, 11
Marching Off the Map. *See* Luccock, Halford
March on Washington, 32
Margalit, Avishai, and *The Ethics of Memory*, 85

INDEX

Marsh, Charles, 207n57
Mason, C. H., 31, 62, 68–69, 111, 115, 211n10, 211n18
Mason Temple, 3, 6, 7, 8, 9, 11, 21, 25, 50, 62–70, 97–108, 116, 138, 155, 204–5n27, 206n39, 211n27, 211–12n28, 220n16; architect (H. Taylor/W. H. Taylor), 13, 21, 67, 212n30; architecture, 63–64, 67–68; tomb, 69
Mays, Benjamin, 51–52, 159, 160, 209n1; and *Seeking to Be Christian in Race Relations* (1957), 198–99
McCracken, Robert, 53; and *Questions People Ask*, 159
McGuire, Barry, and "Eve of Destruction," 34
Memphis Press-Scimitar, 101, 102
Middlebrook, Harold, 107, 217n53
Milton, Clyde, 212n32
Montgomery Bus Boycott, 14, 17, 35, 39, 41, 45, 46, 105, 172, 217n37
Moore, Leslie, 208n31
Moses, Robert, 31, 33
Murray, George, 58, 191–92; and *Jesus and the Parables* (1916), 196–98

NAACP, 6, 8, 10, 25, 27, 212n29
Nash, Diane, 14
New Deal, 75–79, 131, 150
News media, 7, 8, 11, 101–2, 110
Nkrumah, Kwame, 35
Notes on the Parables of Our Lord. See Trench, Robert

"On Being a Good Neighbor." See King, Martin Luther, Jr.: orations
Osborne, Michael, 203n1

"Our God Is Marching On." See King, Martin Luther, Jr.: orations

Parables of Jesus. See Buttrick, George
Parabolic Teachings of Christ, The. See Bruce, A. B.
Patterson, James O., 7, 64
Payne, Larry, 10, 12
Pentecostalism, 64–70; Azusa Street Revival, 31, 65; and biblical Pentecost, 31; and body, 69; and Mason Temple, 23; "speaking in tongues," 31, 65; "tarrying," 69–70
Perrin, Norman, 158–60
Peter, Paul, and Mary, and "If I Had My Way," 34
Pleas, Charles, 212n30
Polsgrove, Carol, 38
Poor People's Campaign, 4, 9, 10, 34, 203n7
Posner, Gerald, 212n28
Pritchard, James, 158–59, 160, 161
Protestant commonplaces, 22, 195–200
Protestant Reformation, 23, 37, 75–76, 131, 132

Raboteau, Albert, 30
Rauschenbusch, Walter, 37
Ricoeur, Paul, 25, 169
Rieder, Jonathan, 207n53
Robinson, Elizabeth "Lizzie," 66
Robinson, Jackie, 14
Robinson, James, 5, 208n31
Robinson, Ruby Doris, 17, 33
Rogers, Taylor, 6
Russell, Penny, 207n2, 207n4
Rustin, Bayard, 8, 14

Sanders, Cheryl, 23
Sanders, James, 96, 169, 209n46
Schwerner, Michael, 47
SCLC. *See* Southern Christian Leadership Conference
Seeking to Be Christian in Race Relations. See Mays, Benjamin
Selby, Gary, 34, 207n52
Selma campaign, 7, 8, 15, 44–45
Selma-to-Montgomery March, 15, 20, 28, 32, 44–50, 71, 125, 130–31, 137, 165–66
Seymour, William, 31, 65
Shuttlesworth, Fred, 8, 17, 22, 31, 32, 33, 36, 165, 167, 208n15
Sides, Hampton, 212n28
Smith, James, 217n50
Smith, Kelly Miller, 32–33, 208n18
Smith, Maxine, 6, 10, 108
SNCC. *See* Student Nonviolent Coordinating Committee
Social Gospel, 28, 37, 173
Southern Christian Leadership Conference (SCLC), 15, 203n7
Spike, Robert, 34
Student Nonviolent Coordinating Committee (SNCC), 72
Studies in the Parables of Jesus. See Luccock, Halford
Sugarmon, Russell, 204n25
Sundquist, Eric, 220n46
Sunnemark, Frederick, 220n46
Sweeney, Marvin, 96, 216n23

Tarrying. *See* Pentacostalism
Taylor, Gardner, 211n4
Taylor, H. (W. H. Taylor). *See* Mason Temple

Teachings of Jesus in Parables. See Hubbard, George
Thompson, Leonard, 144–45, 146
Thurman, Howard, 52–53
Tinney, James, 69–70
Trench, Robert, 210n17; and *Notes on the Parables of Our Lord* (1841), 196–98
Tri-State Bank, 103–4, 217n36
Tri-State Defender, 203n24
Truth, Sojourner, 31
Tubman, Harriett, 30
Turner, Jesse, 6
Tutu, Desmond, 171
"Twelve Gates to the City." *See* Ward, Clara
Two Parables. See Brown, Charles Reynolds

Union army, 30, 36

Vietnam War, 14, 15, 16, 44, 72
Vivian, C. T., 89
Von Rad, Gerhard, 96, 169
Voting Rights Act, 14, 45, 71

Walker, Wyatt, 217n43
Wallace, George, 32
Ward, Clara, 34
Watkins, Frances Ellen. *See* Harper, Frances Ellen Watkins
Watts, Los Angeles, 72–73, 173
Wax, James, 100
Wellhausen, Julius, 163
Wells, Ida B., 38
"What to the Slave Is the Fourth of July?" *See* Douglass, Frederick

"When the Ship Comes In." *See* Dylan, Bob
"Where Do We Go From Here." *See* King, Martin Luther, Jr.: orations
White, Walter, 212n29
Wilkins, Roy, 8, 14
Williams, A. D., 27, 28, 159
Williams, Alberta. *See* King, Alberta
Wilson, Edmund, 145–46
Woodruff, Robert, 104
Wright, Jeremiah, 14
Wurf, Jerry, 220n16

X, Malcolm, 34, 72, 88, 215n55, 217n37

Young, Andrew, 5, 8, 11, 12, 13, 50, 104, 204n27, 206n43, 212n28

Zimmerli, Walter, 169

www.ingramcontent.com/pod-product-compliance
Lightning Source LLC
Chambersburg PA
CBHW030617230426
43661CB00053B/2037